The New Competition

PHILIP KOTLER • LIAM FAHEY
SOMKID JATUSRIPITAK

PRENTICE-HALL, INC., Englewood Cliffs, New Jersey 07632

Library of Congress Cataloging in Publication Data

KOTLER, PHILIP.
   The new competition.

   Bibliography: p.
   Includes index.
      1. Marketing—Japan.   2. Export marketing—Japan.
   I. Fahey, Liam, 1951–   II. Somkid Jatusripitak.
   III. Title.
   HF5415.12.J3K68 1985   382'.0952   84-26596
   ISBN 0-13-612078-4

Editorial/production supervision and
   interior design: Esther S. Koehn
Cover design: Diane Saxe
Cover illustration: Karen Goldsmith
Manufacturing buyer: Ed O'Dougherty

*This publication is available to businesses, organizations,
and resellers at a discount when ordered in quantity.
For information, contact:*

   *Special Sales Representative
   College Marketing
   Prentice-Hall, Inc.
   Sylvan Avenue
   Englewood Cliffs, NJ 07632*

Printed in the United States of America

10 9 8 7 6 5

ISBN 0-13-612078-4 01

Prentice-Hall International, Inc., *London*
Prentice-Hall of Australia Pty. Limited, *Sydney*
Editora Prentice-Hall do Brasil, Ltda., *Rio de Janeiro*
Prentice-Hall Canada Inc., *Toronto*
Prentice-Hall Hispanoamericana, S.A., *Mexico*
Prentice-Hall of India Private Limited, *New Delhi*
Prentice-Hall of Japan, Inc., *Tokyo*
Prentice-Hall of Southeast Asia Pte. Ltd., *Singapore*
Whitehall Books Limited, *Wellington, New Zealand*

Dedication

To Nancy, Amy, Melissa, and Jessica
Philip Kotler

To Patricia, Michelle, and Kevin
Liam Fahey

To my father, mother, uncle, and aunt, who raised me
Somkid Jatusripitak

To the Japanese friends, colleagues, students, and managers
who have provided us much to admire and emulate

Contents

Foreword

American business leaders have prided themselves as vigorous competitors. Indeed they are. They have been particularly adroit competing against neighboring American companies. Each understood the other. Conduct was predictable from years of repetitive experience and expectations. Native mind-sets influenced quality levels. Similar retrenchments in capacity planning were common responses to U.S. cyclic market downturns. Competitive evaluations were made primarily against other American companies.

Foreign competitors looking in from the outside learned and responded to customer readiness for "do differentlies" better than American competitors at times. The Japanese, notably, saw some of these market opportunities sooner and clearer. They did things about what they saw.

Ironically, what the Japanese did operationally then became the greater American preoccupation. Extensive attention was focused here on statistical quality control, their low-cost financing, people involvement programs, and their labor cost and productivity, etc. The American responses to many of these operating factors were effective.

Less evident was American realization of the insight about the customer—the understanding of the market that preceded and accompanied Japan's targeting American buyers.

This book puts the spotlight on the importance marketing played in Japan's trade achievements. The pivot statement in the center of the text reads, ". . .it is equally clear that marketing has played a major role in their success."

The students of American business and the American business leaders were right to emphasize study of Japan's productive processes to meet the challenge. They equally will have missed a key element if they are numb to the role and effect of Japan's world-class marketing, if for no other reason than defense of one's U.S market share.

This fundamental message—the importance of marketing—is clear and emphatic particularly because it is presented from the vantage of Japan's challenge. The presentation here is in balance. The authors accurately portray the mix of factors that the Japanese system, culture, and competences have brought to world trade. In an even-handed way, they account for the role of government re protection, support, and guidance at home; the role of culture re the unity of the people, their sense of survival, and their standards of merit; the role of keiretsus and individual companies as institutions where patient, native skills are practiced well; and the role of customer focus re the inexhaustible gathering of intelligence about the market, the sorting of choices, and filling of needs.

U.S. business managers who aspire to lead and leaders who still wish to learn will carry away from this book practiceable strategies which will enhance the American vigor to compete.

Robert W. Galvin
Chairman of the Board
Motorola, Inc.

———————————————————— *Preface* ——

Surely one of the most impressive economic miracles in modern times is Japan's rise from the ashes of World War II to become one of the world's three great economic superpowers. From its war-torn and destitute state in 1945 when it surrendered to the Allied forces, Japan today stands as the world's most feared and respected economic competitor. Japan not only had to plot its recovery from a war-torn economy but had to overcome four additional handicaps: first, a dearth of major domestic natural resources such as iron ore, oil, and copper, which highly industrial nations critically depend upon; second, a weak understanding of Western culture and business practice; third, a lack of facility in the English and European languages; and fourth, a pre-World War II reputation for shoddy goods. To have overcome these difficulties and now be so universally respected for the quality and variety of its automobiles, motorcycles, consumer electronics, cameras, watches, and many other products, Japan certainly deserves study and explanation.

Japan's understanding and use of "marketing," in our view, has been one of the key contributors to its success in the global marketplace. This raises several questions. Do the Japanese know things about marketing that U.S. and European firms do not know? Have Western corporations forgotten what they once knew about marketing or have they simply failed to put what they know into practice? What can Western firms learn from the Japanese style of market selection, market entry, market penetration, and market maintenance? These questions are being pondered by an ever-growing number of Western executives whose businesses have been hurt by super-able Japanese competitors.

The deep Japanese penetration into world markets is not over. In fact, Japan has been targeting new markets, such as computers, aircraft, pharmaceuticals, banking, clothing, and cosmetics, to name a few. What is more, Japan is only the first of a series of Asian countries that are following the same competitive model or evolving new ones, all of which center on creating quality products at lower costs and lower prices than those produced in the West. Japan's particular success has been marked by a strong business-government partnership; long-term and low-cost loans by banks; management willingness to "buy" market share and wait five, ten, or twenty years for profits; fanatic attention to product quality and service; a drive toward capital-intensive productivity increases; and several other factors. The new Japans—South Korea, Taiwan, Hong Kong, Singapore—are adopting many of these practices and adding some new ones as well. And as we move toward the next century, other Asian countries—particularly China, India, Indonesia, Thailand, Malaysia, and the Philippines—will evolve highly competitive approaches to winning sizeable shares of key global markets. Some observers are going so far as to characterize the next century as the Pacific Century, because they see an increasing share of the world's gross national product originating in that part of the world.

The West, because of its past complacency, is partly to blame for its loss of market position. And its responses to the Japanese challenge are still superficial and inadequate. American and European firms need to start taking this challenge seriously and study the "New Competition."

The New Competition is characterized by the following attributes: (1) a highly intelligent, disciplined, and skilled work force working at lower wages than their Western counterparts; (2) cooperative labor/ management relations; (3) a medium and high-tech orientation in these countries enabling them to compete in the industries that are the mainstays in the West; (4) capital sources that accept a lower rate of return and a considerably longer payout horizon; (5) government direction and subsidization to help business; (6) frequently explicit, and sometimes subtley, protected home markets; and (7) sophisticated concepts of business and marketing strategy.

The question thus becomes: How can Western-based companies that face higher wages and capital costs, worker discipline problems, higher and earlier profit requirements, strong government regulation, and a comparative absence of government support compete successfully with companies that are run according to the principles of the New Competition?

The purpose of this book is to examine the principles of the New

Competition, especially as exemplified by Japan, its leading exponent.

In the first part of the book, we document the impressive record of Japan's economic success, analyze the factors that contributed to that success, and highlight the specific role played by Japanese marketing strategy in achieving such results. In the second part, we describe the range of marketing strategies used by the Japanese to identify opportunities, enter markets, penetrate them deeply, confront opponents, and maintain dominance. The third part will offer major recommendations on how Western-based companies can respond to the marketing challenge of the New Competition. The final chapter draws a host of lessons about where strategic marketing is moving in the twenty-first century.

Throughout the book, we include in-depth descriptions of how the Japanese won specific world markets, including automobiles, motorcyles, watches, cameras, radios, and television, as well as their plans for penetrating several new target industries, including banking, fashion, cosmetics, computers, and aerospace. While our focus is on Japan, the real import of the book is that a new model of global competition has emerged which is being copied by several other countries. This model poses the most serious challenge that Western firms have faced since adopting the principles of free enterprise as spelled out in Adam Smith's *Wealth of Nations*.

Acknowledgments

We began the Northwestern Project on Japanese Marketing Strategy three years ago after observing that various books describing Japan's economic success failed to pay sufficient attention to the role played by Japanese marketing strategy. We felt that Japan's skill in formulating and executing competitive marketing strategies needed to be better understood and highlighted. We wanted to know if the Japanese had discovered new principles of marketing or simply managed to apply these principles better than their Western counterparts.

Included in the Northwestern project were a number of graduate students who searched for available data and interviewed Japanese scholars, business managers, and government officials. We want to thank the following students for their contributions: Lynda Black, Robert Carpenter, Daniel Craft, Jeffrey Day, Philip Eynon, Elizabeth Friskey, Diana Knox, Kevin McDonald, Anurachanee Pingkarawat, and Suvinai Tosirisuk.

We want to express our deep gratitude to two scholars who reviewed our manuscript. Professor Ferdinand Mauser, who has lived in Tokyo and who has taught at Keio University, provided us with excellent insights and suggestions for improving the book. Professor Johny K. Johansson of the University of Washington has published scholarly arti-

cles on Japan and helped us improve the text's accuracy and complete-
ness. We are indebted to both of these scholars for their careful and
detailed reviews. In addition, we want to thank Oscar Collier for his
helpful suggestions on improving the manuscript's focus and clarity.

We also are indebted to Donald P. Jacobs, Dean of the J.L.
Kellogg Graduate School of Management, Northwestern University, for
his continuous support and arranging for contacts with leading U.S.
executives. Our project has also been ably assisted by our secretaries,
Marion Davis, Laura Kingsley, Tracy Ayers, and Julia Taylor, who helped
us move the manuscript smoothly through several successive drafts.

Finally, we want to thank the able staff of Prentice-Hall for their
extraordinary support. We want to single out Elizabeth Classon, our
marketing editor, for skillfully managing the whole project, and Paul
Misselwitz, Tim Moore, Gene Perme, George Stanley, Peter Maloney and
Beverly Vill for their marketing support, and Esther Koehn and Eloise
Starkweather for their production support.

Philip Kotler

Liam Fahey
Northwestern University
Evanston, Illinois

Somkid Jatusripitak
National Institute
of Development Administration
Bangkok, Thailand

PART I
THE MARKETING BATTLEGROUND

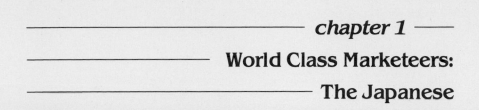

chapter 1
World Class Marketeers:
The Japanese

On August 15, 1945, the entire Japanese nation listened to Emperor Hirohito deliver a message of surrender to the Allied forces. Japan had started a war years earlier to fulfill its needs for resources, land, and power in the Far East and then lost this war, having never before been defeated in war. Japan's economy was in shambles and its people were morally and economically devastated.

In the 1980s, some thirty-five years later, UNESCO published the economic standings of various industrial nations. Here were some amazing facts:

- Japan ranked second as the most economically developed nation in the world.
- Japan ranked second in GNP and fourth in per capita national income.
- Japan's GNP increased more than 200 percent and ranked first among the highly industrialized countries in economic growth rates during 1971–80, a period of great economic difficulty for most countries.

And where did the Allied victors stand some thirty-five years later? France and Britain ranked fourth and fifth, respectively, in GNP among the highly developed countries. Their combined GNPs were lower than Japan's. The USSR, another Allied victor, spent almost three decades in developing its economy without achieving half of Japan's GNP per capita. One might ask, Who won the war?

Japan lost the military war but clearly won the economic war. Military wars have been waged in the past to gain economic prizes. The Japanese painfully learned the lesson that they could win more economic prizes through economic means rather than military means. Too bad they did not know this in 1940.

THE JAPANESE MIRACLE

In 1945, people would have ridiculed any soothsayer who predicted that Japan would be the second most economically developed nation in the world by 1980. Any sane observer in 1945 would have noticed that the Japanese economy was heir to four formidable handicaps, seriously limiting its economic future:

- Japan's factories had been destroyed, its people faced near starvation, its currency was in the throes of runaway inflation, and its political and social fabric was devastated.
- Japan lacked the major natural resources—coal, iron, and oil—necessary for running a modern economy. Furthermore, only 14.8 percent of its land was arable.
- Most Japanese businesspeople only spoke Japanese and knew little about U.S. and Western European markets, cultures, and history.
- Prewar Japanese products had a worldwide reputation for poor quality. To most people, the label "Made in Japan" meant a cheap and poorly made product.

The fact that Japan overcame these handicaps and that its name today stands for "quality" and "value" around the world is a miracle. Their products penetrate deeply into every corner of the world, with names such as Sony, Toyota, Canon, Seiko, and Nikon commanding universal recognition and respect. This turnaround is enough to encourage other developing nations—India, Indonesia, Malaysia—to emulate it. In fact, these countries, as well as many less-advanced European countries, are carefully studying this miracle—and seeing what parts of overall Japanese strategy they can import in the hope of advancing their economies.

In examining the Japanese model for economic development, too many people interpret the miracle as a result of one or a few single factors. Some point to the Japanese government's key role in directing and subsidizing Japanese companies. Others cite the low wages and disciplined work force in Japanese factories. Still others point to the Japanese trade barriers that permitted Japanese companies to charge high prices in the home market while keeping out foreign competitors, thus earning the surplus to finance an export attack abroad. And others cite the Japanese gift for copying—and sometimes stealing—Western-innovated products and improving them in the process. Many other explanations have also been offered.

However, we know that single-factor theories never really explain anything; they are convenient fictions. We will explore in the next chapter the whole set of factors that together produced the Japanese miracle. And by implication, we are saying that other countries will not succeed by copying one or a few elements of Japan's strategy. And they cannot copy all of the Japanese strategies. Every nation and every company, however, can learn from the Japanese. One can extract powerful lessons about corporate strategy from the Japanese experience. We have, in fact, drawn and featured these lessons throughout this book and brought them together in the last chapter. At the same time, each nation and each corporation will have to design its strategy afresh out of its own conditions and opportunities.

Is the Japanese Miracle Over?

One popular, and dangerous, belief is that the Japanese have now won all they will win. Even management guru Peter Drucker predicted recently that "the Japanese will not be a problem in five years." Various reasons have been supplied by Drucker and others. First, the Japanese will face new problems bred by their very success: weakening of the work ethic, higher wage demands, rising infrastructure costs from pollution, traffic congestion, and so on. Second, the Japanese succeeded in the past because of the complacency and blindness of U.S. manufacturers who kept making big cars when a growing number of consumers wanted small cars, analog watches when more consumers wanted digital watches, large copying machines when businesses wanted smaller copying machines, and so on. The argument goes on to say that U.S. manufacturers have "wised up" today . . . they are plugging the holes. The Japanese will not find much more opportunity to expand.

We think otherwise. First, the Japanese social and business culture and drive have not softened. The discipline is still strong, and although wages have improved, so has productivity.

Second, U.S. manufacturers have not plugged all the holes. Many are still not delivering the quality or value provided by their Japanese competitors in cars, motorcycles, cameras, watches, musical instruments, and so on.

Third, the Japanese are now invading a whole new set of markets in which the established U.S. and Western European producers have hardly recognized the threat or bothered to construct counterstrategies. This ignorance allowed the Japanese to advance aggressively into such new industries/markets as fashions, cosmetics, hotels, banking, air conditioning, machine tools, medical equipment, and pharmaceuticals in recent years (discussed in detail later in this book).

THE NEW COMPETITION

Even if the Japanese have shown signs of slowing down in their invasion of world markets, the same thrust will continue but will come from the "New Japanese"—the Koreans, Taiwanese, Singaporeans and the Hong Kong businesses. These people and businesses are copying all or part of the Japanese model and adding a few twists of their own. They are following many of the principles defined by the Japanese for winning world markets:

- Government direction and subsidization of industrial development
- Explicit as well as subtle protection of the home market against foreign competition, enabling high profits in the home market to finance export development
- A highly intelligent, disciplined, and skilled work force working at lower wages than their Western counterparts
- Cooperative labor/management relations
- High availability of capital at low interest rates
- Capital sources that accept a lower current rate of return and a considerably longer payout period, thus enabling business firms to plan for the long run
- An orientation toward medium- and high-tech industries, the mainstay industries of the West, and an active program of phasing out (or down) the "sunset" industries
- A commitment to both high quality and high productivity, and making sure that productivity drives do not take place at the expense of quality
- Sophisticated concepts of business and marketing strategy designed to win global market share leadership in targeted industries

These principles amount to a new model of competition, which we call the New Competition. It is a mix of neo-mercantilism, state direction, and long-term planning. The major objective is to support full-time employment and build up the national wealth. The major means is through stimulating the level of exports while holding down the level of imports.

The New Competition contrasts to the laissez-faire model of competition, which relies on individual companies to pursue their self-interests with a minimum of government interference. Laissez-faire firms aspire for a healthy profit return within a "reasonable time period." Costs have to be held down, especially labor costs, and this turns labor into an adversarial element, where labor is not motivated to high company loyalty and discipline. For funding, management relies on debt and equity suppliers who hope for good returns within a reasonable time period. Laissez-faire management has to deliver reasonable profits in the short run and often is biased against making deep investments involving twenty- or-thirty-year offensive battles to gain ascendency in specific markets.

Not surprisingly, therefore, the sharpest competition in today's world markets is occurring between the U.S. model of competition and the Japanese model, rather than the U.S. model and the USSR model as had been expected. And the leading question in the United States is whether the U.S. model of competition will need modification in the direction of the Japanese model in order for U.S. firms to compete effectively with the Japanese.

Some of these conditions also apply to European manufacturers. Certainly the adversarial attitude of the labor movement in Great Britain—expressed through many prolonged strikes, slowdowns, and featherbedding—has been a major cause of Great Britain's stagnant economy and, ironically, labor's low real income. Even when government and labor are not formal adversaries of business, they often impose conditions that impede business development. Germany's co-determination arrangements allow German labor to veto or retard technological progress and higher productivity in order to save existing jobs. Sweden's high taxes on corporations and businesses to support "cradle-to-grave" social welfare schemes dampen business incentives and diminish investment funds. France's and Italy's operation of some of their economies' largest corporations has failed in most cases to produce entrepreneurially dynamic companies able to establish or maintain dominant positions in world markets. Both European and U.S. firms are thus saddled with many burdens that render them vulnerable in the face of the New Competition.

Nor is the New Competition going to slow down in the 1990s or even the next century. If anything, it will become more formidable. Following the first "Gang of Four" will be a "Gang of Five"—notably India, Indonesia, Thailand, Malaysia, and the Philippines. Each of these countries has a large and talented population—India with more than 670 million people, Indonesia with more than 150 million, and so on. Wages are low, and potential skills, ambitions, and resources are high. These economies need to overcome some traditional problems—corruption in government, a lack of tough-minded politicians and skilled economic planners, a deep need for more business-trained managers, and a poorly developed economic infrastructure. When these nations get their act together, and it may well occur in the mid-1990s, they will flood the world markets with high-quality and low-cost products. Even the Japanese know this and are rapidly establishing factories and joint ventures in these countries to be in a position to keep their production costs low throughout the 1990s.

And then there is China. When this giant finally awakens and stirs, every other country will have to scramble for position. China is already moving rapidly in the direction of liberalizing its economy and decentralizing many businesses.

The message in all of these developments is that we are increasingly facing a New Competition and moving rapidly into a new century that some people are calling the Pacific Century. At least 25 percent of the world's GNP will be generated in the Pacific Basin by A.D. 2000. And U.S. and Western European business interests that dominated the twentieth century will have to prepare for an accommodation to this New Competition as the world moves into the twenty-first century.

EVIDENCE OF THE JAPANESE SUCCESS

How did the Japanese manage to rise phoenixlike from the ashes of 1945 to become the second most economically developed nation in the world by the 1970s? Here we want to provide a picture of their success, and in the next chapter we will explore the reasons for their success.

Rapid Growth of the Japanese Economy

Almost immediately after Japan's defeat in the war, the Japanese people set about rebuilding their war-devastated economy, assisted initially by rehabilitation aid from the United States. By 1954, Japan's gross national product (GNP) had rebounded to the prewar level in real terms. Japan's economy then began to expand from the mid-1950s through the 1960s. Its real GNP grew at an annual rate of 9.5 percent from 1955 to 1961, and 12.3 percent from the end of 1965 to the middle of 1970. Its growth rate

GNP and Per Capita National Income of Selected Countries, 1981

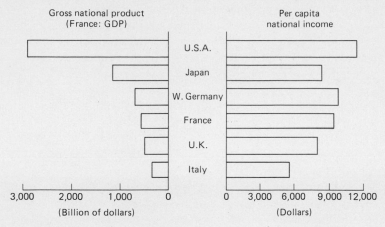

Source: *Nippon: A Chartered Survey of Japan* (Tokyo, Japan, 1983–84).

outstripped that of the United Kingdom in 1966, that of France and of West Germany in 1967, and became second to the United States in the free world, with its GNP exceeding $200 billion in 1970. Today its GNP has already surpassed $1,000 billion, which is twice as large as that of the United Kingdom's and France's combined. Even during the economically difficult years of the early 1970s, Japan was one of the few nations to continue an upward momentum. Japan's economic growth rate during the past decade has remained higher than that of such industrialized countries as the United States, United Kingdom, France, West Germany, Italy, and Canada.

Increasing Productivity

Along with the healthy growth of its GNP, Japan's personal saving rate rose to a remarkable 24 percent while the U.S.'s saving rate declined in the same period to less than 4 percent. The increased saving rate combined with the greater proportion of gross national product spent on capital formation (32 percent of Japan's compared with 18.1 percent of the U.S.'s and 22.7 percent of West Germany's in 1979) and R&D expenditures (Japanese R&D expenses compared with GNP had risen from 1.4 percent in 1961 to 2.3 percent in 1979 while the U.S.'s rate had fallen from 2.7 percent to 2.5 percent) has contributed to a rapid growth in Japan's productivity. Productivity increased 42 percent between 1975 and 1980, which was larger than that in other major industrialized countries. Be-

Changes in Japanese Wages and Labor Productivity, Manufacturing Industries (1975 = 100)

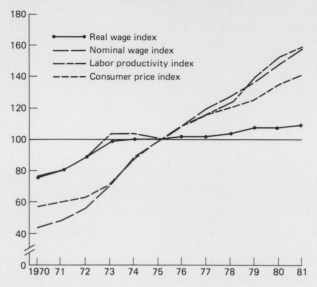

Source: Statistics Bureau, Prime Minister's Office, *Statistical Handbook of Japan*, 1982.

ginning in 1960, productivity grew at a strong 10 percent and evidenced a constant improvement in the manufacturing sector, representing an average annual increase of 9.3 percent during the 1975–80 period. The changes in Japan's productivity along with wage and price indices during the 1970–81 period clearly indicate that labor productivity grew faster than the real wage rate, thus increasing the surplus for capital investment.

Japanese labor's productivity has continued to grow and is now on a par with that in the United States. In some industries, such as steel, electrical machinery, and motor vehicles, Japan has overtaken the United States and Western European countries in terms of labor productivity. It is generally agreed that the improvement of Japanese labor's productivity has been the result of the interplay of huge investments, rationalization, and the quality of Japanese workers.

Industrial Production

The major economic indicators that reflect the extent to which Japan caught up with advanced Western countries can be seen by looking at the changes that took place in the industrial structures and the growth rate of foreign trade.

Before the war, Japan was already highly industrialized, although the emphasis was on light industries such as textiles and toys. After the war, however, great emphasis was shifted to heavy industries such as steel, shipbuilding, machinery, electronics, and motor vehicles.

In 1955, light industry accounted for 23 percent of Japan's GNP but continued to decline to below 10 percent during the 1960s, whereas the rate of heavy industrial production increased from 49 to over 60 percent. The production index in manufacturing alone rose 360 percent between 1955 and 1973. Although the production rate dropped during the first oil crisis, it resumed its steady increase in the past decade.

Japanese Exports

Let us now turn to Japan's external trade. For the Japanese, international trade is not simply pursued because it contributes to economic growth. The fact is that Japan must import to survive. Japan suffers from a shortage of raw materials and is also unable to produce sufficient food for its population. Japan's *dependency ratio* for natural resources was nearly 87 percent in 1979, and for food imports like meat, cereal, and

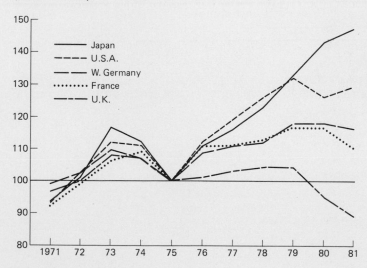

Manufacturing Production Indices of Selected Countries (1975 = 100)

Source: U.N., *Monthly Bulletin of Statistics.*

dairy products it increased from 45 to 56 percent between 1970 and 1979. For these reasons, Japan must relentlessly pursue export expansion in order to gain enough foreign currency to afford its needed imports each year.

Japan's postwar export expansion proceeded rapidly and without geographical or political restriction. Today it exports goods throughout the world not only from Japan but from less-developed countries in Asia, Latin America, and the Middle East to developed countries like the United States and Western Europe; and from free world countries to Communist bloc countries like the USSR and China. Its exports rose from $6 billion in 1966 to more than $129 billion in 1980, a twentyfold increase in less than two decades. As a result of its large amount of trade surplus during the 1970s, protectionism and anti-Japanese feeling spread all over the world. Even so, nothing seems to stop the Japanese expansion. Today Japan exports over $31 billion of goods to the United States, $16.6 billion to European countries, $31 billion to the Asian region, and $9 billion to the Communist bloc.

Japan's exports grew by an average of 16.8 percent annually

Exports By Areas and Countries

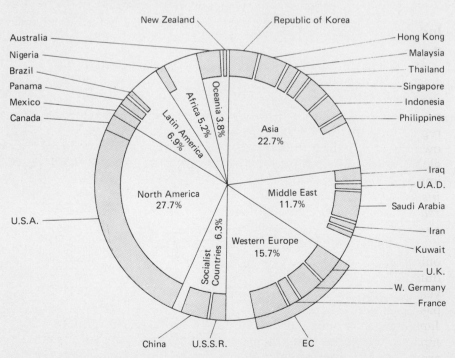

Source: Japan: Ministry of Foreign Affairs, *The Japan of Today*, 1982.

JAPANESE EXPORTS BY COMMODITY GROUP, 1981

	PERCENTAGE
Machinery	65.9
Metals and metal products	14.8
Textile fiber and products	4.7
Chemical products	4.5
Nonmetal mineral products	1.4
Foodstuffs	1.1
Other	7.6

Source: Statistics Bureau, Prime Minister's Office, *Statistical Handbook of Japan,* 1982.

between 1971 and 1981, or at a rate of about 1.2 times that of world exports. Japan's share of world exports by 1980 was 7.1 percent, thus ranking it third, next to the United States and West Germany.

The changing industrial structure at home resulted in a distinct shift in export patterns. Before the war, textiles made up more than 50 percent of Japan's total exports, but by 1981, textile exports had dropped to only 4.7 percent of total exports. Meanwhile, exports of machinery, metal products, and chemicals, which accounted for only 16 percent before the war, had increased to 85.1 percent of total exports by 1981.

Industries Dominated by Japanese Exports

Japan's growing export strength has had a strong impact on the rest of the world. Before 1960, the word *Japanese* meant "cheap, low-quality products." Today, however, consumers in the developed countries highly regard and even prefer Japanese products to those produced in their own countries. Since the early 1970s, Japan has managed to achieve global leadership in industries thought to be dominated by Western impregnable giants: *automobiles, motorcycles, watches, cameras, optical instruments, steel, shipbuilding, snowmobiles, bicycles, pianos, zippers, radios, televisions, audio equipment, calculators, copying machines, and so on.*

The automobile industry is the best example. Japan produced only twenty thousand passenger cars in 1955. Within a decade, seven hundred thousand passenger cars were produced and in subsequent years the automobile industry continued growing until the production of passenger cars reached 3 million units in 1970. By 1967, the output of Japanese automobiles surpassed that of West Germany, and in 1980 Japan overtook the United States to become the world's leading auto producer with a total production of over 7 million units (followed by the

United States, 6.3 million; West Germany, 3.5 million; and France, 2.9 million). Japanese cars have earned a good reputation overseas for their efficiency, high quality, reasonable prices, and trouble-free operation. Under the brand names of Toyota, Nissan (Datsun), Mazda, Honda, Subaru, and Mitsubishi, Japan exported 3.9 million passenger cars in 1981 (followed by West Germany, 1.9 million; France, 1.4 million; and the United States, only 0.5 million). In the U.S. market, Japanese cars had already captured over 20 percent of the small-car market compared with 3.7 percent in 1970. Toyota, in just a few years after making a major commitment to the U.S. market, was able to seize first place in the U.S. automobile imports market in place of Volkswagen. The flood of Japanese autos continued pouring into U.S. ports during 1980 at a rate of fifty-two hundred per day. Japan's U.S. market share would even be larger today if it were not for the import quotas imposed on it in the early 1980s.

In the motorcycle industry during the 1950s, European producers, namely BSA, Triumph, and Norton of the United Kingdom, Moto-Guzzi of Italy, and American producers like Harley Davidson, dominated the international market. By the late 1950s, Honda had become a serious international contender. By the early 1960s, Honda had established itself as the number-one motorcycle brand in the United States. Its lightweight machines with the slogan "You meet the nicest people on a Honda," and an aggressive sales organization and distribution network, all combined to greatly expand the market for motorcycles. Later Yamaha and Suzuki entered by selling small, lightweight, easy-to-ride and low-priced motorcycles, aiming to attract the younger generation. By 1966, Honda, Yamaha, and Suzuki were able to control around 85 percent of the lightweight motorcycle market in the United States. The Japanese success story has been repeated in other countries as well. For example, in the European market the Japanese achieved a 74 percent market share in the United Kingdom, 74 percent in France, 70 percent in West Germany, and 30 percent in Italy by 1974. Japan is now the world leader in both the production and the export of motorcycles. In 1981, Japan produced 7,410,000 units, or 65 percent of the world's total. Japan exported over 4 million of these units.

Let us now turn to high-technology fields like electronics and electrical appliances. At the end of the war, Japan's electrical industry not only had been damaged by the bombing raids but was also technologically backward. Japanese firms began to buy licenses from the West, and they quickly learned how to make high-technology products and in fact managed to improve on them. Whereas in the early 1950s, Japanese radio, television, and tape recorders were inferior to those of U.S. competitors, by the late 1960s, Japan began surpassing its competitors. Major companies like Matsushita, Toshiba, Hitachi, Mitsubishi Electric, Sony, and Sanyo fiercely competed with each other, at first in domestic and then in international markets. The intense competition led to dramatic improvements in design and performance as well as lower manufacturing costs, which in turn sparked further growth throughout the 1970s.

By 1968, Japanese exports of TV, radio, and tape recorders reached $960 million, making Japanese firms the world's leading producers and exporters of these products. By 1980, a little over a decade, their exports of these products jumped to $7.9 billion. The combined exports of TV and radio accounted for almost $5 billion. How did this happen? As soon as the Japanese received a license from the United States to produce transistor radios, they began exporting three-transistor radios to the United States, beginning at first with only one hundred thousand units. By 1963, Japan managed to dominate the radio market. From radio, Japan moved into tape recorders and television. By the end of the 1960s, Japan had conquered these markets as well. In 1973, four of the eleven major TV producers, namely, Admiral, Motorola, Magnavox, and Philip, were forced into merger or acquisition in order to solve market and financial difficulties. Following their TV victory, the Japanese moved into and conquered the videotape recorders and the video-disc market, a business expected to exceed $1 billion annually by the mid-1980s. Today the Japanese enjoy an overwhelming dominance over the entire consumer electronics market.

The Japanese success story is repeated in electric home appliances as well. The appliance industry in Japan became highly competitive

EXPORTS AND IMPORTS OF RADIO AND TV RECEIVERS OF SELECTED COUNTRIES, 1980 (IN MILLIONS OF DOLLARS)

	RADIO			TV		
	Exports	Imports	Of which, from Japan	Exports	Imports	Of which, from Japan
Japan	3,008.9	77.7	—	1,724.7	5.8	—
U.S.A.	90.7	1,679.7	783.0	441.6	691.1	156.9
United Kingdom (1)	52.0	491.3	210.4	126.9	249.1	96.3
W. Germany	283.7	619.7	253.2	1,103.9	427.4	88.2
Italy	31.0	193.8	2.4	174.8	501.3	0.5
Canada	35.2	195.4	58.7	27.2	156.6	21.8
Netherlands	91.6	210.1	42.4	213.3	351.3	13.0
Belgium (2)	172.3	119.6	32.5	307.0	149.9	7.0

Source: U.N., "Commodity Trade Statistics."
Notes: (1) 1979. (2) Including Luxembourg.

as each Japanese company endeavored to carve out its own image for its products. Hitachi, Toshiba, and Mitsubishi, joined by Matsushita, Sanyo, Sharp, and other small producers, marketed their own brands of electric fans, refrigerators, and kitchen gadgets in the domestic market and later in the world market and achieved remarkable growth in sales, outselling their non-Japanese competitors by the 1970s.

In the field of watches and clocks, the Japanese took aim at the Swiss watchmakers, who were number one in the world in the postwar period. Seiko, Citizen, and Orient designed high-precision, high-quality timepieces low in price. Led by Seiko, the Japanese broke into the U.S. market by offering new-product features, pushing the development of the quartz digital watch as an alternative to the mechanical watch. By the 1970s, the Japanese became number one in sales. Such U.S. producers as Texas Instruments, which had plans to dominate the lower-end digital watch market, decided to abandon the market in the early eighties. In the hand calculator market, Casio, Sharp, and others offered various new features and models, such as calculators with melodies, and calculators with clocks. Adopting the strategy of accelerating and shortening product life cycles as well as lowering the price, the Japanese discouraged and outsold their competitors in the hand calculator market.

Japan has also achieved outstanding success in the camera industry. Japan now ranks second after the United States in low-cost cameras. In the field of high-quality, single-lens, reflex cameras, Japan has overtaken Germany, the so-called land of the camera, to become number one, with total exports of $1.29 billion in 1980 (followed by Germany, $0.33; and the United States, $0.28). Nikon, Canon, Pentax, Minolta, and Olympus are among the best-known fine camera makers today. They have had similar success in scientific and optical equipment. The Japanese now dominate this market, with exports of $4.5 billion in 1980, jumping from only $372 million in 1968.

In two heavy industries—shipbuilding and steel—Japan has achieved outstanding leadership. Japan is the world's leader in shipbuilding, with its costs running 20 to 30 percent lower than those of European shipbuilders. While in 1960 Japan had constructed only 20 percent of world tonnage, by 1975 that percentage had risen to 50.1 percent, with a total of 18 million tons of ships leaving Japanese shipyards. In iron and steel, Japan was the fifth largest producer up to the end of World War II, running behind the United States, Germany, the United Kingdom, and the USSR. By 1953, its production had increased to over 7 million tons compared with a mere 0.5 million tons right after the war, and it surpassed the United States in 1961 and West Germany in 1964. From 1964 to 1973, Japanese steelmakers had reduced the needed labor-hours per ton of steel from 25 to 9 compared with 13 to 10 in the United States. Its blast furnaces had an average size of 1.67 million tons, or twice that of the United States.

These are but a few of the major industries in which the Japanese have achieved world leadership. The end is still not in sight.

Industries Currently under Attack by the Japanese

In areas where Japanese competitiveness is lower than their counterparts', such as in computers, construction, chemicals, pharmaceuticals, and machine tools, they are now making strong inroads to be number one.

Among these, the computer industry is the fiercest battlefront, with the Japanese devoting considerable resources to challenge the world's most-advanced and largest producer, IBM. The recent scandal in which some Japanese companies were caught trying to steal some IBM secrets is the best mirror of their ambition. At a recent national computer conference in Chicago, Japan's display of computer prowess has frightened the U.S. industry leaders. Japanese firms showed a broad spectrum of computer equipment, ranging from over $1 million data-processing centers to $250 pocket computers. The majority of the machines were aimed at the fast-growing market for small desk-top computers selling for under $10,000. The implication is that they are planning to do the same thing that their compatriots, Toyota and Datsun, have done—concentrate first on attacking the less-expensive, small-machine end. In just a few years, the Japanese have moved from nowhere to the number-two position in the world computer market. They have already displaced IBM as the biggest seller in Japan. In the U.S. market, the United States currently holds 80 percent of the market while Japan has 10 percent. Though the U.S. firms are much stronger in sales, Japanese firms are noted for matching U.S. technology and often improving reliability and driving the domestic price down temporarily and making U.S. expansion difficult.

In the semiconductor market, although American firms still dominate the world's market, Japan appears to be mounting an all-out offensive. From out of nowhere, the Japanese managed to take a 40 percent chunk of the world market for 16K RAM semiconductor chips. In the United States, Japanese electronics manufacturers kept concentrating on their 64K RAM marketing, thus creating stiff competition among magnetic media manufacturers as the 64K supplanted the 16K RAM by 1982. Nippon Electronics aimed 60 to 80 percent of its production at the United States. Other Japanese manufacturers in the sweep-stakes include Fujitsu, Hitachi, Toshiba, and Mitsubishi.

In robots and machine tools, Japan is now showing considerable leadership. Japan stands today as the industrial robot capital of the world. An estimated 70 percent or more of the robots currently in use throughout the world are concentrated in Japan. It has been predicted that the robot market will grow at least 20 percent per year, absorbing up to fifty-five thousand units worth over $1.3 billion in 1985, compared with nineteen thousand units worth $350 million produced in 1980. In the machine tool industry, from the 1960s through the first half of the 1970s, Japan's tool industry showed remarkable growth to a position equal to that of other industrialized nations. Its annual production in 1979 was around $833 million, a sixteenfold increase from 1960. In 1982, Japan's output of machine tools finally attained the world's top position by surpassing the United States and West Germany.

It seems that the Japanese never ignore any industrial area with great growth potential. In the past few years, the Japanese have been rapidly expanding their aircraft industry. Through their production license for the F-15 supersonic fighter and separate joint ventures with Boeing and Rolls-Royce, Japanese firms are learning how to produce sophisticated aircraft. Western industrial planners fear that Japan will become the world's leader in industrial science within fifteen years. Japan is also rapidly expanding its export of consumer goods and services. It is the world's largest exporter of soy sauce (Kikkoman) and is

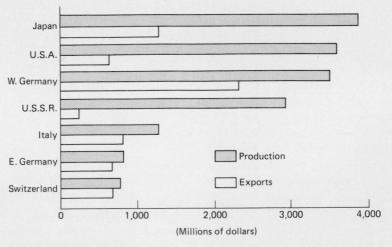

Production and Exports of Machine Tools of Selected Countries, 1982

(Millions of dollars)

Source: *American Machinist.*

increasing its foreign drive into world cosmetics (Shiseido). Japanese hotel interest groups have been building or buying hotels around the world which are noted for their quality and service. And Japan is moving rapidly into world banking, competing vigorously for loans and deposits.

Japanese Direct Investment

These expansive successes of the Japanese have deeply hurt other economies and have led these economies to selectively impose trade restrictions of various kinds on Japanese imports. Not wishing to provoke further trade protectionism, nor lose access to raw material, Japanese firms have responded by considerably augmenting their direct investment in other countries. From continent to continent, Japanese companies are buying up, buying into, or building factories and financial and trading offices. Today Japan's cumulative direct investment stands at over $36 billion, more than half of which has occurred in the past five years alone. The value of Japanese investments in North America in-

Japanese Exports By Principal Commodities

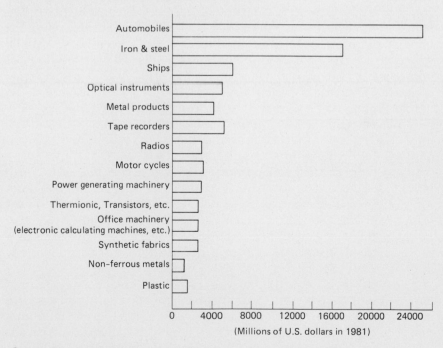

(Millions of U.S. dollars in 1981)

Source: *The Japan of Today* (Japan: Ministry of Foreign Affairs, 1982).

creased from $0.9 billion in 1970 to $9.7 billion in 1981, from $1.0 billion to $6.2 billion in Latin America, and so forth.

It used to be said that when the American economy sneezed, the rest of the world caught a cold. Today this can be said about the Japanese as much as the Americans. The high noon of American supremacy has passed. Someone might argue that this is an exaggeration, but if we consider the whole set of phenomena described above that have taken place in Japan during the past three decades and compare them with Japan's state immediately after the war, it would not be an exaggeration to state that the Japanese have performed a miracle.

Incomplete Explanations of Japan's Success

Many factors have been cited to explain Japan's success. Some argue that the foundation of Japan's success rested on a combined policy of protecting its home market against foreign competition while dumping its goods in foreign markets. With trade protectionism to protect their home market, Japanese companies were able to charge high prices at home and accumulate excess profits that they reinvested in new product and process development and plant expansion. Presumably these companies also received government subsidies, which enabled them to sell their goods abroad at lower prices than at home or even lower than the true costs of producing and selling these goods. This combination of home market protection and foreign dumping has allegedly undermined competitors and established a base toward future monopolization of the market. Zenith Radio Corporation, for example, charged that Japanese television set manufacturers used a "dumping" strategy to enter the U.S. market. At the same time, Zenith could not successfully enter the Japanese market because of trade barriers.

Others argue that Japan's success was largely due to its cheap labor costs. According to an American business leader: "Japan's tremendous gains in the auto export sector can be attributed to the lower wages paid auto workers. Companies such as Nissan and Toyota currently reap the benefits of high productivity, while they pay wages as if those workers were employed in an auto industry with the productivity level of Mexico, Spain, or at best, Italy."

Still others argue that Japan's success was due more to luck and happenstance than to its superior capabilities. A U.S. auto executive noted that Japanese cars were going nowhere in the United States until the price of oil shot up. Had fuel costs not escalated, most Americans would still be driving large cars. The Japanese companies were doubly lucky that U.S. automakers responded slowly, and triply lucky that Detroit's first small cars were poorly designed.

Good fortune and happenstance have indeed played a role. Similarly, no one can deny that Japan's cheap labor in the past played a role, but this hardly holds true today, especially if total labor costs are actually higher and if other costs—raw material, land, etc.—are substantially higher. The Japanese have employed a policy of trade protectionism and dumping in the past but that policy is less relevant today. Furthermore, these same techniques have been used by many developing nations to open up export possibilities, but without the same results obtained in Japan.

An ancient Chinese strategist, Sun Tsu, once observed: "Know the enemy and know yourself; in a hundred battles you will never be in a peril. When you are ignorant of the enemy but know yourself, your chance of winning or losing are equal. If ignorant of both your enemy and yourself, you are certain in every battle to be in peril." If any nation, developed or underdeveloped, or any individual corporation hopes to meet the challenge of the Japanese, there is little to be gained by incomplete analysis and partial explanation. Instead, such nations and corporations should be prepared to evaluate thoroughly and incisively the factors that have contributed to Japan's success and the factors in their own marketing profile that prevent them from competing successfully with the Japanese.

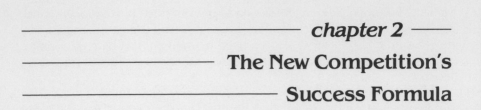

chapter 2 ——

—— The New Competition's

—— Success Formula

We saw evidence for the "Japanese miracle" in Chapter 1, and we must now try to understand it. In recent years, the media have proliferated endless stories on the Japanese miracle, addressing such questions as Why have the Japanese been so successful? How did they do it? How did the United States and Western European nations lose their competitive edge? Can they regain their leadership and, if so, how? Clearly, one must understand the roots of Japanese success in order to know how to deal with it.

Several learned explanations have been advanced. Many scholars attribute the economic miracle to Japanese cultural characteristics, particularly that of "consensus." The phrase "Japan, Inc." expresses the idea that Japan is a consensual society in which government, political parties, industry leaders, workers, and citizens cooperate for the common good. Eugene Kaplan, for example, strongly attributed Japan's phenomenal success to this extraordinary level of cooperation for the common good.

Some scholars have emphasized the supportive behavior of the Japanese institutions in Japan's success. Alexander K. Young has described the role of the Japanese trading companies in facilitating the rapid expansion of Japanese manufacturing and exporting. Chalmers Johnson has described the contributions of the Japanese government through the Ministry of International Trade and Industry (MITI) in masterminding Japan's high economic growth rate. Hugh Patrick, on the other hand, thinks the role of these institutions has been exaggerated and ascribes Japan's strong economic performance primarily to the actions and efforts of private entrepreneurs responding to the opportunities provided in free markets for commodities and labor rather than the supporting role of Japanese institutions.

The most prevalent explanations in the past few years have stressed the role of Japanese managerial style, practices, and strategies. Various authors cite such management characteristics as "lifetime employment," "bottom-up decision-making process," "seniority wage system," "Zen and the art of management," "quality circles," "workers' unions," and "just-in-time production" to explain the Japanese competitive edge.

In contrast to single-factor or limited explanations, we believe that the Japanese success must be understood as the result of a complex

THE JAPANESE SUCCESS MODEL

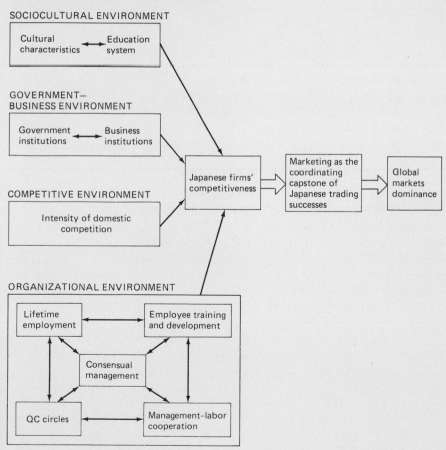

interplay of several important factors. These factors make up the Japanese Success Model and can be classified into four environments, namely, the *sociocultural environment*, the *government-business environment*, the *competitive environment*, and the *organizational environment*. The factors in each environment have contributed to the supercompetitiveness of Japanese companies. Their supercompetitiveness, along with their marketing strategy orientation, has enabled them to achieve dominance in several of the world's most important markets.

We will examine each environment in turn, starting with the sociocultural environment.

SOCIOCULTURAL ENVIRONMENT

Many observers have pointed to Japanese cultural characteristics and Japan's educational system as contributing greatly to Japanese global business strength. We will now examine these factors.

Cultural Characteristics

The culture and personality of a people play an important role in the way they conduct their business. This is especially true of the Japanese, whose business ethos and practices are so closely related to their special cultural characteristics. Their cultural characteristics are to some extent explainable in terms of their land and climate. Japan's scarce agricultural land and mineral resources, its uncertain climate, its natural calamities such as earthquakes, and its long episodes of warfare have profoundly shaped the cultural outlook of the people into a "survival psychology." As a result, the Japanese have a common purpose that pervades their business activity: to overcome life-threatening difficulties in their environment by dedicating themselves to their country and their particular company. To survive is a driving force in the Japanese culture, and it has led to many specific cultural traits that have been integrated into the Japanese ways of doing business.

Among the several cultural traits that observers have pointed out as conferring a special strength in business on the part of the Japanese are the following.

A strong sense of belonging to a group and community. The Japanese derive their sense of self from the groups to which they belong, particularly their community, procreative and nuclear families, and their corporation. As Japanese people, their nationalism is extremely strong.

As family members, they are very devoted to their parents and their wives and children. As workers or managers, they are extremely proud of their companies. They often have little life outside their company, and when they retire, the shock is great. In losing their group, they lose to some extent the sense that they "exist." This is in contrast to Westerners, who feel they have a "self" separate from the various groups to which they belong.

A tendency toward self-effacement and responsibility to the group. In contrast to Western managers who strive for individual distinction and credit for accomplishment, Japanese managers want to avoid "standing out." They do not grab for leadership roles or boast of individual accomplishment. Decisions are arrived at by various members of the group who reflect on proposals and give their assent or suggestions. Therefore the group, rather than the individual, is responsible for the decision. This characteristic leads to a consensual or management system in Japanese companies, as will be discussed later.

A strong sense of "we" versus "they." From this strong sense of loyalty to their group, it follows that the Japanese will see the world as "we" versus "they." Those outside their group are strangers or outsiders. This is why Japanese companies will compete so hard with other companies in their industry. And yet these companies will also cooperate when they face foreign companies. When the Japanese set their collective mind on a goal, there is little that can stop them. They are totally dedicated and cooperate with each other to realize the goal. In the case of economic goals, they go for the highest productivity, the highest product quality, and world domination of certain industries.

A willingness to work hard and persevere toward long-range goals. The Japanese will work very hard to produce the desired results for their group so as not to "lose face." They will sacrifice today's pleasures in order to promote their group's long-run interests. Underlying this is a strong sense of obligation and gratitude for having been accepted as members of the group. The Japanese have a strong sense of duty (*giri*) and returning favors (the norm of reciprocity) to others. When their company falls into difficult times, Japanese managers and workers will frequently sacrifice their short-term benefits for the sake of the company's survival in the long run. They take the long-run view and totally support their companies' objectives.

A strong belief that competence increases with seniority. The Japanese tradition calls for respect for one's elders based on a belief in their great knowledge and kindness. Children grow up with a deferential attitude toward authority figures. In the work situation, the Japanese assume that the more senior people have more wisdom based on their longer experience. They know that they will get better at their work and command the respect of younger workers in time.

Educational System

Education is another important contributor to Japan's phenomenal success. For a nation, no other resource is more valuable than well-trained and highly educated people. In physical resources, Japan is poor, but in human resources, it is rich. Japanese leaders have long regarded education as one of the major tools for building the nation's wealth.

Not only is education highly valued but it is also extremely competitive. University entrance examinations determine which institution of higher learning the student will attend. Since the more prestigious Japanese employers primarily recruit from only the "top schools," such as Tokyo University and Kyoto University, Japanese students experience what is characterized as "examination hell." The pressure is supreme, and suicides among high-school students occur with more frequency in Japan than in most other cultures. The educational system has taken the place of the ancient feudal system in terms of establishing the society's social hierarchy. After graduation, the students will be recruited for jobs through a highly competitive hiring system.

The largest Japanese corporations maintain a fairly standardized recruiting process for university graduates. In *The Modern Samurai Society*, Mitsuyuki Masatsugu explains:

> The company starts sending out its introductory brochure as early as January or February of, say, 1982 to the short list of students to be graduated from first-rate universities the following year. The brochure is intended to attract these undergraduates when hiring takes place in October and November for April of 1983. Only the brightest students are the target at this time of year. The undergraduates select their first and second choices, and perhaps third choices, too. In accordance with the rules of the Ministry of Labor, from October 1 onward, students may make formal inquiry visits to firms. The companies can then officially start their recruitment for the coming year.
>
> Further selection tests and interviews are scheduled for November, but excellent candidates are usually interviewed unofficially and secretly reserved by the companies before October. Such preliminary contact or active recruitment before October 1 is called aotagari (cropping while the rice field is still green). In 1982 the Ministry of Labor relinquished its control over aotagari because the practice had become so widespread behind the scenes. Ministry officials left the situation to a gentlemen's agreement between universities and the industrial society.
>
> Nonetheless, some companies do engage in aotagari behind the scenes by having employees who are alumni of the best schools lure the brightest students over drinks and talk. Those candidates who make every company's mouth water are, of course, the top-notch students

from a sharply limited number of universities who have won a victory over the notorious "examination hell." This group, which includes future high-ranking civil servants, comprises about 3 to 4 percent of the 300,000 new graduates each year.

High-school graduates, on the other hand, are drawn from a much broader geographical range than are the university graduates. Since the more able high-school graduates seek a university education, the high schools are the major source of future production-level, factory-based personnel.

The strong educational system has helped to create the world's most-literate and best-educated population. These highly educated work forces, both white and blue collar, have helped to push Japanese companies to the forefront of world productivity and economic success.

GOVERNMENT-BUSINESS ENVIRONMENT

Postwar politics were significantly influenced by the U.S. Occupation which did not end until 1952, after the establishment of the Japanese-American security structure and the signing of the peace treaty. The period of Occupation was one of numerous reforms. Among these reforms were the revision of the Constitution, the dissolution of the large industrial conglomerates that comprised the Zaibatsu, the political enfranchisement of women, the establishment of the six-three-three system of education, the enforcement of thorough land reform policies, and the establishment of several government institutions and agencies as political tools for accelerating postwar economic growth.

Government Institutions

Through various government agencies established during the immediate postwar period, the Japanese government has aided business in instituting strategic policies and performing services of "administrative guidance." Of these agencies, the one that plays the major role is the Ministry of International Trade and Industry (MITI). American scholars, such as Vogel, have stated that "the key Japanese ministries like MITI have a sense of responsibility for the overall success of Japanese industries in their particular sector. Their job is not to dictate to industry but to work with knowledgeable people in the industries to provide the external environment conducive to a Japanese company's long-term success."

Lockwood adds, "This is the economics by admonition to a degree inconceivable in Washington or London. Business makes few decisions without consulting the appropriate governmental authority."

To understand this relationship, one needs a historic perspective. MITI was founded in 1949 through the transformation of the prewar Ministry of Commerce and Industry and its wartime successor, the Ministry of Munitions. Its major objective has been to strengthen the competitive position of Japanese industry. This, in turn, would lead to economic growth. For example, once the heavy equipment and chemical industries had been targeted as potential catalysts of economic growth, resources and necessary guidance were channeled into these sectors. As Japan's economy grew and more liberal trade policies emerged, MITI began to stress the importance of industrial reorganization in order to increase Japan's ability to compete with the United States and other countries in world markets.

In the mid-1950s, MITI promoted exports as a means of addressing Japan's imbalance of payments. The Supreme Export Council, as well as the Japan External Trade Organization (JETRO), an international commercial intelligence service, was established for this purpose. One of the keys to the Japanese success has been the marketing intelligence provided by government agencies to prepare Japanese firms for export expansion.

Here is a typical scenario of how the government aids industry: The government initially targets an industry as being critically important to the overall economic well-being of the country. The government then undertakes an in-depth assessment of the industry's needs and strategic requirements. Funding is provided by the Japan Development Bank, and licenses are granted for the importation of new technologies. Accelerated depreciation schedules for investment, tax incentives, infrastructure development, and, finally, administrative guidance are pursued to regulate and coordinate the individual firms within the industry. Another step is to develop direct and indirect trade barriers to protect the domestic industry.

One of the key factors underlying the "Japanese miracle" is the government-business "partnership." While in many Western nations, government intervention in corporate affairs is unwelcome or distrusted, the Japanese companies have cultivated a more positive view of such relationships. In Japan, the public and private sectors work in concert enabling the Japanese to achieve the economic objectives that other cultures have failed to attain.

It may appear that Japan has played an unfair game through the utilization of this government-business relationship. But other countries—such as France and West Germany—also show varying degrees of government participation and cooperation.

Japan has thoughtfully incorporated government participation into business planning to help create and sustain its competitive advantage. Japanese business-people view this relationship as being totally sensible, and they see any industry or firm that does not nurture such relationships as trying to assemble a giant jigsaw puzzle without first making certain that all the pieces have been included.

Business Institutions

An important Japanese business institution, the "industrial group," consists of three major entities: the general trading companies (sogo shosha), the banks, and the manufacturing base.

The most striking aspect of a Japanese industrial group—in addition to its size, composition, and magnitude of resources—is the rare degree of functional specialization and cooperation that exists among members. By specializing in domestic and international distribution, finance, and manufacturing, the group is able to achieve certain economies in the areas of marketing, information gathering, distribution, finance, and raw materials acquisition. An industrial group does three things: First, it greatly expands the capabilities/options of the firms, particularly medium-sized establishments; second, it allows Japanese manufacturers to concentrate primarily on their product development and manufacturing operations; and third, it reduces the risk of new ventures because of group support and financing. In contrast, U.S. firms must develop complete capabilities in finance, marketing, distribution, and planning in pursuing their strategies.

We will now examine more closely each of the three entities making up the industrial group.

General trading companies. The Japanese general trading companies (GTCs) are among the most unusual trading organizations in the world. Acting largely as general contractors, the *sogo shosha* play a major role as facilitators of world trade and trade development. The trading companies have also played significant roles in helping many non-Japanese firms become partners in numerous large-scale projects around the world, although they do concentrate primarily on structuring projects with Japanese partners.

In 1980, the nine largest sogo shosha handled an almost infinite number of products ranging from soybeans to aircraft. They accounted for 48.7 percent of Japan's total exports and 56 percent of Japan's total imports. These nine firms totaled over $300 billion in product turnover in 1980. The general trading companies coordinate projects in both the free-world and the Communist bloc countries. Because their volume of business is so great, they have fully developed channels of distribution, warehousing, and marketing procedures for both import and export markets.

The general trading companies provide Japanese manufacturers with up-to-date, precise market information that they would typically not have the resources to secure. They provide detailed information bearing on inventory control, production planning, capital investment, raw material supplies, and country demand and price differentials. Japanese firms can use this information to prepare detailed global strategies. The sogo shosha have been characterized as being a modern leviathan of global communication rivaling the U.S. Pentagon in terms of global reach and significance.

Even though the general trading companies are not financial institutions in the usual sense, they do provide an important financial function in certain industries. Acting as a financial intermediary between the banks and the domestic manufacturer, the sogo shosha are able to arrange loans and loan guarantees to their clients for both the short term and the long term. This tight relationship with the banking industry allows the general trading companies to offer financing packages in the billions of dollars for resource development, manufacturing projects, and trade deals.

Perhaps the greatest service that the trading companies render the Japanese manufacturer is that of risk absorption. The international business environment is risk filled due to problems in currency exchange, different customs from country to country, and language variations, as well as economic and political uncertainties. Through their broad exposure to international markets, the general trading companies can reduce these risks. This risk reduction, in turn, increases the probability of profitability for those firms associated with the GTCs. Through their information network, the GTCs can react with greater confidence when there are significant alterations within any particular industries or countries. Consequently, trading companies have been a key institution in Japan's rapid economic development.

The financial base. The banking industry is another major institution involved in Japanese industrial groups. During the 1950s, the Japanese government adopted an expansionist industrial policy in their campaign to stimulate economic growth. Heavy machinery and equipment industries were targeted as sectors that should receive a significant portion of the available capital, since expansion was thought to be linked to the development of higher technologies and capital-intensive industries. Funds were also needed to repair and replace factories and the basic infrastructure that had been destroyed during the war.

In the postwar period, over 60 percent of the needed capital came from commercial banks' advances; 25 percent was raised through retained profits and the depreciation of assets; and only 10 to 12 percent came from stock and bond issues. As a result of the importance of bank loans, the larger Japanese firms began to group around certain major city banks. Between 1955 and 1962, these banks channeled over 75 percent of their total loans to these larger firms. This preferential loan policy resulted in groups of industrially diversified firms centering around a particular bank as a nucleus. The most powerful groups were centered on four banks: Fuji Bank, Mitsubishi Bank, Mitsui Bank, and Sumitomo Bank. Firms that found themselves in the same banking group tended to do business with each other whenever possible. When the Tokyu Corporation, which operated several mass-transit lines in the Tokyo metropolitan area, needed new electric fans for its train cars, it purchased Toshiba Fans; both Toshiba and Tokyu are part of the same Mitsui banking group. Although these banking groups are not as powerful as they once were, their influence is still a factor when doing business in Japan.

In the mid-1960s, of 671 major Japanese companies, approximately half of them obtained 20 to 40 percent of their total bank loans from a single city bank. This reflects the close relationship that had developed between the larger industrial firms and the larger city banks. Each of these banks tried to strengthen its membership by providing the funds required for capacity expansion, as well as for entry into potential high-growth fields such as chemicals and automobiles.

The Japanese government also played an important role in providing funds to private businesses through its two-tiered structure of government-guaranteed loan supports to the major city banks as well as through government-owned banks such as the Japan Development Bank. In addition, the Bank of Japan played a role in determining the availability of funds for industrial loans available through commercial banks.

Without having to rely on funds obtained from shareholders, as was the case in the West, Japanese firms were able to discount the importance of short-term profitability. As a result, the Japanese corporation could concentrate on plant, machinery, and equipment investments, long-term product development, and research and development. These comparative advantages enabled the Japanese to improve their productivity, technologies, and position in world markets.

Nissan Motor Company is representative of the firms that relied heavily on debt for their financing. At the end of 1975, Nissan's debt totaled $1.1 billion with an equity/asset ratio of 27.9 percent. The major lenders to Nissan included the Industrial Bank of Japan, 15 percent; the Fuji Bank group, 14 percent; the Sumitomo Bank group, 12 percent; the Sanwa Bank group, 6 percent; and the Mitsubishi group, 5 percent. This financing through debt enabled Nissan to expand its production capacity with heavy investments in plant and equipment without the short-term pressure from shareholders. As a result, Nissan has become one of the world's largest automobile manufacturers, with superb productivity and advanced technology in its manufacturing operations.

The manufacturing base. Japanese manufacturers are aided considerably by trade associations, which can be found in almost every industry. These trade associations encourage increased communication and information exchange among their members. In addition, the associations are often responsible for establishing industry quality standards. Perhaps the most important function of these associations, however, is the establishment of *priorities*. In defining priorities, member firms discuss output targets, raw material sourcing, and supplier-related problems and opportunities. All of these functions aid the member firms in the formulation of strategy, and consequently the industries are able to achieve more competitive positions vis-á-vis world markets.

      Another interesting aspect of the Japanese manufacturing base is the supplier-manufacturer relationship that exists. Instead of sourcing through numerous suppliers, the typical Japanese manufacturer utilizes only one to three suppliers for any component part or raw material need. American firms, by contrast, often utilize more suppliers and have less power over each supplier than do the Japanese. Nearly all Japanese second-tier suppliers commit over 75 percent of their capacity to one manufacturer. Not uncommonly, the manufacturer will have a significant equity position in its suppliers. Even if the manufacturer does not hold equity in the supplying firm, members of its upper-management team will often sit as directors on the supplying firm's board. This relatively high degree of control allows the major Japanese manufacturers to achieve greater flexibility in the production process than do their Western counterparts.

COMPETITIVE ENVIRONMENT

The conclusion of World War II marked the end of one of Japan's most powerful commercial coalitions: the Zaibatsu. The Zaibatsu was a coalition of businesses that exercised monopolistic control and influence over virtually all business activity throughout the country.

Hundreds of companies that had previously been subsidiaries of the powerful Zaibatsu were now independent entities competing with each other in the domestic marketplace. The increased demand for consumer and producer goods attracted many new entrants into the various industries. Existing firms found it difficult to raise sufficient barriers to entry. Price leadership, interfirm agreements restricting output, and other strategies associated with oligopolistic industries were not present. Subsequently, during the 1950–64 period, the concentration ratio declined in such industries as textiles, machinery, steel, and electronics.

The intense domestic competition provided the Japanese with the opportunity to formulate and test different production and marketing strategies in their attempt to remain competitive. This competition helped the Japanese to sharpen their competitive instinct. The weaker and less-competitive firms were forced out of the market or were forced to merge with other firms into larger corporations. Firms were encouraged by MITI to merge in order to strengthen their position in global markets. For example, the camera industry went from over five hundred separate companies in the postwar period to only seven large firms today. During the 1970s, nearly fifty Japanese companies produced portable calculators; today only Sharp, Casio, Canon, and Toshiba remain in competition for control of over 90 percent of Japan's calculator market. In the steel industry, only four of the eleven firms that existed immediately following the war are in business today.

Another factor in Japan's competitive strength is that many of its production facilities are significantly more modern than the production facilities of competing countries. This is especially true of capital-intensive industries such as steel, machinery, and automobiles. The Japanese have benefited from their careful study and analysis of Western firms that had been competing in certain industries prior to their entry. The Japanese were able to move out quickly on the respective industry learning curves, allowing them to avoid mistakes that others had made before them. Japan's competitive sharpening on the home front greatly contributed to its miraculous competitiveness in world markets.

ORGANIZATIONAL ENVIRONMENT

In recent years, numerous studies have emphasized the contribution of the Japanese system of management to the Japanese economic miracle. Some American professors of business administration have begun recommending that U.S. companies remodel their management systems along Japanese lines. We will consider four of the most important elements: lifetime employment, employee training and development, consensual management, and labor-management cooperation. Ironically, some of the elements were copied from the Western world.

Lifetime Employment

Lifetime employment is one of the most publicized but least understood elements of the Japanese management system. The concept of life-long employment emerged during the 1912–26 Taisho period. At that time, the firm pledged its loyalty to its employees in exchange for their loyalty and increased cooperation. In 1926, the average life expectancy was forty-four years. Today a firm that offers lifetime employment is clearly offering more than its counterpart in 1926, since the average life expectancy is seventy-three years.

During the Occupation, lifetime employment became truly entrenched in the Japanese corporate system. In an effort to stabilize the fluctuating rate of employment, U.S. forces persuaded the larger Japanese corporations to establish minimum levels of lifelong-employed workers in order to create a more solid base on which to reestablish themselves after the war. Today approximately 20 percent of the work force (thus not everyone) is in the lifetime employment system.

Lifetime employment offers the firm several advantages. The firm is assured a constant supply of labor that can be trained without losing the "investment" to another firm. The realization that certain individuals will be employed for an extended period of time helps the company in its efforts to fully indoctrinate new employees into the firm's particular corporate culture. The workers, in turn, feel more loyal to the firm and see their prosperity as being tied up with the firm's prosperity.

Of course, there are also potential problems with the system. During times of recession or decreased demand, the firm cannot remove the part of its work force that is protected under lifelong employment. The Japanese worker ironically pays a price for this benefit. The manager who wishes to transfer to another firm will have to start at the bottom of the new firm. Lateral transfers are therefore rare in Japan. Furthermore, employees receive promotions as their seniority increases. Very able workers and managers have to wait their turn; there are no "fast trackers."

Employee Training and Development

In developing factory workers and management trainees, the Japanese provide continuing education and broad exposure to various functions. Japanese workers will move from machine to machine in order to become better acquainted with the total flow in their respective plant. This rotation theme is partly responsible for the amazing reduction in setup times that the Japanese firms have realized over the past twenty years. And Japanese managers will move through various functions— manufacturing, sales, purchasing, and finance—to learn the business. Thus a marketing manager will be better able to communicate with manufacturing people because of his own background in manufacturing.

Consensual Management

As a people, the Japanese are highly group-oriented. In the process of decision making, every effort is made to reach a consensus. This consensus orientation typically results in longer than normal planning horizons within the typical Japanese corporate environment. Although the decision-making process requires more time, implementation is achieved with relative ease. The Japanese are considered superb implementors of policy, resulting from the fact that most of the major participants have been included in the decision-making process from the beginning.

The consensual style of decision making in Japan takes on a form in the larger Japanese corporations known as the *ringi* system. *Ringi* is a term composed of two basic elements: "rin" means to submit a proposal to one's superior and to receive approval, and "gi" means deliberation and decision. In combination, the term describes a confirmation/authorization that ensures that all elements of disagreement have been eliminated and that an optimal cooperative effort can be achieved.

When a decision must be made, a lower-echelon employee will draft a plan or proposal called *ringisho*. This ringisho is circulated to those various sections of the firm that will be involved in the proposal's implementation. After each respective manager has affixed his seal or stamp of approval, the proposal will be delivered to the president. Once the president has approved it, the decision is made. If the original proposal is not approved by the president or any of the preceding managers, it is withdrawn and revised. In practice, however, the informal approval of all individuals involved is sought prior to the circulation of the ringisho document. Because most of the management echelons extensively participate in the process of decision making under the ringisho system, "responsibility," "coordination," and "dedication" to accomplish the company's goals are thus deeply rooted in their minds and, in turn, enhance the effectiveness of implementation once decisions have been made.

Labor-Management Cooperation

Japan's impressive labor-management cooperation is widely admired throughout the world. Workers rarely strike as compared with those in other industrial nations. The Japanese do not view hiring as being simply the procurement of an additional unit of labor; instead, hiring a new employee is viewed as admitting a new member into a larger family called the company. From the employee's point of view, work is considered a major part of one's lifetime development and a responsibility rather than an unpleasant duty.

The "company as family" in Japan is the result of religious, economic, and social factors. Zen Buddhism stresses the philosophy of "work as a way for people to deepen and further develop their lives and to give tribute to the Supreme God." Economically, Japan's lack of natural resources has contributed to a sense of insecurity and therefore encourages greater cooperation at every level. And socially, Japan is a nation where "groupism" predominates. The Japanese value their ties to groups very strongly. For the Japanese, working is not merely a way to earn money; it is a mode of entry and dedication to a larger social unit. Japanese employees have a strong bond of loyalty to their companies. Labor unions are formed within companies, and they have a fundamentally cooperative attitude toward management:

> In Japan, unions and companies are in a sort of partnership. Labor relations with management are essentially human relations as opposed to contractual. Efforts are made by each party to understand the other position and to achieve a careful balance that reflects the needs and desires of both sides . . .

Japanese employees do not view their company as an oppressor, but rather an expression of their place in society. Many Japanese managers would sacrifice some current salary if they could present the business card of a more-prestigious firm when they make introductions. The Japanese see themselves as permanent members of a certain company, and this close association fosters a sense of responsibility and concern between management and labor.

Quality Control (QC) Circles

In the late 1970s, the term *QC circles* meant little to Western business-people. Today it is receiving growing acceptance worldwide as a key management tool in upgrading worker productivity and product quality.

The Japanese QC circles are, in fact, a modification and extension of the quality control concept originated in Western economies. While the Western concept of quality control held that success in quality control strongly lay with managers and engineers, the Japanese added the notion that blue-collar workers could also play a significant role in improving product quality and productivity. The Japanese broadened the concept to the so-called total quality control or quality control (QC) circles that involve blue-collar workers from the production lines as well as employees outside the factory such as product designers, marketing and sale staffs, and R&D staffs. The underlying belief is that company-wide quality control cannot be achieved without the participation of the blue-collar workers. Consequently, small groups of factory foremen and workers have been organized (so-called QC circles) in order to partici-pate, discuss, and work together to upgrade productivity and improve product quality, as well as to seek ways to reduce costs and improve customer service.

Because the Japanese strongly believe in the norm of reciprocity (returning favors), and because of their strong sense of duty (*giri*), when these blue-collar workers have been trusted and valued by their com-pany, they work with great attention, responsibility, and pride. The re-sults have been steady and substantial increases in productivity and product quality.

MARKETING: THE MISSING LINK

Clearly, Japan's phenomenal economic performance cannot be attrib-uted to any one factor. Japan's group orientation, education system, government-industry partnership, industrial groups and trading com-panies, intense internal competition, consensus management, lifetime employment, QC circles, job rotation, labor-management cooperation, protected home market, and other factors all figured in its Success Model. Companies in the West cannot hope to duplicate this unique combination of factors. Nor can they automatically achieve success by copying a few elements. Nevertheless, Western companies need to study these factors and consider adopting those that can add value and be fused with the business environment that operates in the West.

While the foregoing factors positioned Japan for strong global competitiveness, this competitiveness was not enough. Strategy, particularly marketing strategy, is also essential. Without it, many of the other advantages disappear. Consider the following:

> In 1959, the Japanese automakers like Nissan and Toyota, after strengthening their domestic market, tried to expand their market by entering the United States. The result was market failure and the Japanese cars were withdrawn from the market in a very short time.

> When Sony first developed tape recorders and recording tape, its company founders thought they could easily make a fortune. Once they started producing the first Japanese tape recorders, they found that they couldn't run the business unless they had the capability to market their products.

Despite its importance, the role of Japanese marketing is still being underrated by American scholars and businesspeople. Competitiveness alone does not bring out economic and trade success, nor does marketing. Only the combination of these two factors does.

When a company wants to play an offensive role in the world marketplace, the marketing edge is a key factor in determining which companies will win. In offensive marketing warfare, an indispensable ingredient is the ability to attack the opponent's mind and strategies. Japan's trade success over the past two decades is the best evidence of this. Japan realized early the crucial role of strategic market planning and made an all-out effort to study and implement the latest marketing concepts and techniques. In the next chapter, we will describe the role of Japanese marketing as the "coordinating capstone" of its global success.

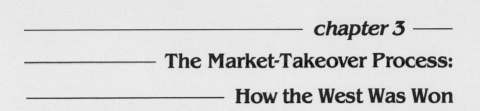

chapter 3 ──

── The Market-Takeover Process:

── How the West Was Won

In 1958, Toyota sold only 288 cars in the United States, but on the twentieth anniversary of its market entry, the company was selling at the rate of five hundred thousand vehicles per year. Toyota became the leading U.S. automobile importer, surpassing its major competitor, Volkswagen, in 1975. In the early 1980s, Toyota became the second-largest manufacturer of motor vehicles, with annual production in excess of 3 million vehicles.

This chapter will examine the "role of marketing" and will demonstrate that effective marketing skills and excellent marketing strategies, consistently applied, have been a major foundation of the Japanese triumph.

The role of marketing has been evident at two levels. First, the Japanese government used marketing analysis to evaluate and select national industries worthy of special treatment and development, industries with expected superior investment returns and international trade benefits over a sustained period. Second, the individual firms within these "target" industries have used the right marketing concepts to design effective corporate strategies for winning markets.

One target industry, automobile manufacturing, has been selected in this chapter to illustrate the critical role of marketing in the Japanese strategic approach. We will analyze the factors that enabled the Japanese auto industry to move from its weak state in the 1950s to global dominance in the 1980s. We will describe the underlying strategic marketing-planning model that the Japanese have used in this and in other industries to achieve success. The overall model will be described here, and its components will be examined in greater detail in later chapters.

The objective of this analysis is to compare Japan's basic strategic marketing philosophy with that of the United States. A fundamental understanding of these issues will lead to recommendations, presented in the final chapters, which Western corporations can use to cope with, and effectively compete against, the Japanese challenge.

HOW THE JAPANESE GOVERNMENT PAVED THE WAY FOR THE JAPANESE AUTOMAKERS

We will start by documenting the critical role played by the Japanese government in assisting the development of the Japanese automobile industry. The Japanese government took early steps to strengthen the domestic auto industry and subsequently adopted other measures to encourage Japanese auto manufacturers to export their cars.

Strengthening the Domestic Motor Vehicle Industry

Government concern for the viability of the Japanese automobile industry was evident even before World War II. Ford (1925) and General Motors (1927) built plants in Japan with a combined capacity of about eighteen thousand vehicles per year. Both companies also established extensive dealership networks and supported rapid development by financing approximately 75 percent of all sales.

These moves by the American companies hurt Japanese automakers and contributed to Japan's deteriorating balance of trade. Unable to compete, one Japanese company was pushed into bankruptcy, and three other companies were saved only by the demand for military trucks. In 1931, the Japanese Ministry of Commerce and Industry created the Committee for the Establishment of the Automobile Industry to formulate a plan for viable domestic vehicle production. Government protection for Japanese automobile manufacturers had begun.

In 1936, the Japanese government limited Ford's and GM's annual production, and import tariffs were raised to 70 percent for completed vehicles. These measures, together with the semiwartime conditions following the China incident, forced Ford and GM to close their Japanese operations in 1939.

In the immediate years following World War II, the American Occupation forces instituted a program known as "Operation Roll-Up" designed to recover and rehabilitate equipment that had been abandoned throughout the Pacific by the hasty demobilization of U.S. forces. Several Japanese auto companies, including Toyota, Nissan, and Fiji, were ordered to rebuild military vehicles by the American authorities.

These American military-supervised production operations provided the Japanese with fundamental knowledge of American mass-production techniques and a means to bridge the huge technology gap that existed vis-á-vis other nations. "Operation Roll-Up" trained Japanese engineers, mechanics, and laborers in the latest production layouts and methods, effective equipment selection usage, and quality control concepts.

As an example of the size of this program, in the Fuji plant of Oppama, 187,000 units were rebuilt over a ten-year period until, by 1958, the plant had earned 18 billion yen ($50 million) from its operations.

In 1949, the Japanese government established a new policy to foster the automobile industry. The government chose automobiles as one of the key target industries to develop for its export potential. The automobile industry was seen as being closely aligned to the fledgling domestic steel and machine tool industries, and thus to industry in general. It was expected to provide a logical synergy between the resources Japan could import and the value it expected to add before export. In the government's paper *Industrial Rationalization*, the role of the auto industry was seen as an integral part of the development of the economy as a whole.

The first step was to protect the domestic auto industry from outside competition. Over time, four different protectionist measures were adopted:

1. *Import tariffs.* An import duty was set on imported passenger cars of 40 percent, and on commercial vehicles and parts, 30 percent. This held until 1968.

2. *Foreign currency regulations.* When in the early 1950s there seemed to be a threat that foreign-made cars would succeed in overcoming the 40 percent import duty barrier because home-produced cars were still expensive and technology was not very advanced, stringent currency regulations were introduced along with general import restrictions. These remained in force during the Japanese depression from 1954 to 1957.

3. *Commodity tax.* To focus the Japanese automobile industry's efforts on small cars (to keep down oil import requirements), the government imposed a commodity tax in 1959 with the following rates:

Engine Size	Commodity Tax
Less than 2000 cc.	15%
2001–3000 cc.	30%
Over 3000 cc.	50%

4. *Control of foreign investment.* Automatic approval of foreign capital participation in existing Japanese enterprises was subject to a limit of 7 percent for an individual and 20 percent in total, beyond which special dispensation was required. This measure was designed to prevent foreign corporations from acquiring control and then benefiting from the rich rewards the Japanese government believed would be forthcoming.

Stimulating Exports

In the eyes of Japanese policy makers, international trade is critical because Japan lacks its own natural resources. Imports required for domestic consumption must be paid for with offsetting exports. As a populous nation, the volume of exports necessary for balanced trade, and the inherent need to trade globally, have focused Japanese attention on industries with significant scale economies and which together comprise a consistent, logical flow of resources into the country for later export with value added.

The automobile industry met these criteria handsomely. Economies of scale not only exist but are especially important in this industry, whose products are infrequently purchased and whose customers are scattered instead of concentrated. Using basic marketing research and forecasting techniques, the Japanese government foresaw tremendous growth in worldwide automobile market demand with plenty of room for additional competitors.

As a result of the prewar dominance of U.S. automobiles in Japan, and the postwar training by the American military, Japanese car designs were readily adaptable to the tastes of Western nations and the attractive U.S. market in particular. Tapping this world market potential would also provide the means to support domestic market growth, which would otherwise require vehicle importation and a significant outflow of foreign currency.

To encourage exports, the Japanese government relied on three classic measures:

1. *Incentives and rewards.* Predominantly financial, these incentives included rapid depreciation and other taxation advantages. For example, companies could write off 150 percent of any investment made for export promotion.

2. *Direct assistance.* These measures included government-inspected quality control over exports, financing, and export insurance. Companies that

failed to meet high standards of product quality were denied export licenses. Automobile manufacturers were among the first Japanese industries to apply Edward Deming's statistical quality control procedures in the operation.

Financing measures provided plenty of risk capital at low rates, and banks were encouraged to hold equity in automobile companies. The Bank of Japan stood ready with 3 percent loan guarantees to support these efforts. Finally, insurance was available to protect companies from the first three or four years of losses in export operations.

3. *Support measures.* Several Japanese government departments stood ready to gather, collate, and disseminate world economic and market research statistics free of charge. Teams of government consultants were available to advise industry in a process Vogel described as meritocratic. In addition, MITI acted to upgrade the low technical level of domestic producers by facilitating the licensing of Japanese automakers for the knockdown assembly of imported cars of foreign manufacturers such as GM and Ford.

This type of support has continued in varying degrees ever since, and the efficiency of these efforts in relation to the Japanese penetration of the U.S. automobile industry cannot be questioned. Prior to 1955, imports' deepest penetration of the U.S. market was less than two hundred thousand units, but by 1976 automotive imports into the U.S. had contributed $16.4 billion to the U.S. balance-of-payments deficit.

THE FIRST EXPORTS TO THE U.S.

In the world market, Japan began with the export of a mere 1,250 vehicles in 1955 out of a total production of 20,000 units; by 1980, it was exporting almost 6 million cars and had become the largest automobile-producing country, building over 11 million cars, or 31 percent of total demand. In contrast, the U.S. automobile production in 1955 was just over 9 million units, but with the economic decline, the United States only produced 8 million vehicles in 1980, 6 million below its highest level.

Japan did not win its success easily. Government, banks, and manufacturers all worked hard to achieve it. The early years were especially difficult, and individual corporate planning was inadequate to meet the Japanese government's lofty objectives. For example, the first test models of Toyota's passenger cars sent to the United States were a disaster. With the unfortunate name of "Toyopet" and a block-shape silhouette, the product was seriously flawed. The engine roared like a truck, the interior was rough and uncomfortable, and the lights were too dim to pass California standards.

Although some of these problems were corrected when full shipment began in 1957, the $2,300 price, compared with $1,600 for a Volkswagen Beetle, meant that the company was only able to sign up five dealers and sell 288 cars in the first year of trading. An improved version, later renamed the Toyota Crown, was introduced in 1959 but fared little better.

In 1960, Detroit introduced new compacts (Falcon, Valiant, Corvair) to compete with the Beetle. Although not the target, Toyota suffered heavy financial losses with the rest of the imports, forcing the company to retrench. The U.S. staff of sixty-five was cut in half while the company prepared to wait the expected five years for the engineers in Japan to research, design, tool up, and produce a car that would meet the needs of Americans. During this period, selling operations became essentially limited to the Land Cruiser, although the company did introduce a stopgap, the poorly received Tiara, in 1964.

REFORMULATION OF MARKETING STRATEGY

The Toyopet defeat forced Toyota back to the drawing board. Toyota's management now had to think afresh about how to successfully enter the U.S. market. They did not institute all at once a comprehensive marketing framework for market entry, takeover, and leadership maintenance, but in retrospect we can recognize the main strategies they followed at each stage and the strategic marketing-planning model they used. We will look at the strategies they pursued at each stage in turn.

Stage I: Market Opportunity Identification

First, Toyota needed to do a better job of identifying opportunities in the United States. The key to this was investing more in systematic information gathering guided by the two concepts of market segmentation and cross-cultural analysis.

The massive market research effort was conducted simultaneously along two fronts: (1) Toyota conducted a complete study of what the U.S. dealers and consumers wanted, and what was not being provided; and (2) it studied foreign car manufacturers' export activities in the United States in order to determine weaknesses and to formulate a superior sales and service strategy.

Toyota used many sources to accomplish its research task. In addition to the information provided by the Japanese government, it used trading companies, foreigners, and its own staff to gather information. Toyota commissioned an American research firm to interview

The Japanese Strategic Marketing-Planning Model, Stages I through IV

Volkswagen owners to determine unsatisfied consumer needs. The firm researched attributes of American styling, road conditions, and customers' tastes for "creature comforts." Not surprisingly, Toyota discovered a product-market gap in the U.S. market due to shifting trends that were being overlooked by Detroit.

Toyota discovered a waning of the traditional love affair of Americans toward automobiles as status or sex symbols. Attitudes had become more practical, and cars were being considered more as a means of transportation. Americans liked the legroom, ease of driving, and smooth ride of American cars but were seeking substantial reductions in the costs of owning an automobile, such as original cost, fuel economy, durability, and maintainability. Toyota also found consumers reacting to the growing frustration of traffic congestion and wanting smaller cars that were easier to park and get around in.

The research also indicated that much of Volkswagen's success with the Beetle was due to its establishment of a superior service organization. By providing maintenance that buyers could depend on, VW had been able to overcome consumer fears that foreign cars were expensive to own and that parts were rarely available when required.

By synthesizing the research results, Toyota was able to accurately profile a consistent demographic and psychographic target. With this precise market segment in mind, Toyota's engineers then developed an appropriate product—an American automobile, only more compact and more economical to drive and repair—the Corona.

The whole process can be summarized as one of Opportunity Identification. The effort has two objectives, market segmentation and cross-cultural analysis.

Market segmentation.   Here the purpose is to spot unserved or under-served market segments. Researchers were also alert to the potential of "window" opportunities—temporary market conditions that require corporations to react quickly or forfeit their chance.

In identifying overlooked product gaps, the Japanese were also seeking opportunities where little competitive reaction could be expected. This approach is consistent with the tenet of Japanese strategic philosophy. Initially, the Japanese avoid confrontation by nibbling away at competitor "corners" until sufficient advantage has been gained for a frontal attack.

Cross-cultural analysis.   The second objective of this Opportunity Identification phase of Toyota's strategic plan is to develop familiarity with every facet of the consumer and cross-cultural differences in the global markets that it intends to serve. "Knowing the customer" is taken very seriously by the Japanese, and great efforts are made to seize every opportunity to serve its market better. The Japanese approach amounted to basic marketing: First identify consumer needs, and then satisfy them.

In contrast, the strategies of U.S. automobile manufacturers totally lacked market targeting and appropriate product development. Instead, a mass-market production orientation and a drive to commonize parts led to reduced real differentiation in the products offered by the U.S. producers.

Stage II: Development of Market-Entry Strategies

For the Japanese, information gathering and opportunity identification and strategizing are a continual process. Japanese management reserves far more time for planning and evaluating policy than in the United States, and far less for day-to-day operating problems. This constant preparation for tomorrow helped Toyota achieve its impressive results. Of course, they were also helped by the failure of Detroit to act.

Exhaust emission standards introduced in 1968 indicated the need for more-efficient transportation. It was government prodding, not reaction to competitor moves, that prompted GM and Ford to build small cars. Chrysler, which did not have a small car on the drawing board, was skeptical about the introduction of GM's and Ford's new compacts. It believed that those cars had only been developed in response to pressure from Washington, which was worried by the rising imports and their effect on the balance of payments. Tom Killefer, then vice-president of finance at Chrysler, stated publicly: "It's pretty stupid to go ahead with a chauvinistic display of patriotism when the cost features aren't there."

Nor did the U.S. auto industry seem concerned about the growing stockpile of unsold cars. By failing to curtail optimistic production quotas established before sales declines, Chrysler, which had lost 2 percent market share in the 1969 model year, was left with excessive and costly inventories. Speaking to a news conference, Chrysler's John Riccardo (group VP for production, later to become president) belittled the importance of the company's ninety-six-day supply of cars by stating, "We planned it that way."

General Motors' President Cole summarized the auto industry's sublime reaction to its problems: "Never has the need for aggressive salesmanship and good management been more critical." By 1971, it was evident that a major trend toward buying small cars was under way. Much of the increased demand to buy two cars was from families migrating to the suburbs.

The U.S. automobile companies ignored these warning signals and continued to build larger and more expensive regular automobiles. This total ignorance of consumer demand led to significant negative car buyer attitudes—a pro-foreign, anti-Detroit syndrome. As Donald Peterson, vice-president of car planning and research for Ford's Product Development Group, observed:

> People believe that we make too many changes for change's sake—i.e., non-functional changes. There's a credibility gap. People don't believe our advertising. It has done more harm than good.

Percentage of U.S. New-Car Retail Sales by Class

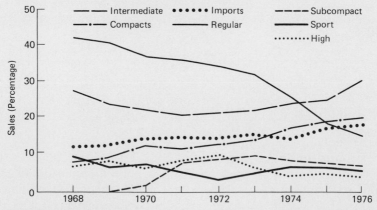

Source: Motor Vehicle Manufacturers Association Statistics.

Clearly, more was required from Detroit than just "aggressive selling."

Based on its research, Japan formulated a comprehensive strategy to reenter the U.S. market. The preceding four years had transformed the strategic posture of the Japanese auto industry. Not only had planning focused on the export challenge but during this period the domestic automobile market had developed rapidly, helping the Japanese companies to build operational experience.

In 1960, there were only 1.3 million cars in Japan, but by 1969 the number had increased to 15.1 million. Even in 1969, only 45 percent of Japan's vehicle production comprised passenger cars compared with averages of 90 percent in other Western nations. With the growth of passenger cars continuing throughout the 1970s, this strong domestic base constantly provided Japan with the means to support its marketing thrust overseas.

The year 1965 appeared to be an auspicious time for reentry into the U.S. small-car market. Compact auto sales were booming with the change in consumer preference, and Detroit had returned once again to building big cars.

Toyota's reentry strategy can be described along the four dimensions of product, price, distribution, and promotion.

Product strategy. Japan's product strategy was to build smaller, improved versions of "Detroit" models because this Americanization would enhance the acceptability of the product. The new Toyota Corona met every specification. It had twice the horsepower and performance of the Volkswagen Beetle, Toyota's principal target. Improved road handling was combined with fuel efficiency and the convenience of a smaller car. Well styled on the outside, the interior provided all the cosmetics Americans desired, such as soft upholstery, tinted glass, and whitewall tires. The car was the only import to have a fully automatic transmission. Almost no detail appears to have been overlooked. Armrests were positioned for longer arms, and seats were adjusted to give more legroom on American models.

Similar careful attention was directed toward less-visible attributes such as quality, reliability, and maintainability. Both before and after market entry, continuous market research was used to iron out difficulties and problems before they became serious. The Toyota Corona quickly established a reputation for quality, and the average number of complaints per hundred vehicles sold declined from 4.5 in 1969 to 1.3 in 1973.

Pricing strategy. The Japanese pursued a strategy of penetration pricing to break into the U.S. market and, later, marginal pricing as volumes grew. The guiding principle was to move rapidly down the experience curve. The Toyota Corona was priced under $2,000, and the next major car introduced, the Toyota Corolla, was priced under $1,800. This aggressive pricing strategy, combined with the low cost of maintenance, provided Toyota with a quality-with-economy image. The company was clearly in the lower-price market, directly competing with Volkswagen.

Distribution strategy.   Toyota's distribution strategy for market entry was predicated on detailed competitor analysis. Both Toyota and Nissan tied their sales efforts to providing a strong servicing and spare parts capability. Toyota had 384 dealers and a $2 million parts warehouse stocked before introducing the Corona in 1965. The sales drive was preceded by the establishment of service facilities in the new operating areas to build a solid marketing support channel.

Toyota focused its strategy on four key West Coast urban market areas: Los Angeles, San Francisco, Portland, and Seattle. Once a beachhead had been established, then "geographical roll-out" could begin. This made it possible to concentrate the sales force, closely supervise marketing activities, and penetrate one area thoroughly before tackling the next. In this way, too, mistakes were quickly detected and corrected.

Toyota recruited dealers on a highly selective basis. It targeted established, reputable dual-line imported car dealers who were experienced with foreign makes and whose customers were partial to imports. By 1967, however, 43.9 percent of the dealers were exclusively Toyota, second only to Volkswagen in single-line, imported car dealers, even though the company had only one model. To build experience within its own sales corporation, Toyota recruited experienced Americans to meet its staffing requirements.

Promotion strategy.   Toyota's initial efforts constituted heavy advertising directed toward its target markets. Initial advertising in 1965 was primarily through TV spots, supported by print. Since no other foreign manufacturer advertised on television, Toyota enjoyed dominance in this medium for the small-car and import category.

Toyota could not afford television by itself, so the company shared the costs of this medium 50:50 with its dealers. Care was taken to ensure that product and service features of quality and economy, promised to buyers in commercials, could be provided. Advertising timing was coordinated with sufficient dealer stocks of both cars and parts. These efforts were necessary to overcome American buyer feelings of dissonance resulting from the purchase of an unusual motor car—a foreign automobile.

Effective penetration of a new product-market, especially against entrenched competition, requires that limited corporate strengths be linked to a unified strategy. As our discussion has shown, Japan has been good at sequencing its strategy to market opportunities. Importantly, these export opportunities also recognized the inherent constraints of Japan's desire to use as many national resources as possible, such as labor.

In planning their strategy, Japanese companies accepted that their investment returns would be far in the future. The failure of the Toyopet would have deterred many organizations, but Toyota and the Japanese government were prepared to sustain their efforts by investing heavily. They approached the opportunities they had identified with a balanced marketing approach involving all four P's (product, price, place, and promotion) and carefully directed it at targeted markets.

Stage III: Market-Takeover Strategies

Once the Japanese had captured a foothold in the U.S. market, they pursued market-share expansion strategies. These strategies will be analyzed in terms of product, price, distribution, and promotion.

Product strategy.   Toyota's market-takeover strategy was marked by a constant refinement of its automobile to meet consumer demand. The Corolla series underwent major model changes in 1970 and 1974 when its body was enlarged, the vehicle's tread was widened, and its stability improved, all to satisfy Western preferences.

As production experience grew, the Japanese were able to include many of Detroit's options as standard equipment. This policy significantly enhanced consumer perceptions of the value of a Japanese car.

For Toyota, these ongoing changes and improvements had to be supported by increased productive efficiency and even greater product quality. Productive efficiency was enhanced by continuous investment in the latest plants and equipment. As for product quality, the Japanese adopted simple, sound industrial-engineering practices and automated production techniques.

The Japanese think of quality as "fitness for use by consumers." Technical innovation is directed toward product emendation from the consumer's view and is not regarded as an end in itself. This approach can be contrasted with that in the United States, where quality frequently means meeting specifications.

By performing extensive research, and paying attention to consumer feedback, the Japanese were able to synthesize consumer needs into broader product offerings. The Japanese offer far less variety in their models, even limiting color and interior selections, and providing options only in group packages, not individually. These actions had the advantage of minimal disruptions of production and the standardization of common parts for maximum scale economies.

Some of Toyota's drive for quality was in response to its fellow Japanese competitors. At Nissan, for example, the staff of engineers included Tyoichi Nakagawa, who had designed the engine for zero fighter planes. Nakagawa used his past aircraft design experience to put similar quality into Nissan's cars, such as tight, secure door latches and good noise control.

At both companies, this effort for improved product quality also focused on quality control in the production process. Various kinds of quality control have been used. The "zero-defect" concept was aimed at identifying root causes of unsatisfactory output until production was almost error free. The "QC circle" technique provided communication channels and a common vocabulary to stimulate employees to suggest creative ideas for product and process improvement.

Cross-trained to do several jobs, QC required workers to begin their work by inspecting the tasks performed at the previous work station. As a result of these measures, quality control inspectors at the end of the line found defects in fewer than 1 percent of the finished automobiles.

The twin drive for quality and productivity extended beyond Toyota's plants. Japan's automakers get their components from separate companies, and vertical integration within single corporations is shallow. The Japanese auto companies cultivate strong cooperative relationships with their groups of suppliers based on high standards of mutual trust and respect.

A significant proportion of a supplier's output is directed to a single original equipment manufacturer (OEM), and these OEMs typically hold directorships and equity in their suppliers. In many cases, these arrangements include the sharing of technical innovation through combined training programs, all aimed toward achieving ever-higher goals of effectiveness and efficiency. For example, Asahi Malleable Iron, which makes malleable iron and aluminum castings for Mitsubishi, also machines its components and mounts tires on its aluminum wheels. Asahi's overhead for these operations is lower than it would be for Mitsubishi. Referring to this cooperation, Asahi managing director Shirgesaburo Asai said, "We are foundry specialists, so every week Mitsubishi engineers come into our plant to advise on ways to improve productivity in the machine shop.

By locating suppliers within the same industrial park as that used by their own operations, the Japanese auto industry was able to adopt the famed Kanban, or "just-in-time," inventory system. The close physical proximity of the production chain reduced transportation costs, minimized transit damage, and substantially lowered necessary inventory holdings. Under the Kanban system, many parts are not produced until hours before they are needed by the next process. Eliminating these stocks also highlighted previously hidden overmanning, undermanning, and machine inefficiences for correction.

The results of this aggressive drive for productive efficiency have been tremendous. In 1958, Toyota was producing 1.5 cars per employee per year. By 1965, the company had raised this to 23; and by 1969, to 39 cars per employee each year.

Although there is the possibility that these numbers are over-stated due to the exclusion of "part-time" employees who only work forty instead of the usual forty-eight hours, the contrast with Detroit is startling. Over the same period, GM was only able to improve its productivity from 8.9 cars per employee to 11.4 in 1965.

Pricing strategy. In order to attract high numbers of new buyers and move rapidly down the experience curve, Toyota and the other auto-

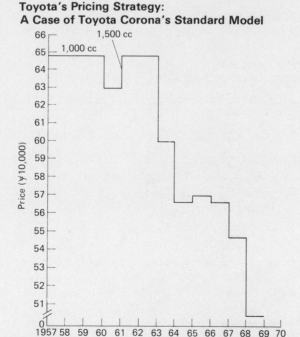

**Toyota's Pricing Strategy:
A Case of Toyota Corona's Standard Model**

Source: John B. Schnapp, *Corporate Strategies of the Automotive Manufacturers—Vol. II: Strategic Histories* (Boston, Mass.: Harbridge House, 1978). Prepared for the U.S. Department of Transportation, National Highway Traffic Safety Administration, p. 149.

mobile companies priced their products substantially lower than their competitors. Since this strategy augmented experience and reduced unit costs, the Japanese were able to further reduce prices, adding a snowball effect to their pricing strategy.

As an illustration of this pricing strategy, the price of Toyota's Corona standard model declined 20 percent over a ten-year period in the Japanese market.

By 1968, technical gaps among Japanese competitors in the small-car market were closing rapidly and campaigns for sales had intensified into damaging price wars. In a step unprecedented by Western standards, Toyota's President Kamiya publicly admonished the industry to try to halt these pricing strategies, and price trends were reversed.

Nevertheless, Japanese prices still remained far below those of U.S. automobiles. For example, the Pinto and Vega were at a $100 to $400 price disadvantage against the Japanese. As we will see later, reevaluation of the yen and the oil supply crises in the early 1970s dissipated much of the Japanese price advantage.

Distribution strategy. In support of the Japanese auto companies' recognition that supply and service were key aspects of their marketing program, Toyota moved rapidly to expand its service outlets and dealer force. From the 384 dealers at the time of the Corona introduction in 1965, Toyota's dealer force expanded to over 1,000 by 1976. During the same period, the number of U.S. manufacturer dealerships, which far outweighed the Japanese, declined by over 5,000.

Although both Toyota and Nissan expanded the number of dealerships, each company adopted different implementation strategies. Contrary to the stereotype of a monolithic Japan, Inc., each of the eleven Japanese automakers has its own distribution approach.

Toyota's geographic roll-out spread east from its beachhead in the California market. The company signed up "well-heeled, politically powerful" independent distributorships and gave them the job of recruiting dealers in the hinterlands not supplied by company-owned warehouses. For example, former California Governor Edmund Brown owned part of the Toyota Mid-Atlantic outlet, headed by Frederick R. Weissman, one-time president of Hunt Foods & Industries, Inc.

Nissan, in a bold move to overtake Toyota, simultaneously set up eight regional company offices in an umbrella strategy to cover the entire U.S. market. This approach, however, was not as effective as Toyota's because the company's stretched resources could not compete effectively against Toyota's strategy of building strength on strength.

Toyota's growth in the number of dealerships understated its distribution strength buildup. The company spent considerable effort in improving dealership quality through selection and upgrading. One key aspect of this program was vigorous education and training throughout the distributor system. By using the information gathered from market entry and continuous feedback, Toyota identified and disseminated the best ideas in training programs and incentive plans for dealers.

With this objective of continuous evolutionary improvement of market performance, Toyota established a Marketing Services Department in 1966. This department's initial responsibilities were to provide unique, consistent dealer signs, sales incentives for Toyota salesmen, auto-show exhibits, and a used-vehicle reconditioning training program for dealers. Later it established sales training and sales promotion groups.

For example, a unique national sales program called Project IMAGE (In-Dealership Motivation and Goal Expansion) was launched in September 1972. Its aim was to help dealer personnel achieve better salesmanship through a deeper understanding of customers and the practice of more personal communications. As another example of improving distribution efficiency, Toyota hosted an international seminar to persuade dealers to adopt a computerized parts management system that the company had developed.

Through continuous research, Toyota identified well-directed marketing channels to support Toyota's targeted geographical segments. In addition, Toyota trained dealers and helped them sell, whereas Detroit twisted arms under the hard-sell approach and squeezed margins during difficult times. Toyota fostered and encouraged its dealers by giving them good margins of approximately $181 per unit, unheard of for small cars and almost the same as margins for a Chevy dealer. Altogether, these steps produced such a dramatic improvement in the average dealer volumes that within five years they were approximately those of Chrysler.

Promotion strategy. During this period, Japanese advertising expenditures were considerable. Compared with the American Motors Corporation in 1969, which spent $12 million to promote 270,000 unit sales, Toyota paid $18.5 million for only 130,000 units, and Nissan $10 million for 87,000. The Japanese advertising expenditures per vehicle consistently exceeded U.S. competitor levels. Against other imports, the Japanese budgets achieved media dominance. In 1971, Toyota accounted for 39 percent of total spot TV advertising of imported motor vehicles, followed by Nissan, with 19 percent. Volkswagen was distant third with 16 percent.

At the same time, Japanese advertising content was cautious, given the growing trade pressures between Japan and the United States. The ads downplayed the Japanese origin of the cars. Nissan, for example, built a campaign around "the imported car with the American spirit" and

played up the American transmissions, produced by Borg-Warner Corporation, on some of its models.

Stage IV: Market-Share Maintenance Strategies

Not everything has gone the Japanese way. The Japanese have had to
weather several setbacks. On July 1, 1971, a strike of longshoremen on
the West Coast shut Toyota's California ports for one hundred days. The
company coped with this by putting into action a contingency plan
already prepared to ship cars through Canada and Mexico.

On August 14 of the same year, President Nixon placed a 10
percent tax on imported products. This measure, together with a 17
percent upward reevaluation of the yen in the fall, raised Toyota's U.S.
prices by 10 percent in the five months before December 1971. Although
this virtually eliminated Toyota's price advantage, Toyota managed to
maintain a high global sales volume. Then in 1973, Japan was harder hit
than the United States by the Arab oil embargo, due to its total reliance
on imported oil.

While these events following the oil crisis threw U.S. automakers
and other imported automakers into marketing and financial difficulties,
Toyota managed to maintain its market leadership with increasing sales.
By 1980, its sales were around 580,000 units, or more than twice its 1975
volume: Toyota accounted for nearly 25 percent of total imported vehicles. Toyota's success was achieved by continuously monitoring consumers' changing tastes toward auto economy and safety and away from
body style and car speed. The Japanese kept searching for ways to
improve the product's performance, features, style, and quality. Toyota's
new models stressed three major points: fuel economy, safety, and less
pollution. Toyota, as well as other Japanese automakers, successfully
developed automobiles that economized on fuel consumption by 25 to 30
percent as compared with the conventional cars. At the same time,
Toyota developed cars that provided excellent accident protection and
accident safety, as well as postaccident safety.

Toyota continued to raise its quality through the increasing use
of automation and robots. It automated not only the final assembly line
but also the interim assembly processes. It incorporated fully automatic,
specialized, multispot welding machines and robots into the production
process. As a result, Toyota acquired a reputation for excellent quality
that helped increase its sales even though it began losing price competitiveness in the world market.

One common thread running throughout Toyota's strategic
thrust has been its appetite for continuous learning and improvement,

Driven by a cultural obsession with learning, the Japanese have never been afraid to learn from their mistakes and from the best ideas of others. The Japanese quest for continuous improvement combined with cooperative industrial relations confers a competitive edge of formidable proportions.

Japanese export autos are specifically engineered for the U.S. market, whereas U.S. manufacturers tend to export surplus production adapted to their own market. Having designed cars to U.S. specifications, Toyota devoted attention to the problem of marine damage. In 1966, this amounted to approximately $18 per vehicle. Determined to cut this dramatically, the company directed substantial corporate resources behind this effort. An import manager (Hiroshi Imai) and team were appointed to research and implement improvements. By 1967, damage had been reduced to $6 per car, and later, through stevedore training and a specially designed corporate shipping fleet, this was lowered even further to $3 per car.

In contrast, as recently as 1982, Jack Barnes, director of strategy and analysis at Ford, discussed the difficulty U.S. manufacturers had homologating cars exported to the Japanese market. Ford had established a modifications center in Japan to repair "less than perfect paint jobs" and rework cars to Japanese specifications. Barnes estimated the average rework cost of "$400 to $500 per car" to be a "nontariff barrier" because it included the installation of a half dozen unique lights required on cars in Japan, and a special warning device required for catalytic systems.

Meanwhile Japanese auto companies began to weather the growing storm of protectionism by starting small assembly operations and buying components in the United States. Toyota voluntarily limited the number of cars shipped to the United States. Nissan similarly restricted its volume but chose to do this by limiting the number of dealers. This approach avoided the difficulty faced by Toyota of some dealers going out of business, not, ironically, because of a lack of demand but because of a lack of supply.

Japan's spectacular success in the auto market can hardly be questioned. The steady growth of Japan's world market share between 1950 and 1980 demonstrates that the large market shares held by U.S. and West German automakers provided no protection against competitors who dedicated themselves to offering a superior value to the marketplace.

MARKETING STRATEGY IS MUCH MORE THAN SELLING

When Toyota introduced the Toyopet, it was merely selling; but during the market-takeover and development stages, it moved rapidly into a

World Automobile Production—Japan, United States, West Germany, 1951-1980

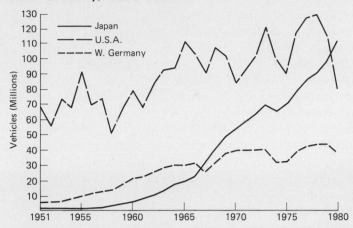

Source: P. Bayres and A. J. Sanders, *Japan: Its Motor Industry and Market* (London: P-E Consulting Group Limited, 1971), Report to the British National Economic Development Office, p. 104; and Nobuyori Kodaira, "Position of the Japanese Automobile Industry in the World," *Journal of Japanese Trade and Industry,* January 1982, p. 17.

marketing mode of thinking. The Japanese set about perfecting their marketing philosophy and techniques with a vengeance. Meanwhile Detroit failed to recognize the difference between selling and marketing. As late as 1974, when the Japanese had already captured a threatening share of the market, Richard Gerstenberg, then chairman of General Motors, said again of the industry's problems, "We've got a selling job to do with the dealer, and he has a job to do with the customer."

The penalty for this attitude was severe. Henry Ford II estimated that "for every 1% of import penetration there were 20,000 fewer jobs available in the U.S." The sad irony is that the Japanese started with American techniques following World War II and developed rapidly while Detroit stood still.

This inactivity contributed greatly to the Japanese success. Even when Detroit automakers did react, their efforts were not well planned. Ford's introductions tended to cannibalize its own models instead of beating the Japanese imports. As *Newsweek* observed in 1971, "Pinto is chewing into the Maverick the way Maverick chewed into Mustang." When GM introduced its own subcompact Vega, the car was of extremely poor quality and did not meet previously announced specifications that the company considered necessary to compete with the Japanese models.

Japanese marketers spent their time continuously refining their marketing strategy. They emphasized market segmentation and targeting; product quality and innovation; pricing according to perceived value; careful dealer selection and motivation; focused and heavy advertising.

These marketing themes were pursued in the context of, and in configuration with, a larger body of strategic thought developed in Japan over a period of several hundred years. Japanese strategic thought was heavily influenced by *The Book of Five Rings*, written in 1645 by Miyamoto Musashi, a celebrated Samurai warrior. Musashi's book emphasizes the extreme importance of taking the initiative and forestalling the enemy at every point. He stresses singleness of purpose, crushing the enemy unrelentingly until he no longer is a threat, and knowing the enemy to the point of thinking like him.

Consider Musashi's specific strategic prescription entitled "To Injure the Corners":

> It is difficult to move strong things by pushing directly, so you should "injure the corners." In large scale strategy, it is beneficial to strike at the corners of the enemy's force. If the corners are overthrown, the spirit of the whole body will be overthrown. To defeat the enemy you must follow up the attack when the corners have fallen.

The Japanese auto companies' market-entry techniques employed this principle. Japan's constant pressure of each element of the marketing mix "injured the corners" of the U.S. manufacturers. Yet for Musashi, the goal of strategy was to "crush" the enemy:

> If the enemy is less skillful than oneself, if his rhythm is disorganized, or if he has fallen into evasive or retreating attitudes, we must crush him all at once. The primary thing is not to let him recover his position even a little. You must research this deeply.

The only way to "crush" the enemy is by direct attack. A formidable opponent's morale and strengths can patiently be eroded by probes and feints—i.e., by "injuring the corners." However, the object of strategy is not attained without the culminating direct attack. The Japanese have not yet accomplished this purpose in the U.S. automobile market, but they have in a host of other industries, as we will see in later chapters.

As strategic planners of the highest order, the Japanese aim their marketing efforts, not at where the competition is situated, but at where they think the competitive battlefield will be in the future.

This action is particularly successful against the essentially defensive and short-run stance of many American corporations. To avoid being further entrapped by "flanking" and "encircling" attacks, American corporations *must* develop a longer-range strategy based on an offensive positioning when facing their competitors.

PART II
FAR EASTERN
MARKETING STRATEGIES:
THE ROAD TO DOMINATION

chapter 4 ——

Identifying Opportunities:
Knowing Where to Strike

To understand how and why many Japanese industries have so successfully penetrated the world marketplace, it is essential to understand the
ways the Japanese handle their marketing. The world did not beat a
relentless track to Japan's door in search of its products. Quite the
contrary, the Japanese label on products signified inferior quality when
Japanese companies started exporting over three decades ago. Yet the
great lesson for other nations is that the Japanese were able to overcome
their postwar reputation of manufacturing shoddy merchandise to become the great marketer whose products today are sold and respected in
every corner of the world.

In the past, many major U.S. corporations got their start by
coming out with the right products at the right time in a rapidly growing
market. Their marketing decisions were typically made without the
benefit of strategic thinking and planning. Wise or lucky, their management decisions carried these companies to where they stand today.
However, intuition or luck alone is no longer enough for succeeding in
today's intensely competitive environment. The declining fortunes of
many large U.S. corporations are the best evidence of this.

Successful Japanese companies are more oriented to formal
long-run strategic planning and marketing implementation. Their marketing starts long before their products are produced and continues long
after their sales are consummated. They first search for attractive opportunities. Then they develop appropriate products that represent a value
to the customer. They choose their market-entry points and timing

carefully with the purpose of gaining a strong initial foothold. Then they shift into market-penetration planning aimed at broadening their customer base and expanding their market shares. When they finally achieve substantial market leadership, they adopt strategies to maintain and defend their market position. This sequential strategy formulation process comprises four components. Each of the four components of the Japanese strategic process will be described in detail in the next several chapters. In this chapter, we will examine the first step, that is, how the Japanese identify and manage market opportunities.

The Japanese Strategic Marketing Process

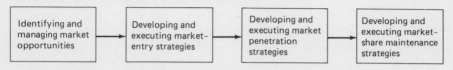

THE CONCEPT OF OPPORTUNITY: ITS ROLE AND IMPORTANCE

The notion of *opportunity management* lies at the heart of Japan's emergence as a world economic power during the past thirty years. By that we mean that Japan as a country organized itself to make some hard choices and to carry through whatever public and private programs were necessary to realize the fruits of these choices.

Specifically, the Japanese ways of opportunity management can be examined at two levels:

1) *Industry Opportunities Identification and Management:* The choice and selection of those industries that were most suited to Japan's resource base and in which Japan obviously thought it could realize a competitive advantage in the world marketplace. This macrolevel identification of opportunities is carried out mainly through the administrative guidance of Japanese governmental authorities.

2) *Market Opportunities Identification and Management:* The micro-level management of opportunities that concerns the choice of specific markets to enter and products to manufacture within a particular selected industry by Japanese companies.

While these choices are obviously interrelated, we will treat them sequentially. Before examining these choices in more detail, we want to consider them in a broader context, that of the history and evolution of the Japanese political economy, especially in the period immediately after World War II.

JAPAN'S NEEDS FOR OPPORTUNITY MANAGEMENT

The Japanese political economy in the late 1940s and early 1950s was in a sad state of disrepair. From 1945 to 1952, Japan suffered the national indignity of being under the direct control of the Occupation forces. Its politics and economics were ruled by a foreign power. Its constitution, educational system, and other administrative structures and processes were fostered—some might say imposed—by the Occupation forces.

The Japanese economy was sadly depleted. During the war, all production facilities had been directed toward the war effort. Toward the end of the war, much of Japan's physical plant had been knocked out of action. Shortages of many raw materials and finished products persisted in the immediate post–World War II years. During the autumn of 1946, when various forms of governmental subsidies ran out, the Japanese economy virtually ground to a halt. As early as February 1946, the cabinet had called for an "emergency economic policy headquarters" to deal with coal and fuel shortages, inflation (which was rampant during this period), the conversion of old yen into new yen, the freezing of credit funds, and new taxes. The war-torn years of the early 1940s gave rise to the period in the later 1940s when Japan was firmly gripped in economic misery and largely dependent on foreign aid for the initial impetus out of that misery.

Continuing well into the 1950s, the Japanese economy faced many constraints: Capital was in short supply, the technologies needed to revitalize many industry segments were to be found only overseas, costs were too high in many industry segments, and balance-of-payments and foreign exchange difficulties abounded because the country imported more than it sold abroad.

Thus, in the early 1950s, the ability to compete internationally was only a dream. Many observers wondered whether Japan would ever be able to provide its people with a standard of living that at all resembled the standard of other nations. Yet the irony of its situation was that Japan had to compete in the international arena if it was to harbor any ambitions of providing a comparable standard of living for its inhabitants. Its dearth of natural resources further heightened its need to travel in the waterways of international trade.

In short, Japan emerged from World War II with a shattered economy and little prospect of contributing much to world commerce. Worse still, it was evident that Japan would become increasingly dependent on the international economy: In order to augment its meager national resource base, Japan would have to import raw materials, energy sources, and even food. Japan, therefore, as many countries before it and since, faced some hard decisions: How was it to pull itself out of its economic doldrums? What industries might or should lead the way? What respective role should governmental agencies and the private sector play in making these choices? In search of the answers, opportunity identification and management emerged as one of the most important factors in this regard.

IDENTIFYING AND MANAGING INDUSTRY OPPORTUNITIES

Identifying Target Industries

Japan's need to rebuild the nation, to control its balance of payments, to create exports, and to manage its economy back to health led Japan to consider selecting certain industries for targeted growth. Perhaps nothing has been more central to the phenomenal economic performance of the Japanese economy than Japan's willingness to commit resources to targeted industries. *A target industry is simply an industry that Japan identifies as being worthy of whatever support is deemed necessary to make it a strong industry domestically and to help it become and remain competitive in the international arena.*

The propeller—the Japanese government. The ideology and history of the United States would have strongly suggested that industrial development should be left to the "free play of market forces." Government's role in the enactment of these choices would have been precluded upon the maxim "The least government involvement is best." However, quite the opposite has been the case of Japan. Again, this reflects Japan's history, culture, and sociopolitical structure, and, in no small way, some of the legacies of the Occupation by the Allies.

One thing is clear: Government has played an important and sometimes decisive role in fashioning Japan's economic recovery, economic growth, and industrial development. Governmental agencies, especially in the form of MITI, with varying degrees of input from and cooperation with business, identified which industries would be designated for special supports and what shape and form these supports might take.

Government is not an abstract entity; its work is carried out by specific governmental institutions or agencies. During 1949–55, Japan put together the institutional instruments that were to catapult it into the economic big league. Unquestionably, the pivotal entity in this institutional structure was MITI.

MITI came into being in 1949. It was an outgrowth of the institutional mix the Occupation forces were trying to put in place. It represented another milestone on the road to Japanese self-government. Even the title *MITI* is significant: The inclusion of international trade is indicative of Japanese intent to guide resources toward the exploitation of international markets.

MITI quite quickly assumed the central coordinating role in guiding Japan's economic destiny. It was the "point-man" in what has become known as the "administrative guidance" of business. It worked very closely with many other governmental agencies; nowhere was this more true than in its close ties to, and its direct and indirect use of, the Ministry of Finance and the Japan Development Bank.

In the late 1950s, MITI had direct leverage points or "controls" to support its "directives," "appeals," or "suggestions." From the early 1960s, its influence was much more derived from long-established business-governmental relations, belief that MITI represented the national interest, respect for its neutrality in arbitrating disputes, and recognition that even without direct controls a governmental agency such as MITI could orchestrate many informal pressure points—something that MITI was not loath to do.

At the core of MITI's roles lie separate though related elements:

1. Establishing objectives and priorities for the Japanese economy
2. Developing the economic (physical) and institutional (commercial) infrastructure
3. Selecting target industries
4. Funneling the necessary capital to target industries and specific firms
5. Nurturing target industries toward maturity
6. Developing the means to regulate all forms of competition within the Japanese economy
7. Controlling the flow of foreign investment into Japan
8. Managing the institutional environment

These elements are examined in the following paragraphs.

Economic goals as priorities.   An overarching function of MITI and, in essence, a raison d'être of administrative guidance has been the establishment of goals and priorities for the Japanese economy. Everything that MITI does and has done, in one form or another, relates to this task.

Development of infrastructure.   Another broad general element in MITI's administrative guidance weaponry has been its role in fashioning the physical and commercial infrastructure to facilitate and speed up the process of industry development. Though it frequently receives little discussion in accounts of the Japanese "economic miracle," this infrastructural development was a prerequisite to many of the other elements in Japan's industrial policy.

Development of the physical environment was an early MITI goal. This was achieved by the Enterprises Rationalization Promotion Law of 1952 that committed the central and local governments to building parks, highways, railroads, electric power grids, gas mains, and industrial parks at public expense and making them available to approved industries. The importance of this legislation and its impact on Japanese economic development cannot be overstated. It unambiguously signaled to Japanese business that MITI, and, more broadly the Japanese government, were willing to embark on long-run measures to advance Japan's industrial interests.

The importance of the Enterprises Rationalization Promotion Law has been well captured by Chalmers Johnson:

> The last provision was perhaps the most important because it drastically reduced production costs. It began the extensive efforts by MITI and the Ministry of Construction over the next two decades not just to build the infrastructure for industry but to rationalize it as completely as possible. The idea behind the provision was the recognition that since Japan's industries had to import most of their raw materials and to export their products, factories and port facilities should be completely integrated. The prewar Japanese steel industry had worked out the rule of thumb that it had to transport six tons of raw materials in order to produce one ton of steel. MITI planned to change that by dredging harbors, building factories at dockside, and locating intermediate processors next to final manufacturers. One of the most famous products of this policy is the Keiyo industrial belt and petro-chemical kombinato, which was built in Chiba prefecture on land entirely reclaimed from Tokyo Bay. The Kawasaki Steel Company alone, which in 1953 fired the first blast furnace of its new, integrated facility (pig iron to rolled steel; at the time, the world's most modern), received some 3 million square meters of free

land from Chiba prefecture. Ichimada, the banks, and Kawasaki's biggest competitors (Yawata, Fuji, and Nippon Kokan) all derided the Kawasaki effort at the time as beyond Japan's capabilities, and needs—something MITI has never let them forget in view of its unexampled success.

Nor was MITI averse to using its formal and informal powers to orchestrate what it considered as desirable changes in the country's commercial infrastructure—i.e., the institutions and practices involved in the acquisition of raw materials and in the distribution and promotion of finished goods. MITI's efforts to develop and strengthen Japanese trading companies are a good example.

MITI helped rebuild the trading companies by issuing laws that authorized tax write-offs for the costs of opening branches and for contingency funds against bad debt contracts. It also worked hard to rationalize the system of trading companies. Through the wide array of weapons available in its administrative guidance arsenal, MITI was able to consolidate well over two thousand trading companies that existed in the early 1950s to about twenty large ones, each serving a large industrial group or a cartel of small producers.

Identification of target industries.   Perhaps MITI's primary impact on Japan's industrial progress has been its role in identifying target industries or, more broadly, serving as the institution that coordinated and integrated the inputs of relevant public and private parties in this decision-making process. In effect, the early bureaucratic leaderships in MITI made it the decision center for the choice of designated industries as well as how they could best be supported.

The choice of target industries, as well as the institutional structure that has evolved in Japan to make and implement such choices, reveals many of the "secrets" underlying that country's prodigious economic performance. We will first identify the target industries chosen and then examine the apparent criteria underlying these choices. While it is not an exhaustive delineation of industries targeted by Japan, it does indicate the scope of the target industries program that Japan has undertaken during the past thirty years. A number of brief comments are warranted.

Choice criteria.   Not surprisingly, the initial industries targeted for special support in the early post–World War II era were those industries that were critical to quickly generating some form of economic momentum. Electric power, coal, steel, and ships were the industries singled out for special development in the late 1940s. The criteria underlying the choice of these industries are fairly self-evident: the need to develop those industries that lay at the heart of the economic infrastructure of Japan, an infrastructure that as previously noted was not present in early post–World War II days.

In the early 1950s, as the economy began to make some headway and as the Occupation forces began to emphasize "recovery" rather than "reform," Japan's own institutions began to play an increasingly important role in determining the direction and nature of the country's fate. The founding of MITI in 1949 provided a vehicle for the exercise of this role. As early as the mid-1950s, the direction of emphasis within Japanese industrial policy under the tutelage of MITI was becoming apparent— movement from labor-intensive to capital- and technology-intensive industries.

Japan in the early 1950s was a country with a relatively large population and a comparatively cheap labor force, but with a quite poorly developed industrial infrastructure. This explains Japan's prewar emphasis on labor-intensive export industries—what an MITI official later called "low-quality textiles" and "masses of gadgets."

However, if Japan's vision of itself in some future time period included anything remotely resembling industrial leadership in the world marketplace, it had little option but to create opportunities for itself to do so. Continued dependence on labor-intensive industries—i.e., exploitation of its inherent comparative advantage—would not transform Japan into a world commercial power. Had Japan chosen to depend on labor-intensive industries as the spearhead of its drive to develop an export-oriented economy, there is no doubt that it could not have achieved the results it did in the late 1950s and 1960s. It would have been much too easy for both the developed and the lesser-developed countries to compete against Japan—something that was well recognized by many key "actors" in Japan.

The essence of the approach adopted by Japan to fashion opportunities for itself on the world economic stage is well captured in the following description by a high official from MITI:

> Should Japan have entrusted its future, according to the theory of comparative advantage, to these industries characterized by intensive use of labour? That would perhaps be a rational choice for a country with a small population of 5 or 10 million. But Japan has a large population. If the Japanese economy had adopted the simple doctrine of free trade and had chosen to specialize in this kind of industry, it would almost permanently have been unable to break away from the Asian pattern of stagnation and poverty, and would have remained the weakest link in the free world, thereby becoming a problem area in the Far East.

The Ministry of International Trade and Industry decided to establish in Japan industries which require intensive employment of capital and technology, industries that in consideration of comparative cost of production should be the most inappropriate for Japan, industries such as steel, oil refining, petro-chemicals, automobiles, aircraft, industrial machinery of all sorts, and later electronics, including electronic computers. From a short-run, static viewpoint, encouragement of such industries would seem to conflict with economic rationalism. But, from a long-range point of view, these are precisely the industries where income elasticity of demand is high, technological progress is rapid, and labour productivity rises fast. It was clear that without these industries it would be difficult to employ a population of 100 million and raise their standard of living to that of Europe and America with light industries alone; whether right or wrong, Japan had to have these heavy and chemical industries.

Inherent in the above description is an emphasis on opportunity creation. Japan was ready and able to commit itself to developing industries. Many of the target industries designated by MITI were at best in their infancy in Japan in the 1950s. Japan was willing to embark on a long-term path: It would not be in the forefront of any of these industries on a worldwide scale for ten, fifteen, twenty, or more years. Of course, there was absolutely no guarantee that it would ever succeed in establishing any of these industries domestically, not to mention making them keen international competitors.

Managing Target Industries

Channeling funds to target industries. The target industries selected by the Japanese government are served, directly and indirectly, by MITI as the source and clearinghouse for much of the capital that was channeled to them. MITI itself was the source of some of these funds, but what in many respects was much more important, it wielded tremendous influence over the banks in their investment decisions.

MITI's own budget hovered around the one percent of national budget and, of that, only about one-half was used for direct subsidies to industry. Thus, MITI itself did not control nearly enough of a resource base to directly shape industrial development. But it did exercise much control over the banks, by far the largest source of capital for Japanese firms.

Intense competition exists among Japanese banks for deposits and loans. The Ministry of Finance exercises strict control over loan and deposit interest rates, dividend rates, opening of new branches, and so forth. Thus the banks find it imperative to do business with growth industries and businesses if they wish to increase their share of the market for deposits, loans, and so forth. In judging what makes a growth industry, banks have relied on MITI's judgment and criteria. The banks therefore found it in their own self-interest to remain close to MITI and not antagonize it.

MITI's relationship with the government banks was more formal and more direct. Six such banks were established between 1949 and 1953. The most important for industrial policy was the Japan Development Bank (JDB). The purpose of JDB "was to provide long-term equipment loans to private enterprise which the commercial banks were not in a position to assume the risks involved." MITI quickly made JDB an important instrument in shaping its vision of economic development. Although JDB had been placed under the Ministry of Finance's administrative jurisdiction, MITI came to wield a large policy-making influence because it was given the duty of screening all loan applications and making assessments of the shortfall between available and needed capital. Moreover, even though JDB's share of the government's supply of capital to industry had declined dramatically by the early 1960s, the bank influenced the flow of funds through the indicative effect of its decisions to support or not to support a new industry. As noted by Johnson, a JDB loan, regardless of its size, became MITI's seal of approval on an enterprise, and the company that had received a JDB loan could easily raise whatever else it needed from private resources.

MITI influence is also reflected in the proportion of JDB's funds funneled to MITI's target industries—electric power, ships, coal, and steel—during the 1953–55 period. Approximately 83 percent of JDB's funds went to these four industries, accounting for 23.1 percent of all investment in electric power, 33.6 percent in shipbuilding, 29.8 percent in coal mining, and 10.6 percent in new steel plants.

Nurturing target industries.   The hand of MITI has been most visible in a plethora of laws, regulations, and actions designed to foster and nurture target industries. It is hardly possible to find any other country in the free world that has placed in the hands of one central economic planning institution such a complete and comprehensive set of tools to aid and nourish fledgling segments of its economy. The types of actions taken were dependent on the extent to which Japan had any prior experience in the industry, the condition of the Japanese economy, MITI's goals at any given time, and the type of industry being supported. It is worth reemphasizing that many in the United States would label these support activities "interferences" in the working of the economy.

MITI and its alignment of relationships with related institutions had at its disposal all the necessary tools to handle the myriad of problems that might inhibit the development of infant industries. Principal among these problems might be a lack of foreign exchange, an absence of technology sources, an inappropriate tax structure, an extremely limited supply of and an excessive cost of capital, an unrestrained foreign competition in the domestic market, and an inadequate access to foreign markets.

A number of devices were employed to help launch designated industries and nurture them through infancy. Control of foreign exchange was especially important during the 1950s. As soon as an industry was targeted for development, foreign currency allocations were authorized by MITI. This entitled the industry to acquire foreign raw materials, components, or technical capability. MITI occasionally provided direct subsidies to emerging industries. MITI also exercised control of access to foreign technology. Licenses had to be granted by MITI for the import of foreign technology. Much of the initial impetus in most of the target industries during the 1950s can be traced to the acquisition of foreign technology. For example, every item of petrochemical technology was obtained on license from abroad.

A complete and variable set of financing, tax, and loan arrangements could be instigated by MITI to spur and sustain target industry development. MITI was not averse to interceding with the banks on behalf of a target industry or individual firms within it to obtain more favorable financing arrangements. Target industries were accorded special and accelerated depreciation on their investments. Special tax breaks were also given to such industries.

Managing competition in particular industries. These financial supports helped supply the nascent industries with badly needed funding. However, MITI and, more broadly, the Japanese government did not depend exclusively on providing industries with preferential financial treatment as a means of fostering their development. They took many steps to directly interfere with the process of competition in order to grant target industries the strongest possible chance of succeeding. In MITI's view, these industries (especially in their early stages) should not fall prey to the whims of competition. Individual firms within an industry, however, could be allowed to go to the wall.

In order to shelter native industry from the potential ravages of foreign competition in its own domestic market, MITI did everything possible to keep imports out of Japan. Goods that competed directly with domestic products were particularly targeted. A complete system of tariffs and quotas was put into operation by MITI. Part of the rationale for the installation of import controls was initially provided by the need to conserve foreign currency. In the late 1960s, however, long after the foreign exchange problem had been solved and Japan had come under intense foreign pressure to liberalize its trade laws, a variety of import controls centering on quotas were still in existence.

MITI had a number of much more direct controls over competition. It could exercise its powers to form cartels or mergers in an industry. Much of MITI's activity in the 1950s revolved around its efforts to prevail on other governmental agencies and private interest groups to allow cartels or "cooperative behavior" (which became the public euphemism for a cartel) among firms in a given industry.

MITI could either initiate movement toward a cartel itself or merely signify its approval of a cartellike behavior that was already taking place. Cartels or cooperative behavior could assume many forms: limiting production and sales, sharing technological know-how, rationalizing production lines, joint consulting on investment plans, and sharing of distribution and sales capabilities. Many of the early MITI-sponsored cartels were aimed at overcoming excessive industry segmentation and reducing industry cost structures. The underlying presumption was that correction of both of these "problems" would better position these industries to compete internationally.

MITI could also go beyond initiating and supporting cartels: It could effect mergers. In so doing, its "persuasive" powers were tested to the limit. MITI needed all its direct and indirect "controls" to consummate some mergers. If MITI decided a merger was in "the national interest," it pursued it doggedly. Steel, automobiles, and computers are those major industries in which MITI successfully instituted mergers.

Cartels and mergers reveal much about the underlying operating philosophy of MITI. In the early 1950s, it had feverishly pushed the enabling legislation, resulting in September 1953 in revisions to the Antimonopoly law (which had been created by the Occupation forces, in part, to prevent any movements toward what they deemed anticompetitive practices). MITI wished to protect the export sector at all costs, even if it had to impose protective measures. Economic stability was preferable to the results that might be unleashed by unfettered competitive forces: overinvestment in some industries, lack of investment in others, unnecessary cutthroat competition, and the inability of some firms to reach a viable scale of operation.

Controlling foreign investment. For many years, MITI played a decisive role in appraising and controlling almost all forms of foreign investment in Japan. Even in the 1950s when Japan was particularly capital-poor, MITI exercised its discretion whenever it suspected that foreign investment did not fit with its vision of the workings of the Japanese economy. All forms of investment were carefully screened. Even financial investments in the form of loans and debts were not subject to automatic approval.

Foreign investment control was linked to opportunity management most directly through its impact on industry structure and competition. Foreign companies could not acquire Japanese firms. Nor could they establish a wholly owned subsidiary in Japan unless they could provide essential raw materials, technology, or finished products that Japan might have severe difficulty obtaining elsewhere. Joint ventures with Japanese firms were thoroughly scrutinized. Joint ventures had a much better chance of being approved if the foreign firm provided access to technology or raw materials.

Managing turbulence. MITI's dominant role in economic decision making has contributed heavily to arguments supporting the existence of "Japan, Inc." Yet the history of MITI, full as it is of institutional wrangling, political in-fighting, and "turf" wars, suggests that Japan is and has been a far cry from a homogeneous, monolithic society. MITI itself was for many years a political football. It became a parking lot for political and governmental appointees, giving rise to much internal political and bureaucratic disputes. Even the founding and continued existence of MITI were bitterly opposed by some political and governmental leaders. It is always important to note that MITI's role and dominance in Japan's economic policy making has followed a checkered path, revealing a number of peaks and valleys.

MITI has always had to fight other governmental agencies, political and governmental leaders, and industrial constituencies to have its views prevail and sometimes even heard, fights that MITI has not always won as it would have liked. For example, MITI's plan to develop and structure an automobile industry was initially intensely opposed by the Bank of Japan, the Ministry of Transportation, the Ministry of Finance, and some elements in the automobile industry. MITI had to pull out many of its formal and informal weapons to get its plan of action off the ground. Even so, many lingering pockets of doubt were still being heard in the late 1950s.

MITI's commitment to cartels and mergers brought it into frequent confrontation with the Fair Trade Commission. It was the latter's responsibility to administer the Antimonopoly law. Many forms of MITI's "informal" advice to industries and individual firms were also frequently challenged by the Fair Trade Commission. Not surprisingly, MITI's actions or plans were also frequently bitterly opposed by factions in industries who believed they were being slighted or were not receiving due support from MITI. In short, MITI's success in no small way stemmed from its ability to manage its relationship with a vast array of constituencies. Its capacity to shape some degree of consensus out of well-entrenched conflicts was a sine qua non of its policy-making success from the late 1950s or when many of its direct controls (e.g., control over foreign exchange) no longer existed or were less significant.

In summary, primarily through the auspices of MITI, Japan has designated a series of industries for special development and nurturing. These industries were aided through financial, tax, and technology supports and were sheltered from foreign competition in the domestic market. An institutional infrastructure was erected to foster these industries at home and to help them break into foreign markets. In short, Japan has not depended and does not now depend on the "invisible hand" or the free flow of market competition to generate market opportunities. The very visible hand of the Japanese government or, more precisely, business-government relations has been the dominant driving force in transforming the sheltered economy of the early 1950s into one of the three major players on the world economic stage.

IDENTIFYING AND MANAGING MARKET OPPORTUNITIES

The tasks of identifying and managing business opportunities did not rest solely with the Japanese government but depended at least as much on the initiative of the Japanese companies themselves. This section will investigate how Japanese companies identified and managed their market opportunities in the particular industries designated as target opportunities by the government. Five strategic approaches to opportunity identification and management will be discussed.

Strategy I: In Search of Provided Opportunities

In most of the industries selected as targets for Japanese entry, Japanese firms sought to identify market segments that had been ignored or poorly served by other firms. The Japanese committed themselves to establishing a solid presence in these unserved market segments. After achieving success in these initial market segments, they would move toward the larger part of the market. This has been the dominant strategy in almost every industry in which the Japanese now compete worldwide.

The Japanese chose entry points into the U.S. market where U.S.

competition had been weak, complacent, or nonexistent. American producers were concentrating little attention on small autos or motorcycles; cheap, easy-to-carry radios or television sets; or copiers suitable to the needs (in terms of both function and price) of small businesses. The Japanese entered the U.S. motorcycle market by picking out the ignored segment—the small lightweight motorcycle—as their target while other strong competitors such as Harley Davidson, B.S.A., Triumph, and Norton of the United Kingdom focused on the higher-price and bigger machine. The Japanese invaded the copy machine industry by offering the small-copier market a new, small, plain paper model to attract small-business customers who had never considered purchasing a big copier, as well as those copier users who were dissatisfied with the older-model, coated-paper copier that was less efficient. This strategy of exploiting the unserved or ignored market segment is the best illustration of how the Japanese exploit "provided" opportunities.

These opportunities are much more clearly seen as provided when we consider U.S. responses to the initial Japanese entry into these unserved markets. Many U.S. competitors publicly decried the Japanese for their efforts to nurture these markets. Honda's first small motorcycles were depicted as "toys." Sony's first small televisions were depicted as "playthings."

This attitude no doubt reflected U.S. firms' beliefs that these segments were small and would remain small and therefore did not constitute opportunities for significant profits. This is well illustrated in Harley Davidson's view of the end of the small motorcycle market that Honda attacked:

> We believe that motorcycles are sports vehicles, not transportation vehicles. . . . It is generally for leisure time use. The lightweight motorcycle is only supplemental. Back around World War I a number of companies came out with lightweight bikes. We came out with one ourselves. We came out with another one in 1947 and it just did not go anywhere. We have seen what happens to these small sizes . . .

Of course, the real acid test of a "provided" opportunity goes beyond the beliefs and attitudes of U.S. firms. They did not respond to the entry of Japanese firms by producing similar-type products and going head-to-head against the foreign invaders. Rather, the Japanese were given a number of years to exploit their chosen market segments before they encountered direct U.S. competition. The Japanese found these "windows of opportunity" and made the best of them. Success did not come quickly. Patience, diligence, and persistence were the Japanese trademarks. As we will see in later chapters, the Japanese were not idling as they sought to penetrate these niches: They were improving their products, stretching their product lines, and learning about the U.S. market. They were positioning themselves for the market battles which they knew lay ahead. The opportunity for them to do so was provided them by U.S. firms.

Strategy II: Created Opportunities

At the opposite end of the opportunity spectrum are what we will term *created* opportunities. These are opportunities that the Japanese have fashioned through their own research and technology development. Their products are no longer scaled-down imitations of U.S. products, and they assume much more the role of market leader and innovator. Rather than confrontation avoidance, which is a key element in "provided" opportunities, created opportunities almost inevitably bring about some form of competitive confrontation because they usually entail taking existing or potential market positions away from U.S. firms. Created opportunities, then, involve competing in existing product-markets broadly defined or establishing new product-markets where competition can be expected to appear quite quickly.

The essence of created opportunities consists of seeking and establishing new product-market niches in the face of stiff competition. New market needs or wants are created and fostered. In so doing, products are significantly modified or improved or both. Sometimes, even products new to the market may be introduced.

A good illustration of created opportunities is the watch industry. The Japanese watch industry has secured a position of world leadership as a result of its pioneering quartz technology that created new opportunity in the watch market. The big break for the Japanese watchmakers was in the early 1970s when Japanese quartz oscillation watches and clocks powered by midget electric cells began to upgrade precision watchmaking technologies and replace conventional mechanical watches with longer-lived and more-accurate watches. Due to this technology as well as the slowness of the Swiss watchmakers to respond to the new challenge, the Japanese created their opportunities and swept to the top of the world market. Citizen, one of the leading Japanese watchmakers, created its own place in the market by offering a highly accurate quartz crystal wristwatch; it then introduced the world's first solar cell analog watch; and it later introduced the world's most precisely accurate high-frequency quartz watch "Citizen Quartz Mega" with an error ratio of three seconds per year, an ultrathin quartz watch and a multifunction with both digital and analog time indication. These product innovations helped build a strong market share for Citizen in the U.S. market.

Japan's initial success in the U.S. TV and radio market was due to its strategy in entering the lower-end market; but its dominance over the consumer electronic industry, particularly in audio and video, came about through its innovations. Whereas the transistor technology dominated the development of the electronic industry during the 1950s and early 1960s, the Japanese expansion into IC and semiconductor know-how helped open up new areas of opportunity, particularly in video electronics. For example, Sony has long realized that without building something new and better, it would be hard to outcompete its U.S. competitors. As a result, Sony's management places major emphasis on R&D that leads to product innovation. The development of the tape recorder, magnetic tape, Trinitron color TV, and Betamax videotape recorder is the result of creative innovation.

The 1970s and 1980s have witnessed a transition on the part of the Japanese: They have moved from exploiting provided opportunities to manufacturing created opportunities. They were the first to introduce on a large scale solid-state television, quartz watches, and plain paper copiers. Computers, semiconductors, and pharmaceuticals are industries where they have clearly begun to create opportunities in the 1980s. In the space of a few short years, they have assumed a dominant position in the semiconductor industry, and many are predicting that a similar fate awaits the computer industry.

Strategy III: Create Opportunities
through Marketing Creativity

Technology breakthroughs are not the only key to succeeding at competitive product development. What is really required is product and market creativity.

Sony's Walkman success is an excellent example. The Walkman audio system is not a technological breakthrough but rather a creative version of a standard product. Sony knew that a lot of people like music and want to take good stereo sound with them wherever they go, not just in their homes. But to bring a radio or tape recorder with them is cumbersome, so why not produce a product to satisfy them? Sony developed the right product and was able to sell over 4 million units of Walkman in the United States.

Sony's marketing creativity can also be seen in the personalized TV market. Sony decided to produce a five-inch TV so that people who liked to watch television could have TV available anywhere. This was at a time when U.S. TV producers were concentrating on making bigger-screen television. Sony introduced its portable TV and had great success in the market.

If we compare Sony's products with those of other Japanese producers such as Matsushita (Panasonic), we might wonder why Sony is able to price its products higher than others in the U.S. market and exploit this advantage even though their prices are at parity in Japan and their quality is nearly the same. The secret is Sony's creative marketing. Sony realized that when product performance and quality as well as other modes of distribution are almost the same, image may be the only source for differentiation. Sony has long invested more heavily in public relations and promotion to build up its product image as the superior quality product than its competitors in the United States. The resulting image difference provides the opportunity for Sony to price its products at around 5 to 10 percent above those of its competitors.

Another good example of creative Japanese marketing has occurred in the camera industry. Because of the sluggish sale growth of the single-lens 35-mm reflex cameras that were designed for photographers who know how to operate sophisticated cameras, Canon made this kind of camera simple to use by introducing its AE-1, the automation 35-mm model, in 1976. Until then, the industry wisdom held that 35-mm cameras were sophisticated items for professional photography only. Instead of promoting its product to this limited target group, Canon broke the old tradition and promoted its product with a multimillion-dollar TV campaign, a medium that did not seem appropriate for a 35-mm model. It was a big gamble for Canon, since never before had this kind of camera been advertised on TV, but Canon's objective was to create new opportunity by broadening the market to other target groups. With the first catchy commercial showing tennis star John Newcombe snapping action photos with the new camera, this gamble paid off. Canon's sales skyrocketed and hardly kept up with demand.

Strategy IV: Adapting to and Changing
Customer Preferences

The Japanese have demonstrated a notable capacity for adapting to customer preferences. Unquestionably, a central element in opportunity creation and management is understanding what the customer wants (or might want) *and* is willing to pay for. Of course, this is the heart of the marketing concept: *anticipating and satisfying customer needs and wants at a profit.*

This is clearly shown in the case of color television. Around 1975, demand in the U.S. market began to shift toward the high-quality portable and table models. The U.S. firms, however, still concentrated on the production of console models and ignored the quality of their products but relied on heavy advertising, since they believed that only a strong brand name would hold the loyalty of American consumers. In contrast, Sony and Matsushita took this shifting demand as their opportunity. They rapidly developed portable color TV models to serve this emerging demand and attended to quality as the first priority. As a result, U.S. firms lost their color TV market to the Japanese within a very short time period.

Clearly, in both provided and created opportunities, the Japanese have also shown a capacity to change customer preferences. Honda labored hard to get more Americans to consider buying and driving a motorcycle by making it fun to ride and by selling the idea that "You meet the nicest people on a Honda." Toyota labored hard to sell the idea that small, fuel-efficient, high-quality automobiles make sense for American drivers.

The Japanese have never allowed themselves to be seduced by the economist's notion of "revealed preference"—i.e., customers' preferences are revealed by what they spend their money on. They have always shown a tendency to go beyond *current* preferences. Opportunities reside in unserved preferences—the meat of both provided and created opportunities. Stated differently, the Japanese are master practitioners of market segmentation—i.e., trying to identify clusters of customers who might buy a different product or buy the same or a similar product for a different reason.

Strategy V: Learning from Competitors to Create Opportunities

The Japanese have not limited opportunity identification to a better understanding of their customers. They have focused on a better understanding of their competitors: how their competitors conduct their business, what products they sell, what strategies they pursue, how they manufacture their products, and so on. They study competitors' weaknesses and limitations to identify possible vulnerabilities.

Learning from and through U.S. competitors has been a well-mastered practice of the Japanese. As a means of entering the U.S. market, they have frequently used potential U.S. competitors to distribute their products. While the U.S. firms are helping to develop a market position for the Japanese products, the Japanese are learning all they can about how the U.S. firms do business—how they distribute, promote, and sell the product, what kinds of relationships they develop with the trade, and so on. Of course, they also learn a good deal about the market—what customers appreciate and value, where they buy, and so on. The Japanese fashion this learning into opportunity. Once they develop a market position for their products and they feel they have learned enough about the market, they establish their own distribution and sales system, sell under their own brand name, and begin to compete directly with the U.S. manufacturers and distributors who helped them gain an initial toehold in the U.S. market.

The following example illustrates the Japanese penchant for studying their competitors and putting that knowledge to use. In the home appliance industry, one of the major Japanese firms, after learning about its competitor's success in developing an automatic dishwasher, took the competitor's dishwasher to its laboratory. It assessed the competitor's model in terms of product performance, the number and variety of parts, and cost structure. The machine was stripped down to examine each component in order to identify design improvements as well as to learn about the competitor's technological capabilities. The competitor's factory, production facilities, and distribution system were investigated. Through this process, the Japanese firm was able to design a dishwasher that outperformed those of its competitors, and it also developed a more-effective distribution system.

THE ROLE OF MARKETING INTELLIGENCE

All of the opportunity identification and management activities impose extensive information requirements. Indeed vast amounts of different types of information are required. Understanding the U.S., European, and even broader Asian markets involves learning new cultures, new institutional arrangements, and new ways of doing business. Japan, however, has been equal to the task. It has clearly distinguished itself in its voracious appetite for information collection, analysis, and dissemination.

Japan's institutional infrastructure has greatly facilitated its information-gathering and management process. Some institutional elements were put in place specifically to perform these tasks. The Japanese trading companies, MITI, and JETRO have each established a worldwide market intelligence system. All of the large Japanese firms have developed their own information intelligence system. Not only is the scale of these data networks peculiar to Japan, but the degree of information exchange among and between these information collection entities far outstrips anything found in any other country.

The role of the general trading companies in foreign commercial intelligence, and in aiding individual Japanese firms (and sometimes even industries) to transform such intelligence into product-market opportunities, cannot be overstated. Each of the nine general trading companies (GTC) operates on a worldwide scale. Each has been organized into worldwide product divisions characterized by a country-product matrix system so that each division will have an in-depth knowledge and experience in a particular country-product. A large number of personnel are trained in handling certain products or groups of products, with particular emphasis on a country or group of countries. Each division manager has been sent abroad for a stay of between three and five years in order to learn the language, culture, and markets in these countries. The trading companies send and receive via telex tens of thousands of pieces of information each day. The volume of information delivered by GTC exceeds that exchanged daily by the country's Ministry of Foreign Affairs.

With their worldwide network of intelligence systems and their large number of specialists, the GTC are the Japanese firms' major vehicles for appraising and identifying overseas opportunities. The use of GTC marketing information by large Japanese firms varies a great deal depending on the kind of industry. For example, industries with homogeneous products like steel rely heavily on the services provided by the general trading companies. High-technology firms tend to depend less on the trading companies.

Among governmental agencies, JETRO is the most significant. JETRO is a semiautonomous organization under the supervision of governmental authorities. It functions as a national center of market information for Japanese business firms. Its main function is largely informational and includes such activities as publishing periodicals and monographs on foreign trade, collecting international market intelligence, collecting and disseminating current worldwide market data, sponsoring market research, and organizing trade fairs and seminars. Perhaps most significant of all is the fact that at the request of business firms or trade organizations, JETRO helps pay the cost of market research. Such a policy of underwriting research costs is extremely beneficial to smaller-sized firms that otherwise cannot afford the cost of information activities. The breadth of information gathered by JETRO ranges from general data and trends on individual countries to custom-tailored market studies. Detailed market information, competitors' activities, political and legal conditions, and suggestions on product strategy are indicative of help provided to JETRO clients.

JETRO now operates seventy-five offices around the world, and its officers are specially trained in handling market opportunities. This organization has been closely interrelated with MITI. Its early scope and direction were precisely shaped by MITI. In fact, many of its key personnel have been MITI transferees.

IN SEARCH OF FUTURE OPPORTUNITIES

Since World War II, Japan has been quick to establish and modify its institutional structures to manage institutional conflicts and societal turbulence. It artfully employs both formal and informal structures and processes. One important example in the context of industrial opportunity management is the Industrial Structure Council (ISC). Founded in the early 1960s, the ISC is an advisory organ that discusses and deliberates on the direction of MITI's policies. It is composed of different interest groups: industry, academia, consumers, and labor unions.

During the past twenty years, the Industrial Structure Council has prepared three reports that have served as guidelines for MITI's policies. The first report, "The Industrial Structure in Japan," appeared in 1963; the second report, "The Vision of MITI's Policies in the 1970s," appeared in 1971. Finally, for the 1980s, the council prepared "The Vision of MITI Policies in the 1980s," which was published in 1981. The last report reveals much about the current focus of Japanese opportunity creation and management. Technology will serve as the major force in Japan's drive for domination of new-product markets. This 1981 MITI report, which reveals the searching of future opportunities, is worth quoting from extensively, as shown below.

The Vision of MITI Policies in the 1980s: Toward a Technology-Based Nation

PHILOSOPHY

(1) Technological innovation is a source of progress for Japan as well as the world. Great expectations are therefore placed on technological innovation providing the key to solution of various problems in the 1980s. Japan must strive to develop its creative capacity and contribute, as an innovator, to world progress.

(2) As technological development is a means of attaining economic security by strengthening a country's bargaining power, Japan must stand on the ground of technology.

(3) The now prevalent apprehension is that the technological progress is

about to stagnate. In the 1980s, however, the following types of techno-logical efforts will be made: (a) new application and combination of existing technologies, (b) flowering of new technology resulting from a new application of science and technology, and (c) the preparation for the next generation's epoch-making technological innovations expected in the years after 1990. If these efforts are successful, the economy and society are expected to move into a new, prosperous stage.

OBJECTIVE OF TECHNOLOGICAL DEVELOPMENT IN THE '80s

The principal tasks for technological development to be stimulated by economic and social necessities in the '80s are the following:

(1) Energy

(a) Energy-saving technologies such as magneto-hydrodynamics (MHD) power generation, highly efficient gas turbines, fuel cells and a waste heat recovery system.

(b) Alternative energy technologies such as nuclear power, coal, solar energy and geothermal energy.

(c) New energy technologies such as nuclear fusion for commercial application in the 21st century.

(2) Improving the Quality of Life and Community Facilities

(a) Social systems related to personal and community life including a medical information system.

(b) New energy-saving housing systems and artificial ground for intensive use of land.

(3) Knowledge-Intensive and Innovative Technologies

(a) Knowledge-intensive production systems equipped with microcomputers, and upgraded resource-saving and energy-saving technologies.

(b) Innovative technologies such as new materials, optical communication, VLSI (very large scale integrated circuit), and laser beam technology.

(4) The Next-Generation Technologies

(a) In the field of life sciences: treatment of cancer, genetic manipulation, investigation into a photosynthesis process and its application for food production.

(b) In the field of energy: nuclear fusion and MHD power generation.

(c) In the field of data processing: applying newly discovered principles such as the Josephson effect.

(5) Among the above themes, particular emphasis must be placed on three areas:

(a) Development of technologies inventing new materials.

(b) Development of technologies, applying a large-scale system including those for alternative energy sources.

(c) Development of technologies related to a social system, including that in the field of personal and community activities.

NEW PHASE IN POLICY ON TECHNOLOGY

The principal role of the government policy for the development of technology is to encourage development efforts in the private sector. In the past, the Japanese industry achieved brilliant results in improving and applying imported technologies. In the '80s, however, it will be essential for Japan to develop technologies of its own purpose. For this purpose, it is necessary to systematically pursue policies with an emphasis on the following three points.

(1) Development of Creative Technologies

(a) Switchover to "forward engineering": Now that it has become increasingly difficult to find specific goals of development of imported technologies, Japan needs to press ahead with projects for the research and development of original technologies through trial and error and the accumulation of basic data.

(b) Training of personnel capable of achieving technological breakthroughs.

(c) Establishment of a system to encourage taking risks and squarely facing new challenges.

(2) Systematic Promotion of Technology

(a) Technological developments must be promoted by presenting a "Long-term Vision for Technological Development," which identifies the priority goals for technological developments, as well as systems for development and funding.

(b) In the area of energy-related technologies and in other pressing areas requiring a large amount of development funds, the government must launch national projects on its own initiatives.

(3) Increased Allocation of Research and Development Funds

(a) Efforts must be made to increase the budget available for research and development of technologies.

(b) The share of government expenditures for R&D in total R&D expenditures is in the order of one-third in Japan, compared with around a half in Western industrialized countries. This share should be raised in spite of the expected deficit in the national budget.

(c) Recognizing that research and development of technologies are the nation's best interest, the government must make every effort to find a new source of funds for financing such projects.

LESSONS AND IMPLICATIONS

Based on this review, some key lessons about opportunity management are:

- Companies should not wait for market opportunities. They need to know how to systematically search, choose, and manage them.

- Companies must pay attention to whether the government will support or impede the opportunity. The attractiveness of an opportunity is magnified when the government plans to support the sector in which the opportunity is found, through such means as trade protection, administrative assistance, and subsidies.

- Companies can identify "provided opportunities" by examining unsatisfied customer needs, competitors' weaknesses, and company strengths.

- Companies can create new opportunities by stimulating internal creativity and by actively monitoring the changing environment.

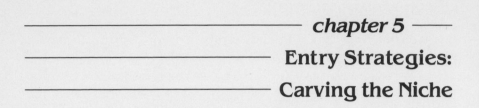

chapter 5

Entry Strategies:
Carving the Niche

Any organization wishing to compete in a particular marketplace has to face the question of how to enter the market successfully. Foreign market entry, in particular, requires more study and ingenuity than do new entries within the domestic market. Throughout the past decades, the Japanese have demonstrated a high degree of proficiency in developing effective entry strategies to penetrate every market selected as a target. The market-entry strategies are not original with the Japanese, but they do exhibit the Japanese capacity for painstaking implementation of classic marketing techniques developed elsewhere.

How the Japanese enter foreign markets can be discussed in two distinct steps: (1) their pre-market-entry activities that help identify the target product-market to enter and (2) the specific marketing strategies and tactics used to gain entry into the market.

PRE-MARKET-ENTRY ACTIVITIES

Successful Japanese companies do not simply export their existing domestic products to the new markets. On the contrary, they spend much time analyzing market opportunities and acquiring a deep understanding of how consumer and organizational markets work in the specific target market they are considering.

Market feasibility studies and marketing research are the two important pre-market-entry activities undertaken by the Japanese. They send study teams to the country, and these teams spend several months doing a feasibility study before making their recommendations. Their sales subsidiaries and personnel are stationed in various countries. Japanese trading companies and JETRO are the two major institutions that help provide numerous valuable insights and market information to Japanese companies. Graduate students are sent by some Japanese companies to gather data in overseas countries. These different sources of marketing intelligence are channeled to their parent companies where this information serves as a data base for analyzing and identifying market opportunities before any market entry will be done.

In the U.S. market, for example, the invasion of Sony and Matsushita Electric into this market provide excellent examples of this pre-market-entry activity. Before entering the United States, Sony sent specialist teams of designers, engineers, and so forth, to the United States to study how to design its product to suit American consumers' preferences. Matsushita has stationed full-time personnel in the United States since 1951 to gather market information before entering the U.S. market. These companies then hire American industry specialists, consultants, and executives to help them figure out how to enter the market. Ironically, much Japanese marketing strategy in the United States has been formulated not by the Japanese but by the American executives working for them.

Toyota's entry into the American automobile market illustrates the careful approach taken by the Japanese. Toyota knew it would enter the small-car segment of the U.S. market, not the large-car segment. The small-car segment was dominated by Volkswagen (VW). Toyota knew that its success depended on challenging and displacing the VW. Although Japanese producers do not always attack the most successful competitor, they always study the most successful competitor or competitors to learn the reasons for the success. In the case of VW, Toyota commissioned an American marketing research firm to interview VW owners and determine what they liked and disliked about their VWs. VW owners wished that their cars would heat up better in the winter, would have more room in the back seat, and would have more attractive interiors. The Japanese went to the drawing board and designed a Toyota that offered all the advantages of the VW with none of the disadvantages. To clinch the offer, Toyota put a lower price on its car, spent a higher amount on advertising, and gave larger commissions to its dealers than did Volkswagen. Not surprisingly, Toyota hit the market right and gradually moved into the top spot at VW's expense. Toyota went after the right market (small cars), identified the key complacent competitor (VW), and formulated a superior offer of value.

Nissan Motor, before its decision to enter the United States, conducted its pre-market-entry activity through two Japanese trading companies. Marubeni Corp. took charge of market surveying on the Pacific Coast while Mitsubishi Corp. concentrated on the Atlantic Coast. Nissan's decision was to follow Marubeni's proposal. A project team then was sent to the United States to learn about the market conditions and consumers' tastes. Even though Nissan could not make a success in its first entry, it never stopped studying the market. As early as 1960, official teams were sent again to learn about American motor vehicles and production techniques as well as a car designed so that its previous shortcomings could be eliminated. Through this premarket activity, Nissan successfully reentered the U.S. market in the early 1960s by offering the "Bluebird," which was soon joined by the "Sunny."

In contrast, many American companies tended to ignore the wisdom of "situation appraisal." When General Foods and Revlon tried to crack the Japanese market, they totally exported American taste to Japan without modification. They did not carry out thorough market research. They would send a few staff people on an inspection tour, and these individuals would bring back only simple and superficial knowledge of market conditions, degree of competition, and Japanese consumer taste. The results were that both General Foods and Revlon failed to penetrate the Japanese market.

MARKET-ENTRY STRATEGIES

After identifying and carefully studying an opportunity segment, the Japanese will proceed to design a strategic market-entry plan that integrates all the marketing elements—product, price, distribution, and promotion. We will describe Japan's entry strategies in the 1950s and 1960s as well as some of the more recent strategies they have been using to enter new markets.

Product Strategy

When the Japanese began to enter foreign markets, their main objective was to gain strong market shares in each market. The Japanese had to face strong U.S. and European competitors that dominated many world markets at that time. Japanese products could not match their competitors' products in terms of either technology or global marketing networks. The main hope was to compete on price because of the Japanese labor cost advantage. In addition, the Japanese had to overcome their pre–World War II reputation for manufacturing shoddy products. Accordingly, in the 1950s and 1960s Japan placed especially heavy emphasis on designing, producing, and exporting three categories of products for their foreign market entries: (1) lower-cost products, (2) products with innovative features, and (3) high-quality products. This emphasis is also evident in their more recent market entries.

Lower-cost products.   While American firms concentrated on producing sophisticated products carrying high prices and high profit margins, the Japanese were content to produce simple, small, and more-standardized products at lower prices and profit margins. Their strategy aimed to build volume and drive cost down early in the product life cycle.

In the motorcycle industry, for example, Honda and Yamaha entered foreign markets with smaller and easier-to-operate machines; in the copy machine industry, Ricoh, Canon, and Sharp introduced much smaller machines than Xerox's; Sony and Panasonic, in the consumer electronics industry, entered foreign markets with smaller and standardized radios and television sets. This product strategy was also evident in other industries, such as automobiles and home appliances. The strategy is also clearly evident in recent market entries into knowledge-intensive industries, such as computer and medical electronic equipment. In the latter case, the Japanese entered the U.S. and world markets with a low-cost, stripped-down version of competitors' equipment. Toshiba, for example, introduced an X-ray computerized CT scanner at 40 percent less than GE's model and without some costly features that customers would not necessarily miss, whereas American manufacturers preferred to build sophisticated features and charge customers more.

Products with innovative features.   Although the majority of Japanese firms have employed low-cost product strategies in their foreign market entries, there are some exceptions. Some Japanese companies entered foreign markets by offering products with more features and functions than their competitors did. This product strategy was frequently applied in the case of technical products with short life cycles where new product development was the key to success. For example, in the hand-held calculator market, Casio, Sharp, and others offered various new features (e.g., calculators with clocks, with melodies, etc.). Casio's strategy was to bring out new models by changing and adding new features that their competitors' products did not have. Shortly after marketing its 2-mm-thick card-size calculator, Casio rapidly lowered the price and brought out a new model—a calculator with melodies. It aimed to accelerate and shorten the product life cycle to discourage competitors from following with a similar product. Seiko pursued a similar strategy in the watch market by bringing out many new features made possible by quartz technology.

Products with high quality and service. In their entry into foreign markets, especially the U.S. markets, Japanese companies placed heavy weight on two other product attributes—quality and service. Smallness (in product and price) alone does not guarantee continued product sales. If products break down frequently and customers cannot get service, competitors will enter and fill the void. The early Japanese entrants therefore had to devote considerable attention to the issues of product quality and after-sales services, especially because of the poor reputation of Japanese products before World War II.

Quality is a multidimensional product attribute. *Reliability* was heavily emphasized by many new Japanese entrants. Honda and Yamaha were at pains to get across to the American consumer the high reliability of their new small motorcycles, and similarly for the auto, copier, stereo, and television manufacturers. *Functionality*, or "fitness for use," has also been emphasized. Thus smaller motorcycles are convenient modes of transportation, smaller copiers can be used almost anywhere, and small TVs can easily be moved from room to room or viewed in places where it would be inconvenient to place the large "consoles."

Japanese entries in the 1970s and 1980s have also been marked by an emphasis on multiple dimensions of product quality. The entry of Japanese firms into the U.S. computer and semiconducter markets is a particularly noteworthy example. Japanese firms in these industries have been quite vociferous in proclaiming superior product quality. They have been aided in this claim by many U.S. firms, particularly in relation to semiconducter chips. In the late 1970s, American firms purchasing chips, notably Hewlett-Packard, emphasized that the quality of the chip shipments from U.S. suppliers was much worse than that of the chips from Japanese firms; it cited defect levels of up to ten times higher in the U.S. products.

In semiconductors, some critics have alleged that Japan may have gained an undeserved reputation for high quality by shipping 16K chips of atypically high quality to selected U.S. customers. Tests by some U.S. semiconductor manufacturers and users indicated that Japanese 16Ks sold to some less-favored customers were of a lower quality than U.S.-made 16Ks.

Japanese firms also paid attention to *service*. The Japanese are highly service minded and go out of their way to accommodate customers who have a problem. American buyers have found that service from Japanese manufacturers is at least as good as that provided by

American manufacturers. Nissan Motor, for example, after deciding to enter the U.S. market, carefully studied the experience of European imports—especially Volkswagen—and this study clearly showed that adequate provision for parts and services was vital to the success of imported cars to the United States. Nissan digested this lesson and developed its parts and services networks to assure customers of prompt and efficient service. It upgraded parts requirements for dealership, insisted on well-balanced inventories and well-trained parts personnel, with adequate and neat-appearing parts departments capable of providing courteous, prompt, and efficient service. Service departments have been established to develop good consumer relationships, handle consumer complaints, give direction and advice to dealers on design of service facilities, and so forth.

Pricing Strategy

Pricing strategy is one of the most important elements of the marketing mix in helping a company achieve its marketing objective. In entering foreign markets in particular, managers must decide on a pricing policy that will enable their company to attain its several goals in the target country-market it planned to enter. However, as Kotler pointed out, most U.S. companies still do not handle pricing well enough. Pricing is set independently of the rest of the marketing mix rather than as an intrinsic element toward achieving their ultimate marketing objectives. Very often the pricing strategy used by U.S. companies for their foreign market entry is too cost oriented (cost plus margin) and is aimed at achieving merely profitability rather than long-run market shares.

On the contrary, if we examine the Japanese marketing strategies, we can see that nothing has been more contentious about Japanese market-entry strategies (and market-penetration strategies) than their pricing behavior. In every target country-market the Japanese have entered, they have applied a so-called market-share pricing strategy which deliberately uses a low entry price to build up market share and establish a long-run dominant market position. The Japanese almost always set the prices of their products much lower than their competitors to attract potential customers, and they feel content to accept losses (in some cases) in the early years because they view them as an investment in their long-run market development. As a result, throughout the past two decades, the Japanese have been accused by many of their competitors of "dumping" their products, especially on the U.S. market—i.e., selling way below cost—and more generally, of selling their products in the United States at prices below those charged for the same products in

Japan. Both sets of charges have been upheld by the U.S. administrative and regular courts.

This aggressive pricing strategy to build up market shares is evident in almost all Japanese entries. All of their entries built around scaled-down versions of standard products came in at much lower prices than those being charged by U.S. firms. Honda's first motorcycles sold for $250 compared with the $1,000–$1,500 price tag on the then much-larger American machines. According to Harley Davidson, its Japanese makers charged as much as 139 percent more for the same bikes in Japan than they did in the United States. Japanese firms introduced three-transistor radios at $14 each when U.S. firms were selling six-transistor radios at $60 each. They eventually dropped their price down to $3.75, which at least partially contributed to many U.S. firms exiting from the market. Komatsu has priced its farm, construction, and mining equipment much lower than Caterpillar, the world's largest manufacturer of construction equipment.

Seiko entered the watch market by introducing a quartz model as an alternative to mechanical watches and selling these models in the price range of $65 to $350 to avoid a direct challenge to Swiss watchmakers, the longtime market leader who emphasized higher-priced watches. In order to gain a market foothold, Seiko relied on its quality and competitive price strategies. The strategy that Seiko used to produce high-quality watches, at relatively low prices, was the downward vertical integration of watch manufacturers. Many of the world's major watchmakers—Daini Seikosha Co. and Suwa Seikosha Co. for example—were linked to K. Hattori & Co. to produce timepieces for Seiko. These companies were fierce rivals, each having an integrated operation with its own component-making affiliates and research development units that turn out technical innovations and new designs. They competed vigorously in designing high-quality, low-cost products for their acceptance by Hattori. The result was that Seiko achieved an image for high-quality, wide-choice, reasonably priced watches.

Even in high-technology-based entries, the Japanese are not loath to use aggressive pricing. Although Japan is undoubtedly the industrial robot capital of the world, Japanese firms have relied heavily on price as the major weapon in their entry into the world market. In the early 1980s, a number of Japanese firms introduced many low-priced models—low priced by comparison with U.S.-produced robots.

The aggressive Japanese stance on pricing fits with their broader business and marketing strategy. The Japanese focused on high-volume products, thus allowing them to drive costs down, derive "experience effects," and push for market share. Lower prices also allow them to promote their products as giving greater value for the money.

Both of these short-run goals—use price to build volume and promote value—are, in turn, outgrowths of a broader goal: the attainment of a substantial market share over a number of years rather than more-immediate profitability goals. In pursuing volume growth, Japanese firms are not encumbered by the restraints imposed by the demands from corporate stockholders for high margins and high profits in the short run. Japanese firms can thus play a different game than has typically been experienced by U.S. firms in entering markets—i.e., the ability to live with low prices and profits in the short run in order to gain market share and position in the long run in the expectation that the latter will result in considerably enhanced future profitability. It should be noted, however, that this has not always been the case for Japanese firms in the U.S. marketplace.

Linking price, quality, and service. A noticeable feature of Japanese entry strategy is that they link price, quality, and service as three distinct attributes of their offer compared with the competition. The integration of these three attributes is well exemplified in the entry strategies of Japanese machine tool manufacturers. They have consistently priced their products below the prices charged by U.S. manufacturers. Initially, the lower price was designed to attract the attention of U.S. customers who had long depended on U.S. manufacturers. The Japanese manufacturers, however, also recognized that price alone would not sell their machine tools. Hence they placed tremendous emphasis on product quality: the advanced technology and the high degree of precision and reliability shown by their machine tools. They also recognized that downtime had to be kept to a minimum. Thus, immediate repair and maintenance services had to be built into the "package" offered to the customer. A network of service stations and spare parts centers was established right from the beginning in order to create a sense of confidence in U.S. customers.

Distribution Strategy

No matter how excellent a product or how low its price, it will still not sell unless and until it can be distributed to those who can purchase it. Distribution of their products provided a major challenge to Japanese firms trying to break into the U.S. market. They did not know the U.S. market, they had a poor-quality image and reputation, and many of them did not have the resource base to develop their own distribution channels. Nor were U.S. channels of distribution clamoring for Japanese products—in short, U.S. distributors were going to have to be sold before they would take large quantities of Japanese goods.

For these reasons, the Japanese approach to distribution was eclectic and strategic, where they chose whatever means had the best chance of gaining market access. They did not rely on time-honored distribution solutions used in Japan, Western Europe, or the United States. Some examples of Japanese strategic distribution are described below.

Initial market focus. Given the entry barriers facing them in foreign markets, the Japanese chose to concentrate their energies on specific market segments and entry points. In the U.S. market, for example, they did not try to blanket the United States as soon as they arrived. *Instead they focused on a particular geographical market, specific distributors and dealers, and/or individual customer types, and they "rolled out" their market penetration from this base.*

The constrained geographical focus was highly evident in many of the early Japanese entries. Toyota and Honda, for example, concentrated their efforts on California. It was there that they learned about the U.S. market, its tastes and preferences, and the way to handle U.S. distributors and dealers.

A selective initial market focus is also manifested in more-recent entries. The entry of Japanese banks in the past decade is a good example. They first focused on specific regions, such as California and New York. They concentrated on trade financing by serving subsidiaries of Japanese companies in the United States. In the middle 1970s, however, they started to consider U.S. customers. They first concentrated on high-volume, low-spread lending to those medium-sized U.S. companies that were anxious to borrow short-term money. Thus the Japanese came in with much lower spreads to serve their target customers than did other foreign banks, whereas U.S. banks tend to restrict their relationships to a few business firms with which they have built up relationships over a long period. The Japanese thus targeted those underserved medium-sized companies. To gain access to these customers, Japanese banks relied on their relationship with Japanese companies in the United States to introduce them to their U.S. suppliers and customers. They would then offer cheap yen loans to these multinational firms' subsidiaries in Japan in return for some business from these firms in the United States. In addition, the Japanese banks, through their home offices in Japan, would provide cheap yen funds to the Tokyo branch of American banks in exchange for participation in syndicated loans to highly rated U.S. companies as a means of gaining access to big U.S. companies.

Selective distribution. Japanese firms also focus on specific distribution channels and dealers. They will seek out those outlets that will give them large market coverage. Thus many television, radio, and audio equipment firms initially sold through large retail chains. Over 80 percent of Toshiba's early television sales went through Sears.

In the watch industry, Seiko signed up fifteen exclusive regional distributors to set up a strong nationwide marketing program instead of building its own national sales forces as its competitors did. Most of these distributors had long experience in business and had a certain position in the jewelry community that allowed Seiko to gain access to important outlets in selling watches. Through this distribution strategy, Seiko was able to gain a strong foothold in the quartz watch segment and employed it as a base for market expansion.

Selective distribution is also characteristic of recent entries. Japanese apparel producers in the higher-priced end of the U.S. market have relied heavily on high-fashion stores in large cities, such as New York and San Francisco. In medium-priced apparel, they have selected a wide range of geographically dispersed U.S. retailers. Japan's JETRO has also assisted the Japanese makers by sponsoring a Japan Fashion Fair in large cities in the United States to introduce U.S. buyers to Japanese apparel.

In cosmetics, Shiseido, the leading Japanese producer, entered the United States in the late 1960s but did not have much success. However, Shiseido has been trying hard in recent years to break into the U.S. market. It conducted product testing in several carefully selected test markets. Shiseido then began selling through high-quality department stores such as New York's Lord & Taylor, Washington's Woodward and Lathrop, and Houston's Neiman Marcus. The intent was to position its products as high-image and high-quality products in the U.S. market.

The Japanese are also not averse to targeting select customers for special attention. They then use their reputation with these customers as a means of gaining success and influence for the next layer of customers. In fact, U.S. firms have sometimes charged that the Japanese treat their U.S. customers better than they do their Japanese ones. Claims abound of the Japanese offering lower prices to particular U.S. customers as a way of penetrating the U.S. market.

One-tier distribution system. In some U.S. markets, the Japanese did not copy the distribution channel pattern of U.S. rivals but instead developed a distribution system more suited to their preferred long-term marketing mix. For example, when the Japanese first entered the U.S. television market, they employed one-tier distribution systems rather than the two-tier systems then being used by most U.S. manufacturers. When some new Japanese entrants launched a major onslaught on the U.S. copier market in the mid-1970s, they sold their products through independent office equipment dealers rather than through a direct sales force, as had been the practice of Xerox, the industry's long-term leader.

A common element in Japanese entry strategy is to use independent U.S. distributors and dealers as the primary means of getting the product to the end customers. This approach was adopted in industries where after-sales service was important—autos, motorcycles, watches, calculators, copiers, and medical equipment. Use of the independent distributors and dealers relieved the Japanese of the problems involved in developing their own distribution and sales arm—until they learned enough about the market and had penetrated the market to the point where they believed they could establish their own distribution and sales capability.

Exploitation of competitors' strength. Many Japanese firms gained access to U.S. markets by having U.S. firms distribute for them under American brand names. This strategy was very effective in overcoming the distribution problems or barriers to entry previously noted. It was especially prevalent in the early years of Japanese entry. Sony began exporting its transistor radio through American companies in the 1950s before it established its own distribution network. Ricoh, the first major entrant in the copier market, initially distributed its machines primarily through Savin Corporation. Yamaha sold its pianos through a U.S. manufacturer, the Story and Clark Piano Company of Wilmette. Even in the late 1970s, a number of the early entrants in the high-technology areas went this route. Fujitsu and Hitachi entered the U.S. market by selling their small computers through American producers such as Amdahl and Intel, respectively.

Establishing local sales organization. When the Japanese first started entering foreign markets, they relied heavily on foreign distributors or intermediaries to handle the distribution of their products because they lacked knowledge of foreign markets' distribution practices. Many Japanese companies simply exported their products to these foreign intermediaries without getting involved in managing distribution in the foreign markets. However, the Japanese soon realized the weakness of this approach. By totally depending on foreign intermediaries, they lacked the power to control and manage their own distribution functions that would be more important once their foreign market shares started growing. Without a company's own sales organization and distribution network in foreign markets, long-run channeling policies and strategies cannot be fully utilized to achieve their ultimate marketing objective. Thus the Japanese began to establish their own overseas sales subsidiaries shortly after their initial market entry had taken place. In this way, they were able to gain their own managerial experiences and thus be better able to strengthen their marketing efforts in foreign markets through directly controlling local marketing functions. These established sales subsidiaries, in turn, were the centers for their further development of overseas marketing networks, which will be discussed in detail in Chapter 9.

Dealers' wealth came first; company's later.   Irrespective of who distributed and sold the Japanese products or their degree of direct control over them, the Japanese offered higher middleman commissions and margins than did competitors in order to generate product push. They firmly believed in giving their distributors and dealers as much incentive as possible to push their products. In effect, this became a major competitive weapon for the Japanese in markets where their brand names were largely unknown, when they were still suffering from a poor-quality image, and when they wanted to develop a strong reputation for quality and service.

Promotion Strategy

The Japanese approach to promoting their products in the early stages of market entry reflects their commitment to establishing an initial market presence. Japanese firms will frequently work with their distributor to promote their products to the first few customers. They will provide the distributor with assistance and advice on how to "sell" the product.

Heavy advertising.   To back their product as well as to support the "push" strategy of their distribution channels, the Japanese sometimes spend heavily on promotion, especially on advertising. This has been particularly true of those Japanese firms who, from the beginning, were intent on selling under their own corporate or brand name. In many of their market entries, they have supported their products with heavy local or regional advertising. In many instances, Japanese firms have engaged in joint promotional programs with their distributors and dealers.

Brand name promotion.   Many Japanese firms have promoted their own corporate and brand names from their initial entry. Sony, Toyota, Nissan, Matsushita (Panasonic, Quasar), Mitsubishi, and Casio pushed their own name and tried to develop their own image and reputation. While there were major marketing risks inherent in this approach and success came slowly to most of these firms, they did begin to establish a consumer franchise and corporate identity. The identification of these names with customer value was a major driving force for many of these Japanese firms.

SOME EXTENDED ILLUSTRATIONS
OF JAPANESE MARKET-ENTRY
STRATEGY IN THE U.S. MARKETS

We will now focus on Japanese entry strategies in two industries: motorcycles and semiconductors.

Motorcycle Industry

In the motorcycle industry, Japanese producers entered the U.S. market in 1959 by aiming at the lower-price, small lightweight motorcycle market that had been ignored by major producers such as Harley Davidson, BMW, Norton, Triumph, and other European and American companies. Most of Japanese machines were under 500 cc, whereas their competitors put more concentration on heavyweight motorcycles and viewed the small machines as toys.

Honda was the Japanese company that pioneered this market. It set its objective in terms of sale volume growth rather than short-time profitability. To achieve its objective, Honda introduced a lightweight motorcycle of higher quality than the lightweights being sold at that time. Honda's motorcycle was small and easy to handle, with three-speed transmission, automatic clutch, and 5 horsepower when compared with the 2½ horsepower of U.S. products. To gain market acceptance, Honda placed the greatest weight on product quality and performance. More than seven hundred design engineers worked on this project. Having developed a good product, Honda priced its product aggressively by selling under $250 retail compared with more than $1,000 for larger U.S. machines. Honda set up its own sales subsidiary, American Honda Motor Co., in Los Angeles instead of relying on local distributors. From this base, Honda lined up 125 distributors, moving region by region, starting from the West Coast and moving eastward. Once its distribution networks had been established, Honda launched a marketing campaign to eradicate the bad image of motorcycle users. Honda conducted a major advertising campaign to cultivate the idea that Honda motorcycles were socially appealing and acceptable to the average family with the theme "You meet the nicest people on a Honda" in *Time, Life,* and *Look* magazines as well as other media. In 1965, Honda spent about $4 million on advertising. In addition to the nationwide campaign, Honda promoted its distributors' sales through regional advertising, with estimated expenditures of around $150,000 in 1965. Honda also stressed the importance of after-sale service. To ensure adequate service, Honda invested in retail missionary sales persons, generous warranties, service support, and quick spare parts availability to back up its marketing message. With these strategies, Honda's sales in the U.S. market rapidly expanded to nearly $77 million in 1965 compared with only $500,000 in 1960.

After Honda's successful penetration, Yamaha, another Japanese manufacturer, decided to enter the U.S. market. Its first step was to study the leaders' major weaknesses, which included several dealers who had become rich and lazy, discouragement of franchise-seeking dealers, and a neglect of promoting the mechanical aspects of their motorcycles. Yamaha also aimed at the lightweight machine, which implied competing against Honda but put more emphasis on the off-road machine. Yamaha developed its own distribution network, offered franchises to the best of Honda-rejected franchisees, and built an enthusiastic sales team to train and motivate its dealers. It continued to improve its products until they could claim and demonstrate mechanical superiority. Yamaha also spent liberally on advertising and sales promotion programs to build buyer awareness and dealer enthusiasm. When motorcycle safety became a big issue, Yamaha designed superior safety features and advertised extensively. These strategies successfully propelled Yamaha to gain a strong market share in the lower-end motorcycle market.

Another good example of Japanese market-entry strategy is Kawasaki, which came in after Honda and Yamaha were well established in the U.S. market. Kawasaki's initial step was to introduce its small bike, Omega, into the market, and it established a one-employee office in Chicago that was later transferred to California. In California, Kawasaki searched for and signed up strong dealers. It conducted a market survey to determine American customers' demands. The information was sent to the parent company in Japan to design a suitable product for American tastes. The result was an introduction of a 31-horsepower motorcycle with a five-speed transmission, a quick cycle designed for the American market. This product strategy stressed speed and performance. Kawasaki kept on improving its product and finally developed a three-cylinder machine that was faster than the biggest Harley. Shortly after that, Kawasaki launched a big cycle machine, almost as powerful as Harley's but closer in price to a smaller Honda. With its high-performance product, Kawasaki started to promote its product with a heavy advertising campaign and its advertising budget jumped from $300,000 in 1970 to $1.5 million in 1971. This was followed by a nationwide campaign with the theme "Kawasaki lets the good times roll," on which Kawasaki spent $12 million from 1973 to 1976. To support this campaign, more dealers were added and its distribution networks were expanded to other regions. To enforce the company's reputation of quality and reliability as well as adequate service, Kawasaki located parts warehouses in key areas, namely, in Lincoln, Nebraska, and in the East and West Coast areas. As a result, Kawasaki gained brand recognition followed by strong market-share growth.

Semiconductor Industry

The increasing sophistication of consumer electronic products during the 1970s helped push the development of Japanese semiconductor industries. Whereas the main semiconductor source for U.S. firms has been the computer industry, the Japanese also had a strong demand for chips from their consumer electronic ventures. For the Japanese, consumer electronics absorb 50 percent of their total semiconductor output, whereas only 15 to 20 percent of U.S.-made chips are used in consumer equipment.

As a result of the rapid market growth of electronic products, Japan was able to lower its costs on semiconductor components production. Most leading Japanese producers of electronic products—such as NEC, Hitachi, Toshiba, and Matsushita—initially developed their semiconductor production as captive supplies to their large consumer electronic divisions. The large consumer electronic market is Japan's "cash cow" source for funding its developmental research in semiconductors. The Japanese consumer electronic companies developed their semiconductors by acquiring U.S. technology and then improving the received technology. Once the Japanese semiconductor industry reached technological sophistication and met internal requirements, it turned to exporting.

In 1976, the Japanese started to make inroads on the U.S. market by producing the 4K memory chip. Shortly thereafter, they shifted their focus to the 16K RAM market when U.S. suppliers were not able to adequately supply their chips to serve the increasing demand. The Japanese—led by NEC, Hitachi, and Matsushita—rapidly took this opportunity to supply the market with their chips. Whereas American companies concentrated on building more complex chips to cram more memory capacity onto the fingernail-size silicon chips, the Japanese stuck with producing relatively simple chips. They squeezed the circuitry of four of the earlier-generation, U.S.-designed 16K chips into a single chip. They sold their product in the market with the same approach as that used for their earlier 16K and built a strong market share while the U.S. firms' share eroded. The Japanese priced their product so low that it triggered charges of illegal dumping. A survey showed that the 16K price in Japan was 30 percent higher than that of the same product sold in the United States. They lowered their price further once sales volumes had started to increase. In just one year, 1980, the 16K price fell from $20 to only $2.

Even though price was the strongest Japanese weapon in penetrating the U.S. market, their other weapon was quality. The Japanese reputation for quality grew out of their efforts to improve the U.S. design. Quality control was stressed. Toshiba spent up to 50 percent more than its U.S. rivals for production marks to lay down the circuit pattern on chips, a process that cut their rejection rate to only one-tenth that of U.S. lines. Automation was adopted to reduce human error in assembly work. Japanese quality has been widely accepted even from the U.S. firms themselves. Hewlett-Packard complained that U.S. chips were worse than the chips from Japan; it cited defect levels of up to ten times higher in the U.S. products. While U.S. firms have improved their quality level, the defects are still about four times higher. In addition to better quality, Japanese firms have been described as rendering better service. Reportedly, the Japanese treated their U.S. customers even better than their Japanese ones.

One factor enabling the Japanese to sell their high-quality but cheaper-priced semiconductors is that the major Japanese firms are highly diversified, vertically integrated electronic-equipment manufacturers, including in their product mixes a wide variety of home appliances, data processing, telecommunication, and so forth. Because of their vertical integration, Japanese makers can draw on cash flow generated by downstream products to sustain heavy capital investment as well as R&D in semiconductor production. In the meantime, highly diversified downstream production provides a ready demand for these chips, which ensures production economies of scale and enables firms to gain learning curve economies more rapidly. These resulted in the Japanese ability to sell their 16K RAMs in the United States at 20 to 30 percent below those offered by American makers. With their lower-price, higher-quality product, the Japanese employed two approaches in their distribution strategy. The first approach was through direct marketing to original equipment manufacturers (OEMs), and the second one was the indirect approach through U.S. distributors. NEC, for instance, employs thirty American distributors for nearly 20 percent of its products sold in the United States while the rest are sold directly to OEM businesses, mainly the U.S. mainframe manufacturers.

JAPANESE ENTRY STRATEGIES: SOME
COMMONALITIES AND DIFFERENCES

Japanese market-entry strategies from the 1950s through the early 1980s reflect the maturing of Japan as an economic power and the growth in technological and market sophistication, skills, and capabilities of its individual firms. Although there are some key differences in Japanese entry strategies between these early and later periods, there are also some key commonalities.

A major difference in the entry strategies pursued by Japanese firms in the 1950s and 1960s compared with the 1970s and 1980s revolves around product positioning. Their early entry strategies sought to avoid direct competition with U.S. competitors. They addressed unserved or poorly served market niches. Low-cost, simple, small, and standardized products, whether by intention or accident, became a means of avoiding head-to-head confrontation with U.S. competitors. By contrast, Japanese entries from the early 1970s tend to confront existing competitors more directly, though frequently they do not take competitors head on. Thus the Japanese entry strategies have evolved from predominantly exploiting "provided" opportunities to much more by way of exploiting created opportunities.

Japanese entries in the 1970s and 1980s tend to be much more upscale and upmarket by comparison with their early entries. No longer are they solely pursuing the markets for small automobiles and motorcycles or cheap radios. Rather, they are entering the office computer systems market, the high end of the cosmetics and fashion markets, and a broad array of technology-oriented markets.

The movement from avoiding competition in unserved markets to challenging competitors in served and upscale markets reflects an evolution in Japanese products. They have progressed from small, simple, and standardized products to complex, innovative, and technically oriented products. Even though they still frequently emphasize product standardization, their products manifest a high degree of technical sophistication. They have gone from largely good imitations to innovative products and are now increasingly moving into inventions. In short, their market entries reflect the dramatic technological strides of the Japanese economy over the past thirty-five years.

As Japanese firms found themselves having to confront U.S. competition that was much less inclined to provide opportunities, and as they sought to protect themselves by entering more technologically advanced markets, they needed to catch up with and, in many instances, use competitors' technologies and established distribution systems. During the 1950s and 1960s, Japanese firms had largely relied on acquiring technology by licensing it from U.S. firms. Increasingly, corporation R&D and government-supported R&D replaced licensing. During the 1970s and 1980s, however, joint ventures emerged as a major entry strategy for Japanese firms. Joint ventures help the Japanese to overcome technological barriers, lessen distribution problems, and reduce potential competition. For example, joint ventures constitute a major plank of the Japanese entry into the aircraft industry. Ishikawajima-Harima Heavy Industries (IHI), Mitsubishi, and Kawasaki have formed a joint venture with Rolls-Royce of Great Britain, and Nissan has entered into a joint venture with Boeing. In the early 1970s, twenty Japanese firms produced semiconductors, about a third of them in joint ventures with foreign firms, mostly U.S. firms.

Yet it would also be misleading to overstate differences in Japanese entry strategies as their products have moved upscale, as they have gone from exploiting provided to created opportunities, and as their products have increased in technical sophistication. When Japanese firms are at a major disadvantage compared with U.S. firms, they still try to avoid or limit competitive confrontation by focusing on less well served and, sometimes, the lower end of the market. A good example is the Japanese entry into the computer market. Recognizing their limitations—the entrenched positions of competitors, the absence of name recognition and distribution systems—many Japanese firms concentrated on the small office system markets, an area on which the U.S. firms had placed little emphasis.

Also, in many markets when the Japanese have entered in more direct competition with U.S. competitors, they have often utilized a low-priced standardized product with additional features and outstanding service—a strategy that was much in evidence in the 1960s. Such has been the case in computer printers. A number of Japanese entrants employed this strategy in the early 1980s, and in the space of two years quickly assumed a leadership position in a market that had been dominated by U.S. firms.

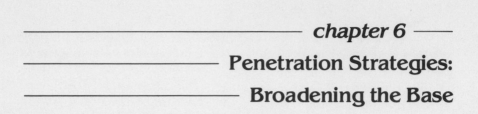

chapter 6

Penetration Strategies:

Broadening the Base

The real challenge encountered by the Japanese firms, even when they had entered the right markets and entered them right, was how to penetrate the U.S. market in the face of anticipated U.S. competitive retaliation and changing market conditions. The magnitude and scope of the challenge may very well have been exacerbated by their choice of entry position in most U.S. markets. Entering in market niches such as small automobiles, televisions, and copiers meant that they had to develop those markets themselves (they could not ride on the coattails of U.S. producers), and they had to move from those niches to larger and more profitable market segments if real market penetration and dominance were to be achieved. Understanding how the Japanese have so successfully penetrated so many U.S. markets not only reveals much about Japanese marketing but also allows us to learn much about the behavior and goals of U.S. firms during the Japanese infiltration.

The Japanese drive for product-market penetration has two focuses: *product development strategies* and *market development strategies*. Each reveals distinct aspects of the Japanese approach to market penetration. It is the effective integration of the two that makes the Japanese such formidable competitors.

PRODUCT DEVELOPMENT STRATEGIES

Japanese firms pursue three strategies in managing their product lines: product line stretching, product proliferation, and product improve-

104

ment. While the Japanese frequently pursue all three simultaneously, each deserves separate attention for its role in the Japanese pursuit of market share and competitive position.

Product Line Stretching

Once Japanese firms have gained an initial foothold in the U.S. marketplace, they diligently set about filling out their product line in order to reach an increasingly broader segment of the total market. They clearly recognized that a broad product line was necessary for long-term success against U.S. competitors who were already occupying the more profitable product-market niches. If they confined themselves to their initial market-entry segments, they could at best achieve only limited penetration of most U.S. markets. Not everybody would want small automobiles, motorcycles, televisions, and so forth.

The early Japanese entrants into the United States gradually stretched out their product line offerings. For many of them, this process unfolded over many years. Toyota's penetration of the U.S. market, for example, was marked by a sequence of product introductions, many of which represented product line extensions. Indeed, Toyota can well be expected to continue extending its range of product. Toyota seems clearly poised to enter the top of the market segment and begin competing against Mercedes, BMW, Volvo, and the upper-tier products of the U.S. producers.

One-way stretching.   For almost all of the early entrants and also for many of the entrants during the 1970s, product line stretching went one way: from the bottom end to the middle and higher ends. Automobiles, motorcycles, televisions, radios, and copiers exemplify this approach. Motorcycles are a good example. The Japanese began with very small low-priced bikes. Throughout the 1960s, Honda, which had pioneered the Japanese entry into the U.S. motorcycle market, stretched its line from under 125 cc. to 1000 cc. machines. Other Japanese companies such as Yamaha followed Honda by coming out with 500, 600, and 700 cc. models and also introduced a three-cylinder, four-stroke shaft-driven motorcycle of high displacement to compete in the heavyweight touring bike market. Kawasaki also launched a series of motorcycles, including its 900 cc. 2-1 model that was later upgraded to 1000 cc.

The copier market in which a number of Japanese firms entered in the mid-1970s furnishes another good example of the Japanese upgrading of their product line. Once they had gained a foothold in the small-simple market end, they rapidly brought to market a range of new medium-speed copiers. The Japanese have now moved into the larger end of the copier market and are competing head-to-head against the major U.S. producers.

Two-way stretching.   In pursuing market penetration, many Japanese firms adopt a strategy of two-way product stretching—moving simultaneously toward the lower and higher ends of the market. In the watch industry during the late 1970s, the Hattori group under the Seiko brand name began to stretch its product line by moving into both the upper and the lower market ends. In the late 1970s, a market niche for lower-cost but highly accurate digital watches began to emerge. Seiko penetrated downward to this lower market end by introducing a series of lower-priced watches under the brand name Pulsar. During the same period, it moved upward to penetrate the high-price and luxury end of the watch market. A set of higher-priced watches, produced by Jean LaSalle, a Hattori-acquired Swiss subsidiary, was introduced. Recently, a razor-thin watch costing around $5,000 was launched to attack the very high priced end of the market, which had long been dominated by Swiss watchmakers.

Product Proliferation

Whereas product line stretching changes product line width, product proliferation introduces a multiplicity of product types or models at each point in the product line. The Japanese have used product proliferation as a major market-penetration strategy in many industries.

Product proliferation serves a number of purposes for the Japanese. First, it allows them to appeal to a large number of market niches: As they proliferate their lines, they appeal to different tastes, preferences, and income levels. Second, the greater the number of products, the greater their capacity to tie up distribution channels and retail stores. This makes it tougher for U.S. and other producers to gain access to channels and to scarce retailer shelf or floor space.

Japanese consumer goods especially manifest product proliferation. Sharp and Casio, for example, introduced a wide array of models of hand calculators with different styles, functions, and features. Many model changes per year was the norm. Japanese watch manufacturers perhaps best exemplify extreme proliferation. Seiko offers over four hundred models in the United States, both quartz and mechanical. Worldwide, Seiko manufactures and sells more than twenty-three hundred models, with many of them slowly entering the United States.

Canon's success in cameras has revolved around a long line with multiple models. Canon achieved a major success with its AE-1 35-mm single reflex model; it then sold many varieties of this basic model by varying the features offered. Canon's marketing thrust is indicative of many Japanese firms: Whenever a new product goes on the market, the next one will be on the way.

Product proliferation is also well exemplified in Honda's product strategy. Honda as an organization has been deeply driven by a commitment to R&D and the most advanced manufacturing processes. A major manifestation of this commitment is Honda's successful track record in introducing considerably more and varied products than its competitors. In 1975, Honda introduced fourteen models for the under-125 cc. market in the $304-$899 price range, six models for the under-350 cc. market in the $897-$1,175 price range, two models for the under-450 cc. market in the $1,176-$1,443 price range, and three models for the under-750 cc. market in the $1,555-$2,112 price range. Harley Davidson introduced only three models for the under-125 cc. market in the $495-$749 price range, two models for the under-350 cc. market in the $930-$1,130 price range, and six models for the over-750 cc. market in the $2,675-$3,375 price range. In the late 1970s, Honda moved into the heavyweight market by introducing the 1000 cc. Goldwing model.

Furthermore, Honda tried to widen its product line by broadening its offering to serve all the off-roads and combinations between on-off road markets. For example, Honda launched seven models for the on-road market, thirteen models for the combination, and six models for the off-road market in 1975. This strategy has been followed by other Japanese companies. By 1975, within the engine size ranging from under 125 cc. to under 750 cc., Yamaha, Kawasaki, and Suzuki had around twenty-nine, twenty-two, and twenty-four models, respectively, compared with only eleven models of larger bikes for Harley Davidson, four models for BMW, and seventeen models of other imported motorcycles.

Changes in the number of automobile models were a major factor in discriminating between the Japanese and their major competitors, especially the German imported cars, during this stage of market expansion and penetration. Volkswagen significantly reduced the variety within its product models while the Japanese substantially increased the number and diversity of their offering. During the 1965-76 period, the Japanese increased the number of models at an average rate of 15 percent per year while the German rate declined at an average of 8 percent per year. The Japanese also increased the rate of their product differentiation to almost twice that of the Germans. During the 1970-76 period, when the Japanese began to dominate the U.S. imported car market, Toyota offered the market eighty-two models, followed by Nissan's fifty-six models, compared with forty-eight models for VW and thirty-one models for BMW.

Product Improvement

Few aspects of the penetration of U.S. markets by Japanese firms are so evident as their capacity to continually improve their product offering: They enhance product capability, extend product functionality, lower product breakdowns, extend product warranties, and improve product service. Every industry we examine where the Japanese have been successful is marked by their capacity to furnish a sequence of product improvements in performance, function, style, features, and quality. The Japanese have apparently long understood that a good product is crucial but that it is only a beginning: The product must be constantly developed and improved.

Japanese devotion to product improvement is reflected in their commitment to listening to and learning about their customers. They will spend long hours in discussion with customers about what limitations and weaknesses exist in their present product offerings, how products might be improved, and how the customers might react to possible product modifications. Once collected, these perceptions, complaints, and suggestions are extensively analyzed and critiqued for insight into user needs and potential product development.

Competitors' products have also been the source of much inspiration for product improvement by the Japanese. The stories are legion about Japanese firms taking apart and meticulously examining competitors' products. Indeed, many Japanese firms for a long time copied U.S. and European products but with few significant improvements.

Many of the improvements in copying machines have originated with Japanese firms. Canon's product introductions represent a series of product improvements. During the 1960s, Canon developed a copier drum with an insulating layer that permitted the use of a more photosensitive chemical than the one on which xerography had depended, thus enabling Canon to be completely free from Xerox patents. The lack of a sales organization and market experience prevented Canon from exploiting this product advantage. In the early 1970s, however, Canon introduced a so-called liquid dry system, using plain paper and a liquid developer that turned out dry copies. This time, Canon made a marketing mistake by licensing the technology to other manufacturers.

After these market fumbles, Canon successfully brought out its compact-size NP-200 copier, a machine controlled by a microprocessor which included a single-component dry developer and fiber optics to replace bulky conventional lenses and mirrors. Canon priced its product cheaply and heavily promoted it through advertising. Less than half a year after the product was launched in the U.S. market, sales grew nearly fivefold. Canon continued to emphasize product improvement and developed its Super-X series, which gushes 135 copies per minute and is faster and consumes less energy than any other big machine sold in the marketplace.

The Japanese are really devoting their attention to product improvement, especially in quality. The result of this quality consciousness is that Japanese products are accepted as being of higher quality than their counterparts. In the air-conditioning industry, for example, a recent study showed that the quality of Japanese air conditioners is much higher than that of American-made conditioners. On the average, the Japanese had seventy times fewer defects. The reason is that the Japanese have been trying to improve their production to bring out quality. Their plants combine quality with high productivity, with up to four times as many units per labor-hour as the American plants. They spend 1.3 percent of their total sales income on quality control while the U.S. firms spend an average of three times as much. The Japanese set up meetings daily to review their quality performance, compared with the best U.S. factory, which has only ten meetings per month. There is not Japanese innovation, but the difference is that the Japanese demand high quality. They demand high quality in the overall manufacturing process, maintenance of equipment, and training of workers.

Continuous attention to product improvement also characterizes Japan's penetration into high-technology markets. Semiconductors are a good example. Product improvement and development is the name of the game in semiconductors. When the Japanese entered the 16K RAM market in the United States, they were still playing catchup to the superior U.S. technology base. They devoted intense R&D efforts to bridging the gap. They especially emphasized the need to develop quality products—i.e., products that would not fail. A Japan Trade Council Report claimed in 1980 that quality was the key factor affecting semiconductor sales in Japan, and that quality was much more important than price, delivery, or technical support.

Their attention to product improvement along two dimensions— enhancing product capability by moving from 16K to 64K to 128K and improving product performance—is especially noteworthy for two reasons. First, U.S. firms had encountered serious problems with regard to product quality and performance. Thus U.S. customers of U.S. chip producers were only too willing to move to more-reliable suppliers, irrespective of where they came from. Second, much of the development work done by Japanese firms represents improvements in technology adopted from U.S. designs. In the words of one Motorola executive, "They have taken the work that was done in the U.S. on quality control and then beat us at our own game."

Extensive R&D work including cooperative research projects

between the government and firms such as Fujitsu, Hitachi, NEC, and Toshiba eventually bore fruit when Fujitsu became the first firm to announce the commercial production of the 64K chip. Hitachi, NEC, and other Japanese firms soon followed. Japanese penetration of the U.S. market was such that by the end of the first half of 1981, they had shipped almost 1.7 million 64K chips, two and one-half times the volume of U.S. firms. By late 1981, Japanese firms had captured 60 to 70 percent of the 64K world market. A result of their R&D programs is that the Japanese have set yield, quality, and reliability standards in the manufacture of chips and in chip performance in such areas as power consumption and timing sequence.

Their relentless pursuit of product improvement is also manifest in nonconsumer goods. A good example is the steel industry. While many U.S. producers have looked for ways out of what they see as an unpromising industry, a number of Japanese producers, in contrast, have tried to create new market demand by adapting and improving their products. Nippan Kokan, K.K., Japan's second-largest steel producer, has developed a steel for use in natural gas pipelines that can withstand pressures of eighty thousand pounds per square inch, which is ten thousand pounds higher than the current pipeline industry standard. This firm is now busy working on lighter steels and composites of steel and plastic for such future uses as more fuel-efficient automobiles.

MARKET DEVELOPMENT STRATEGIES

Product development never occurs in complete isolation. Products are developed and modified with particular markets in mind. It is not necessary that the conception of the market and its evolution be explicit and detailed. Evidently such was not always the case as the Japanese improved, stretched, and proliferated their product lines.

However, Japanese firms do seem to employ some very specific market development strategies. They clearly engage in various forms of market segmentation, and they sequence their market entries and penetration efforts. What is even more evident is their market flexibility. They adapt their marketing mix to prevailing market and competitive conditions.

Market Segmentation and Sequencing

Market segmentation and sequencing provide much of the impetus and direction for Japan's market development efforts. For many Japanese firms—and this is especially true of the 1970s and will be even more true of the 1980s—products are created for and fitted to evolving markets. In other words, the Japanese are playing an increasingly important role in developing markets: They are increasingly engaging in market development strategies.

The history of Japanese penetration of the U.S. marketplace is, in many respects, a textbook illustration of the successes that accrue when markets are segmented and the mode of entry and penetration of these market segments is carefully sequenced and orchestrated. Of course, we must be careful not to overly attribute Japanese success to their marketing prowess and skills. Their success was in no small measure aided by the initial complacency and miscalculations of many of their U.S. competitors and a variety of factors related to the structure and dynamics of their political economy. Yet it is equally clear that marketing has played a major role in their success.

Relating Product Improvement to Market Segmentation and Sequencing

Product improvement, product line stretching, and product proliferation are, at a minimum, implicitly predicated on some conception of the dimensions and characteristics of an evolving market. To what degree the Japanese explicitly detail and critique multiple facets of the evolution of the U.S. market for their products *and* then endeavor to match products to specific and precise market (customer) attributes and needs is probably debatable. What is not debatable is that as the Japanese improved, stretched, and proliferated their lines, they were segmenting the market (whether unwittingly or by intent is largely irrelevant—the results were the same), and they seemed to pay particular attention to when and how market segments were entered and penetrated, that is, the sequencing of market entry and penetration.

Japanese product strategies can be related to market segmentation and sequencing in a number of ways. We can use the notion of market needs and preferences as a means of tying their product thrusts to the marketplace. As the Japanese improve and extend their product lines, they are inherently appealing to an increasingly wider array of market or customer needs, preferences, and tastes. As watches, calculators, radios, motorcycles, and so forth, emerge in varying sizes, shapes, and designs with varying features, styles, and functions, larger and larger slices of the potential customer base are drawn into the purchasing net.

It should be noted that each of the product strategy elements—improvement, line stretching, and proliferation—contributes to finer segmentation of the market and permits some sequencing of market-penetration moves. The Japanese commitment to continuous product improvement opens up those market niches where product functionality and performance are of paramount importance. The "value for dollar" appeal of many Japanese products would not have been possible without continuous product improvement. This was especially the case for the early Japanese entrants into the U.S. market, since they had to battle the initial perception of Japan as a source of poor quality—a perception amply supported by the poor performance of many and, indeed, ultimate withdrawal of some of their initial product entries into the United States.

Product line stretching and proliferation may also be interpreted as further supporting evidence of Japanese market orientation. Their proclivity to stretch and proliferate their lines may reasonably be interpreted as an effort to reach even wider market segments but which implicitly involves market sequencing. As they stretch their lines—e.g., moving to higher-priced watches, calculators, autos—and proliferate their offerings, they appeal to higher-income brackets, customers seeking more aesthetic appeal, performance capacity, or peculiar features.

Market segmentation and sequencing—as elements in market penetration—are perhaps more readily transparent when we use geography as a basis of demarcation rather than customer needs and preferences. Indeed, the two are frequently combined in market-segmentation efforts. However, when we focus on geography as a segmentation mode, it reveals much about the approach adopted by many Japanese firms in penetrating the U.S. market.

Many Japanese firms entering the U.S. in the 1950s and early 1960s initially concentrated on one geographical region. Once they had achieved some penetration there, they set out to acquire complete coverage of the United States in a series of geographical moves. Toyota and Honda clearly employed this approach. The initial focus for both was California. Once they had established an initial position there, they began to establish their presence in adjoining states and continued in this path until they had attained geographical coverage of the United States.

From Product Improvement to Market Development

Product improvement, of course, sometimes evolves into product development and, consequently, to the creation or emergence of new product-markets. The initial entry of many Japanese firms, even in the 1950s and 1960s, involved the development of new product-markets—small motorcycles, etc. During the 1970s, however, many Japanese firms were becoming increasingly involved in what is more typically referred to as "product development." The Sony "walkathon," videotape recorders, and home movie systems are indicative of their product development efforts.

As the Japanese move from simple product improvement to product development, they unavoidedly assume more of the challenges and problems inherent in market development. They must develop the market: assess customer needs, predict customer responses, forecast market size, and develop channel incentives and promotional packages aimed at the end user—all of which may sometimes involve developing innovative marketing programs. They can no longer "piggyback" on existing products and markets. Imitation is no longer sufficient—a charge that is still frequently leveled at the Japanese. However, as they move toward product and market development—and they increasingly are—there is less and less merit in this assertion. Indeed, those who adhere to the belief that the Japanese are predominantly imitators are only adding another layer to the "mythology" that probably pervades their conception of the Japanese.

JAPANESE PENETRATION OF THE COMPUTER INDUSTRY: AN ILLUSTRATION OF MARKET SEGMENTATION AND SEQUENCING

The recent emergence of Japan as a major force in the computer industry provides a good illustration of Japanese market segmentation and sequencing practices at work. The Japanese have come from nowhere in the past fifteen years to where they are now the major threat to U.S. dominance of the industry. Their onslaught on the U.S. market, which has only occurred in the past few years, has been carefully orchestrated and managed, but its origins date back two decades or more.

Beginning in the mid-1960s, Japan began to place heavy emphasis on the development of its computer industry. A major stimulant to this effort was IBM's introduction of its large 370 series of mainframes in 1970. MITI provided much of the drive and direction for the development of a Japanese computer industry. Under MITI's leadership, Japanese computer manufacturers were organized into three groups: Fujitsu and Hitachi would focus on large IBM-compatible mainframes; Mitsubishi and Oki Electric Industry Co. would focus on smaller IBM-compatible computers; and NEC and Toshiba were told to design their own computer architecture.

Thus the early Japanese thrust was the development of a line of computers that were 100 percent plug-compatible with IBM. The initial market for these computers was, of course, their own domestic market, Japan. The initial target customer base was the large number of sophisticated companies that owned IBM equipment but wanted to get more value for their money. The computer offerings from Japanese firms were frequently 40 percent lower in price. "Reverse engineering"—i.e., copying and imitating the prevailing dominant design—was the driving modus operandi of this embryonic Japanese computer industry.

Japanese firms gradually infiltrated their domestic marketplace and eventually achieved a 20 percent market share. In the process, they gained valuable experience about the industry; they learned about customers' needs, what it required to "sell" computers and what it took to manufacture them. Furthermore, as in so many other industries, Japanese computer firms found themselves embroiled in a fierce competitive struggle in Japan—a baptism of fire that was to stand them in good stead when they embarked upon winning foreign markets.

It is in their approach to the world marketplace that market segmentation, sequencing, and development become especially noteworthy. Although many Japanese firms are locked in a competitive battle at home, they apparently have a tacit understanding not to compete internationally except in the United States. The firms deny that any formal territorial restrictions exist. Rather, they contend that each firm focused on particular foreign markets in Asia (these were the first foreign markets entered by the Japanese) and that each market came to be dominated by the first Japanese firms to stake a claim there.

The sequencing of foreign market penetration reveals a distinct pattern: Japanese computer manufacturers each began exporting close to home and then radiated outward. After acquiring know-how in nearby markets, they will move elsewhere—step by step. This incremental approach to market sequencing and development allows the Japanese to test and develop their product line, establish their own brand name and reputation, and better understand customer proclivities before they move on to their ultimate goal—the United States and other developed countries.

The role and importance of market sequencing is well reflected in Fujitsu's approach to entering the U.S. market. Fujitsu has concentrated heavily on Australia. It is using Australia as a test market because Australia resembles Western markets and yet is isolated from the West, so that any mistakes will not necessarily be broadcast elsewhere. Again, the intent is product development and acquisition of market insight. Thus, when Fujitsu attacks the U.S. market, it is coming from a position of strength compared with where it would have been had it set its sights on the United States many years earlier.

Beginning in the late 1970s, Japanese firms began to enter the U.S. market. In their attack on the U.S. market, market segmentation and sequencing are evident. They first addressed the OEM market. They initially gained entrance through deals with original equipment manufacturers (OEM) or systems houses for large microframes and peripheral equipment. They also focused on computer periphery. In only five years, Japanese companies captured 75 percent of the U.S. market for computer printers costing under $11,000 and 70 percent of the high-speed facsimile unit sales.

While the Japanese presence in mid-size and microframe computers is just beginning to be felt, Japan's greatest effort is currently being put into small, low-priced computers. It has entered both the personal computer market and the small business systems market. The overall Japanese strategy seems to be to make a major entrance via small personal computers and business systems and then move up into larger computers—ideally trading up customers into larger systems. A classic example of a firm that is starting in the low end and moving up into more sophisticated equipment is Sharp. Sharp's plan is to begin marketing personal computers through selected U.S. dealers, then roll out small-business computers, and then eventually sell a complete system for a large office or small business.

Part of their market sequencing is moving from OEM's and private labels to their own brand names. They progress from merely selling their equipment to also selling their name (and its attendant image and reputation). It reflects a movement away from entering the U.S. market by "going the American way" to penetrating the market by increasingly going the Japanese way—i.e., assuming more and more of the marketing activities themselves. It is only in the 1980s that Japanese firms have begun selling computer systems in the United States under their own brand names. Yet some have not yet done so, and Hitachi, as recently as late 1981, denied having such a plan. "First we must get a good reputation among U.S. customers, then, we can increase our market share," said a Hitachi executive.

MARKET FLEXIBILITY

The adroit sense of market segmentation and sequencing exhibited by the Japanese is accompanied by a shrewd appreciation of market flexibility. They do not seek one best way to enter and penetrate markets, and once they have found an approach that succeeds, they do not blindly stick with it. Rather, Japanese firms are adept at using a multiplicity of competitive weapons with varying degrees of emphasis—price, promotion, product quality, product features, service, distribution, product line stretching, and proliferation—to penetrate and win markets.

Many U.S. firms, of course, are also noted for their market flexibility. However, in the case of Japanese firms, the proclivity to be flexible may very well be cultural. Buddhist thinking emphasizes that nothing is permanent, that life is ever changing. Samurai warriors in Japan learned several martial arts—judo, karate, aikido—always choosing the best means to attack or defend. A Japanese company will sometimes attack with a karate blow aimed at a competitor's weakness and at times with an aikido side step, taking advantage of the force created by a competitor. The game of GO, originated by the Chinese and perfected by the Japanese, provides a mental training in long-range strategic thinking, the principles of indirect attack and encirclement, and the need for opportunistic replanning. Thus Japanese culture provides deep models for flexible marketing warfare.

Variation across the Marketing Mix

The emphasis within the mix of competitive weapons is typically adapted by the Japanese in accordance with market evolution, their degree of penetration of the market, and their overall strategy. For instance, product line stretching, proliferation, and improvement reflect broad *product* strategies which are adopted as the market evolves *and* as Japanese firms succeed in penetrating the market. Indeed in many markets, much of the market evolution—i.e., customer wants, preferences, usage, or saturation rate—is a direct consequence of the product strategies of Japanese firms. The option to purchase small televisions and small motorcycles was not available to the U.S. consumer until the Japanese entered the market. Having entered the U.S. market and gained some success, they devoted strenuous efforts to stretching and proliferating their product lines. This same thrust is still very evident in many markets in which the Japanese now dominate: Their product development efforts have not stopped in consumer electronics, cameras, watches, and motorcycles even though they now hold the lion's share of these markets.

Their market flexibility goes much beyond concern with product development and adaptation. They differentially emphasize elements in the competitive mix depending on their degree of market penetration. In early efforts to achieve market penetration, the Japanese emphasized low price to the ultimate customer and high margins to the distribution chain. Such was the emphasis in almost all the early entrants to the United States: televisions, radios, calculators, automobiles, motorcycles, stereo equipment, and watches. These were the days when the Japanese were trying to overcome the image of poor quality and were trying to overcome the resistance of U.S. distributors to carrying their products. Many Japanese firms went the route of private labeling in order to gain access to the U.S. market. It was the cheapest and easiest way for them to build volume, gain distribution, and learn about the U.S. marketplace.

As these markets matured and as the Japanese gained market experience, their emphasis within the competitive mix also changed. Brand identification became much more prominent. Those firms that initially sold exclusively under private labels now began to sell and promote under their own brand names. Some continued their private-label business as well.

Implicit in the move away from private labels is that much more extensive distribution also became the norm. Japanese firms gradually rolled out their distribution coverage in order to reach larger segments of the market. They typically entered the market through those distribution channels (large distributors and large retail chains) that would give them the largest initial coverage. Then they would work their way down through the next ranks of retail outlets until finally reaching small independent stores.

Although the Japanese have always professed that service was important, its role and significance in their competitive mix increased as they found themselves competing more directly and more openly against U.S. firms. Japanese auto manufacturers discovered that service was a major criterion along which U.S. consumers differentiated auto producers—in favor of U.S. firms and against Japanese and other foreign producers. Japanese copier producers found that as soon as they began to sell under their own names and utilize their own distribution systems, sales service dramatically increased in importance.

Flexibility in Individual Marketing Variables

A theme running through the above discussion is that Japanese marketing flexibility is also exhibited in their handling of individual marketing variables. Their approach to pricing is a good example. The Japanese raise their prices as their products gain acceptance. For a number of years, Sony priced its television sets below American prices but moved much closer to U.S. prices as it gained market position during the early 1970s. By the late 1970s, Sony televisions were the highest priced in the market. Mazda introduced its handsome RX-7 sports car in the United States at a low price of $8,000, causing much word of mouth and queue formation at its dealerships. The initial low price reflected promotion-oriented pricing to gain attention and early purchase, only to be followed by profit-oriented pricing later.

MARKET PENETRATION: THE CASE
OF TOSHIBA IN MEDICAL EQUIPMENT

Many of the elements of these product and market strategies can be illustrated by examining the penetration approach adopted by Toshiba in the U.S. medical equipment market. This is an illuminating example for a variety of reasons. The Japanese penetration of this market is not particularly well known. Indeed, it is in its early stages. Yet it is broadly indicative of the approach adopted by many Japanese firms across a variety of industries.

Toshiba's major medical equipment product line is CT scanners and ultrasound equipment. Its product line reflects continuous improvement and development. Toshiba has extended what was once simply medical equipment in the 1960s into medical electronics in the 1970s. And, for the 1980s, Toshiba is renewing its medical efforts "to reflect exactly what they do—medical engineering."

Toshiba is now selling the fourth-generation CT scanner. This continual advancement in technology presents a problem in ensuring updating capability for older models. Updating in many cases comes down to rebuilding, since the early models cannot be updated to the technological sophistication of the current fourth-generation model.

Even in Toshiba's first foray into the U.S. market, the Japanese willingness to adapt products to the market was evident. Toshiba began manufacturing medical equipment fifty years ago, after its successful development of the X-ray tube. It initially entered the U.S. medical equipment market by becoming involved in the X-ray tube replacement market. Upon entering the U.S. market, Toshiba quickly determined that some product modifications were needed due to the larger American body sizes. So, a stronger, larger X-ray tube was manufactured for the U.S. market.

The initial objective of Toshiba in the U.S. CT scanner market was to gain a niche for itself by providing low-cost, stripped-down variations of the competitor's equipment. In April 1981, Toshiba unveiled a CT scanner that was 40 percent cheaper than its rival GE model. Toshiba planned to build from this market-entry position and develop its own highly innovative products.

Toshiba's X-ray tubes and other more-sophisticated diagnostic equipment were initially sold through U.S. distributors. One major distributor was used as well as several smaller distributors. However, Toshiba became unhappy with the arrangements with the major distributor in the mid-1970s and decided to establish its own medical equipment sales operation within the United States. A number of reasons seemed to have inspired this move: Toshiba's belief that local distributors only cooperate in sales promotions and marketing programs to the extent that they are profitable to themselves; Toshiba's desire to gain more control over retail prices, sales development programs, advertising, and sales personnel; and Toshiba's recognition of the need to improve after-sales service. An underlying rationale was Toshiba's conviction that it was in a position to begin its own sales operation in a market that it saw as having strong growth potential.

Toshiba's transition to its own sales and distribution organization reveals a number of elements common to many Japanese efforts to establish a strong presence in the U.S. marketplace. It established four regional offices throughout the United States with the headquarters for the medical equipment division located in Los Angeles. A major problem was staffing the new organization. Toshiba needed a sales force and distribution team that knew and understood the customers, had experience in selling the product, and were familiar with competitors' offerings. To overcome these potential problems and to avoid losing valuable momentum, Toshiba invited ten to twenty of the ex-distributor's salespeople to join the Toshiba staff. Toshiba made very attractive offers to experienced local salespeople, who not only knew the Toshiba product line and the U.S. medical equipment industry but were well acquainted with the medical community—an important ingredient for success in this industry.

Japanese commitment to understanding the customer, to product improvement and development, and to marketing flexibility is evident in many ways. They tenaciously pursue market penetration: It is not a stop-and-go activity. Toshiba's efforts to get close to and understand the customer and adapt products to customers' needs are indicative of its desire to be market rather than product driven. Let us briefly examine what is involved in selling medical equipment to hospitals.

Purchasing a CT scanner is a complex and expensive decision. Service contracts average $50,000 to $125,000, and CT scanner parts and labor cost approximately $75,000 per year. Warranties are typically six months to one year, depending on the type of equipment and the negotiated settlement. The purchase decision is heavily influenced by physicians. Hospitals and physicians almost always insist on having the latest available technology—if they do not, it may give a major competitive edge to those hospitals that possess it.

Toshiba approaches this marketplace quite differently from most U.S. firms. Toshiba charges that U.S. manufacturers try to tell physicians what they need to care for their patients. They convince doctors that they need equipment with numerous sophisticated specifications, some of which are unnecessary and add considerable costs. In the words of one Toshiba executive, "It is like convincing someone that he needs an eight-cylinder engine to run a go-cart." Once the U.S. manufacturers have convinced their U.S. customers that they need all of these "bells and whistles," the physicians begin to demand similar specifications from the other manufacturers involved in the competitive bidding.

Toshiba finds itself in the difficult position of having to confront this "specification strategy." It has decided to meet the U.S. competition head on. It looks at the specifications being demanded by its U.S. customers and then goes back and tries to convince these customers that all the specifications are not necessary.

The Toshiba philosophy might well be summed up by the following: "We don't want doctors to tell us what they need. We want them to tell us their most difficult problems. Then we can come up with solutions that are far more imaginative than they could dream up because we know the vast and expanding capabilities of the technology."

Although Toshiba might not see it as such, market segmentation and sequencing are also in evidence. Toshiba tries to install its equipment in influential, well-known teaching hospitals in the United States. Emerging physicians will therefore become familiar with its products. Relatedly, Toshiba looks for "famous" doctors who will become spokespersons for its equipment. Toshiba hopes that these "medical champions" will influence other physicians enough to join the fold of Toshiba equipment users.

Successful product and market development strategies involve tangible and intangible elements. Reliability and quality picture reproduction are the two most critical tangible product characteristics—Toshiba believes them to be the most salient product features to the medical equipment customer. Toshiba prides itself on manufacturing high quality, sophisticated electronics equipment. The microprocessor is the core of Toshiba's medical equipment. With its own in-house semiconductor operation, Toshiba has a major advantage over many of its U.S. competitors: It has the ability to manufacture every component of its equipment and thus control the supply-end quality of its own components.

However, the "product" that Toshiba is selling goes beyond mere physical attributes. For example, after-sale service is a key product feature. Toshiba recognizes that it is not as strong in this area as it ought to be and is currently improving its service capability. An industry norm is that quality of service can be measured by the serviceperson-to salesperson ratio. The industry average is four to five servicepersons to one salesperson. Toshiba's ratio in mid-1982 was 1.25 to 2.

Toshiba's concern with developing an image and reputation (two other intangible product attributes) for reliable and competitively priced medical equipment led it to seek more direct contact with its customers and therefore more control over its distribution and sales promotion activities. Toshiba recognized that it would have to do what all other medical equipment manufacturers were trying to do if it were to succeed in this market—i.e., develop a reputation as a reliable supplier of quality, competitively priced equipment *and* develop solid working relationships and trust with the medical community. In essence, Toshiba found that marketing flexibility would have to include much more attention to managing its customer relationships.

In summary, Toshiba's entry and penetration of the U.S. market reflects product development and market development strategies. It also reveals Toshiba's dedication and commitment to gradually establishing a solid market presence. Nor is Toshiba afraid to be innovative in its product and marketing tactics when it might secure a competitive advantage.

CREATING AND BENEFITTING FROM CHANGE

The Japanese have not used any one approach to extend their presence in U.S. markets. There is even significant variation across Japanese firms within most industries. Yet there are a number of distinct common elements: The Japanese improve, extend, and proliferate their product lines and they engage in market segmentation, sequencing, and flexibility. Furthermore, they manage market penetration with long-run rather than short-run interests in mind: They are dedicated to learning what are the right things to do and how to do them right, even if it means making mistakes in the process.

In short, the Japanese "learn by doing." They develop and modify products, introduce them, and then watch how the market reacts. This observation or learning provides the basis for the next round of product development or modification, introduction, and further learning. It is a trial-and-error, heuristic, incremental process. It is only by initiating actions and learning from them that continued progress toward customer satisfaction can be maintained.

The essential implication of "learning by doing," market flexibility, and strategic incrementalism is the need for constant improvement in products and market position. Since the competitors will constantly be searching for "holes" in the market, standing still would mean suicide.

Any organization that wishes to attain long-run success must continually enhance its product offerings and its appeal to current and new market segments.

Incremental product and market improvements accumulate. They can gradually wear down the enemy. Furthermore, cumulative improvements may reach a point where they represent a "point of inflection" or revolutionary advance or thrust. They constitute a "big bang." Competitors will likely be surprised to discover they have been overtaken. Japanese penetration of many product-markets in the U.S. during the 1950s, 1960s, and 1970s clearly followed this pattern: Incremental improvements provided the springboard from which major product and technology advances were possible.

The incremental thrust of Japanese product and market development points up a "truth" we can so easily forget: Any firm's strategy must be continually adapted to the external conditions confronting it and the firm's own resources and capabilities. Initially, the Japanese used U.S. organizations to distribute, advertise, promote, and service their products. Frequently, they did not even sell under their own names. Even if they had the resources to do so (and many did not), they would have found it extremely difficult to obtain cooperation from U.S. organizations and U.S. customers.

Another "truth" that surfaces is that products and markets must be considered simultaneously. Product developments and improvements make little sense unless targeted at clear customer segments. Furthermore, market segmentation, sequencing, and development presume product variation, differentiation, and ongoing improvement. Consequently, there is a need to think in terms of "product-market evolution" rather than in the simpler but misleading terms of "product life cycles." Describing the life cycle of a product does not necessarily reveal what is happening at the market or customer end.

A focus on product-market evolution helps managers avoid marketing myopia. If leads them to consider how the market (not the product) will evolve and its impact on their strategy. The Japanese infiltration of U.S. markets is really a story of managed market development: segmenting markets, sequencing product introductions, and adapting the marketing mix to individual markets as these markets evolve.

While there is undoubtedly a product orientation in Japanese firms, we believe that this orientation is less prevalent than in U.S. firms. Japanese firms seem to spend more time on detailed studies of customers, preproduct introduction search, and continuous product adaptation. They seem to be more market- and customer-driven rather than product- and technology-driven.

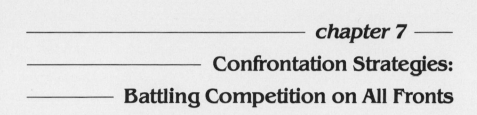

————————————— *chapter 7* ———
————————————— Confrontation Strategies:
————— Battling Competition on All Fronts

In the preceding chapter, we described the product and market strategies that Japanese firms employed in penetrating the U.S. marketplace.
Here we want to place market penetration strategies in a more generic
context. This chapter uses the language of military warfare to distinguish
different types of strategies that firms may adopt as they enter and
endeavor to penetrate any given market. Specifically, five types of strategies are discussed: *flanking, frontal, encirclement, bypass,* and *guerrilla.*
Each strategy type is illustrated with Japanese examples. An understanding of these generic strategy types not only furnishes better insight into
how and why Japanese firms have so successfully penetrated so many
U.S. markets but also provides a framework for thinking about counterattack strategies by the West.

FLANKING STRATEGY

The historical record indicates that few Japanese firms waged a frontal
attack on U.S. companies in their initial efforts to penetrate the U.S.
marketplace. Japanese firms first developed a foothold in product-
markets where U.S. firms were weakest and, in many cases, almost
nonexistent. They then "rolled out" their strategic thrust, building their
product base and market position in order to take on their U.S. competitors in frontal or direct competition at some later time.

Confrontation Strategies

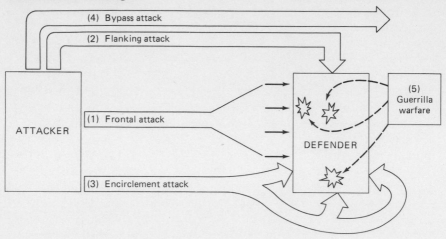

This broad approach to market strategy is best captured by the notion of a flanking strategy. Its essence is to engage competitors in those product-markets where they are weak or preferably where they have little if any presence. Its guiding principle is to pit your own strength against their weakness. Its overarching goal is to build a market position sufficient to launch a major onslaught on the competition at a later time. A flanking strategy is, of course, also premised in the hope that it will not awaken some sleeping giant; the hope is that the firm can avoid head-to-head competition or at least will not be enticed into such combat until it is ready to do so.

A flanking strategy is truly a "niching" strategy. Japanese firms chose particular niches or domains within a broad product-market or industry and focused their marketing efforts on these comparatively narrow "windows of opportunity." As they achieved success in these initial niches, they improved and upgraded their products, broadened their market focus, extended their distribution channels, and promoted their own labels—in short, all the steps necessary to upgrade and extend their product line and penetrate successive segments of the market.

Types of Flanking Strategy

If we focus on Japanese firms competing against U.S. firms in both the world market and the U.S. market, we can identify two broad forms of flanking strategy: geographical and segmented. Of course, both of these can be used simultaneously.

Geographical flanking.   In a geographical flanking strategy, firms attack areas within a country or the world where the opponents are either nonexistent or not very strong. In the chosen geographical segment, opponents are not performing very well, if at all: In short, they are highly vulnerable—their flanks are exposed. The geographical-based strategy is most evident in the case of Japanese firms when we use the world market as our purview, but it is also evident when our focus is the U.S. market.

The history of the past 35 years is replete with examples of Japanese firms focusing their initial onslaught on the world market in areas where U.S. firms were particularly weak. The Japanese computer industry's approach to capturing major segments of the world market exemplifies geographical flanking strategy. They rolled out their geographical penetration, first attacking countries in neighboring Asia, then Australia, and finally Europe and the United States. The U.S. and European manufacturers were weakest in Asia and much less concerned about defending their positions there than they were in the United States and Europe.

A similar story can be told for almost every Japanese industry. Japanese automobile and motorcycle firms first concentrated on Asia and then moved outward from there. Japanese pharmaceuticals and medical equipment firms have placed heavy emphasis on South America. Japanese copier, home appliance, musical instrument, and many other firms have flanked their competition by geographically segmenting the world and building a market presence where U.S. and European firms will find it most difficult to retaliate.

Segmented flanking.   A geographical flanking strategy may be built around selling products that are identical or broadly similar to those of the competition and thus satisfying an identical or broadly similar market need or niche. A segmented flanking strategy is quite different. In this form of flanking attack, the strategy revolves around identifying market niches or needs that are not being served by competitors within a given geographical area. Segmented flanking strategies are potentially much more powerful than geographical flanking attacks: They are inherently built upon satisfying market needs and doing something different from the competition. Most Japanese firms employed this type of flanking strategy in entering the U.S. market.

Time and time again, the Japanese identified unserved market niches in the United States and focused their attention and resources on serving them. They brought to market products that were distinctly different from those of the market leaders and aimed at market needs or customer segments that were neglected. Smaller and/or stripped-down versions of established products, more features for the same or lower price, private labeling and fewer features at a lower price are classic flanking strategies.

Flanking strategy is another name for identifying and, at times, initiating shifts in market segments or market evolution and rushing in to fill these gaps and developing them into strong segments. Instead of a bloody battle between two or more companies trying to serve the same market, flanking leads to a fuller coverage of the market's varied needs.

Conditions Facilitating a Flanking Strategy

The conditions that contribute to the choice of a flanking strategy are strongly evident when we examine the circumstances relating to the early penetration of U.S. markets by Japanese firms. Three market and competitive conditions are pivotal to the choice and potential success of a flanking strategy:

1.   The attacker can identify substantial market segments that are distinct from the prevailing dominant product-markets and are not being served, or served well, by the dominant producers. All of the market-entry strategies previously noted reflect Japanese efforts to enter the U.S. marketplace in market sectors where they did not directly confront their U.S. competitors.

2.   Flanking strategies are greatly facilitated where there is substantial growth in the market or in the industry as a whole. It is therefore a positive-sum game (i.e., gains are not at the expense of competitors' growth) rather than a zero-sum game (i.e., one firm's gain is another firm's loss). Thus, as many Japanese firms began to succeed in penetrating the U.S. marketplace, U.S. firms in the same industry were still experiencing growth in sales and profitability in their sectors of the industry. Such was the experience in the automobile, television, copier, motorcycle, audio equipment, and other industries.

3.   Flanking strategies are also facilitated where the entrenched competitors are complacent and generally consider the new entrants as "upstarts" who will not be able to stay the distance in a competitive battle. Many U.S. firms treated Japanese entrants in their industries with, at best, benign neglect: The Japanese were entering product-market sectors that were "obviously" small by comparison with the established firm's market segments—small in terms of both potential unit volume and profitability.

The choice of a flanking strategy is a function of more than simply market and competitive conditions. The firm's own resource base and capabilities must also be taken into account. If a firm does not have the resources to go head-to-head, or to develop a major onslaught on the market, a flanking strategy is usually the firm's best option.

Corporate resources need to be assessed not only in terms of functional skills and capabilities such as marketing, finance, manufacturing, and R&D but also in terms of the firm's knowledge level of the markets it serves or wants to serve. The initial entry and early penetration efforts of many Japanese firms into the U.S. marketplace demonstrated a lack of understanding and insight into their prospective market. A critical resource, namely, market knowledge, was grossly deficient and ought to have been sufficient to make many Japanese firms tread carefully and warily as they entered the U.S. market for the first time.

Given these market and competitive conditions and their inferior market position, a flanking strategy was a natural choice for Japanese firms. Indeed it may well have been the only strategic choice available to them in the 1950s, 1960s, and perhaps even in the 1970s. They did not have the resource base, market knowledge, and, in many cases, the required products to take on the dominant U.S. firms in direct competition, not to mention surpassing them in product and technology advances. Thus many Japanese firms were compelled to adopt a flanking strategy. It was not a "choice" in the conventional decision-making sense, since they did not possess any second alternative. However, the important point is that they made the best of the "choice" or option: They exploited it and turned it into a strategic success.

Risks in Flanking Strategy

A flanking strategy is not risk free. It is predicated on the existence of a substantial, and often emerging, market niche. If the flanking strategy is directed at a very small market or a nongrowing market, it may fail to repay the effort.

A related risk is that the competitors being flanked may retaliate by invading the niche. The flanking firm may succeed only in creating a market opportunity for the larger firms in the relevant product-market areas. The flanking firm must assess whether and how it would defend itself if the larger firms attack the niche.

In summary, flanking is in the best tradition of the modern marketing philosophy that holds that the purpose of marketing is to "discover needs and serve them." Flanking attacks also have a higher probability of being successful than frontal attacks. This is borne out in military history. In his penetrating analysis of the thirty most important conflicts of the world from the Greek wars up to World War I (which embraced more than 280 campaigns), Liddell Hart concluded that in only six campaigns did a head-on assault produce decisive results. So the strategy of indirect approach has overwhelming support from history as the most effective and economic form of strategy.

FRONTAL ATTACK

Success with a flanking strategy ultimately results in a more direct form of combat. This is usually a consequence of one of two things or both. As newer entrants into the market extend their product lines and begin to infiltrate larger and larger portions of the market (i.e., the end-customer base and distribution channels), they find themselves moving closer and closer to the domain of the previously dominant firms in the industry. At the same time, the dominant firms may engage in countermoves to meet the new competitive threats—i.e., introduce products that are much closer to the products of the new entrants.

Once the Japanese had successfully established themselves in market niches and started on the path to expansion, they found themselves in direct frontal competition with U.S. firms. They were now playing a distinctly different "game" than that which had prevailed during their flanking days. They were now hitting the U.S. firms where it hurt. Market penetration or share gain was now at the expense of U.S. firms. The positive-sum game had now become transformed into a zero-sum game. Japanese and U.S. firms were now attacking each other, matching power with power, strength with strength.

For many Japanese firms, the transition from a flanking to a frontal strategy did not take place overnight; it was a consequence of their penetration of the market over a period of years. Honda had been in the U.S. market for more than ten years before it began to compete directly against Harley Davidson in the large-motorcycle end of the market. It took about the same length of time before Japanese television manufacturers began to take their long-established U.S. counterparts head on. In many instances, it is difficult to specify precisely when a flanking strategy becomes a frontal strategy.

Types of Frontal Strategy

Pure frontal attack. All variants of frontal strategy are modifications of a pure frontal attack. In a pure frontal strategy, the aggressor matches its competitor product for product, price for price, promotion for promotion, and so on. The aggressor goes after the *same* customers as the other firm. It is fundamentally a "me-too" or "look-alike" strategy. The aggressor believes that it can "outgun" the competitors in "head-on" competition. Superior resources are presumed to be sufficient. It should be said, however, that corporate graveyards are full of firms who thought this way. Unless the firm enjoys some form of competitive advantage, its chances of outgunning the competitor or even fighting to a stalemate are slim in the long run. The aggressor will expend extensive resources and will have little to show for it in terms of market-share gain or profitability or both. Thus, modified frontal strategies are preferable to pure frontal onslaughts, since they are predicated on the creation and maintenance of some form of competitive advantage. A number of modified frontal strategies can be noted.

Limited frontal attack.   One modified frontal strategy occasionally employed by the Japanese is to focus on specific customers and do everything possible to lure them away from competitors. This focused customer strategy may take place at any time after market entry. For instance, in semiconducters, it occurred quite soon after market entry. Japanese firms identified select U.S. customers and pursued them with tremendous intensity. They provided product demonstrations, offered very favorable price deals, and committed themselves to after-sales relationships. Thus they addressed specific customers and tried to out-compete their U.S. competition along a number of dimensions simultaneously.

Price-based frontal attack.   A more common frontal strategy is a price-based frontal attack. In this market thrust, the aggressor basically matches the competitor on other counts but beats it on price. Price-based frontal strategy has often been used by the Japanese. It is perhaps the most common theme in their frontal strategies. It is evident in almost all the industries and product-markets previously discussed—watches, automobiles, motorcycles, copiers, televisions, radios, medical equipment, and so on. The Toshiba strategy in medical equipment discussed in the preceding chapter is a good example. Toshiba matched or surpassed its U.S. competitors on all dimensions, but its marketing package was built around competitive pricing.

   A priced-based frontal strategy works if competitors do not retaliate by cutting price or if competitors do not convince the market that its product offers real value. Thus it is in the aggressor's interest to devise a strategy that buffers it from competitive retaliation. One such strategy is an R&D-based frontal attack.

R&D-based frontal attack.   In an R&D-based frontal strategy, the attacker tries to imbue its product with attributes that may allow a number of different frontal attacks in the marketplace. One form is to invest in *process* R&D to achieve lower production costs and thereby facilitate an attack on competitors based on price. It is much more difficult for a competitor to respond to an R&D-driven, price-based strategy by cutting price because of its higher-cost structure. The Japanese emphasis on process R&D and, relatedly, manufacturing efficiency is a frequently cited reason for their lower-cost products *and* superior product quality in terms of performance and reliability. Process R&D-driven, price-based frontal strategy has been especially noticeable on the part of the Japanese in the 1970s. It is central to their marketing strategy in semiconductors, personal computers, and consumer electronics.

It is, of course, important to note that process R&D (with particularly heavy emphasis on development) has been a primary concern of the Japanese since at least the early 1950s. Even as they acquired product technology from the United States during the 1950s and 1960s, they paid much more attention than did U.S. firms to seeking and developing improvements in how these products were manufactured.

Product R&D-driven frontal strategies, on the other hand, result in value-based (rather than price-based) frontal attacks. Value is imbued into products by creating product improvements and establishing features not found in competitors' products. The intent is to achieve product differentiation based on factors other than price.

The 1970s have witnessed an upsurge in Japanese product R&D-driven, value-based frontal strategies. What were previously flanking strategies have assumed much more of a frontal attack, in large measure due to advancements in product R&D. No longer are they simply developing product technology acquired from the United States; they are initiating much of it themselves. Much of the Japanese success in the consumer electronics industry has resulted from product R&D, value-based frontal strategies. In television, the Japanese were the first to go to all-solid-state sets, led by Toshiba in 1969 and soon followed by all the other Japanese firms. Many U.S. firms did not do so until the early 1970s.

Conditions Facilitating a Frontal Strategy

A number of conditions are conducive to a successful frontal strategy. These conditions must be carefully assessed, since an unsuccessful frontal attack is most likely to result in major financial loss and the disintegration of morale.

First, the firm needs sufficient resources to underwrite the frontal strategy. More precisely, it requires comparable or superior resources to the firms being attacked. Von Clausewitz, in his *On War*, claimed that the attacker should have at least three times the resources of the enemy if it wants to be assured of victory. To the extent that head-to-head battles become endurance tests, resource availability may prove to be the deciding factor.

Second, the launching of a frontal attack is usually predicated on an assumption by the attacking firm that it can create and sustain a competitive advantage over the "prey," or other firms. A frontal attack, to be successful, requires that the aggressor be capable of eventually distinguishing itself in the marketplace. It should be able to develop a "better" offer to the target market than its competitors can.

Third, frontal attacks hinge on whether the attacker can lure customers into initially trying its product. Unless product and/or brand loyalties can be overcome, the likelihood of a frontal strategy succeeding is slim. Not only must the presumed competitive advantage of the attacking firm be real, it must also be perceived and understood by those who distribute and purchase the product.

Risks in Frontal Strategy

The overriding risk in a frontal strategy is that it will provoke intense retaliatory competitive response. It may serve to awaken sleeping giants. If the attacking firm does not have the resources to sustain a long-drawn-out war, it runs the risk of substantial losses. It may also create losses for all participants—that is, less profit for the industry as a whole. In short, the risks are high unless a frontal strategy is built on superior competitive advantages and resources.

In summary, frontal strategies capture the picture of competitors directly attacking each other. Frontal strategies make the most sense when the aggressor has adequate resources and a strategy that is price-based, cost-based, or value-based. Otherwise the frontal attack is merely a contest of wills and resources, a matter of brute force.

ENCIRCLEMENT STRATEGY

A frontal strategic onslaught will lead the competitor to counterattack. However, if the aggressor encircles the competitor's position—e.g., produces many more types, styles, and sizes of products including those that are less and more expensive—the competitor's possible retaliatory responses are correspondingly reduced. The enemy aggressor stands ready to block the competitor no matter which way the competition turns in the given product-market.

The strategic goal of encirclement is simple and straightforward: to force the competitors to protect their front, sides, and rear all at once. The intention is to disperse the enemy's coverage so that its concentration of resources will be diluted. This attack strategy over time results in a more fluid front line or marketplace that can more easily be pierced at a number of points and potentially developed into new market segments for the aggressor. This corresponds to the military offensive principle that states:

> If he prepares to the front his rear will be weak, and if to the rear, his front will be fragile. If he prepares to the left, his right will be vulnerable and if to the right, there will be few on his left. And when he prepares everywhere he will be weak everywhere.

Types of Strategic Encirclement

There are basically two types of encirclement: product encirclement and market encirclement. Although these are closely related and may be the same under some circumstances, they are conceptually distinct.

Product encirclement. Product encirclement consists of launching products in a multitude of qualities, styles, and features to swamp the opponent's product line. Honda and other Japanese motorcycle manufacturers have clearly encircled Harley Davidson. Japanese electronic firms have encircled their U.S. competitors in such product segments as televisions, radios, hand-held calculators, and audio and stereo equipment. Seiko has so stretched and proliferated its product lines in watches that it now encompasses the bottom to the top of the watches in terms of price, quality, and special features.

Market encirclement. Market encirclement consists of expanding the firm's offerings to almost every adjacent market segment. Japanese manufacturers extend and proliferate their product lines to appeal to different buyer needs and preferences. Market encirclement goes beyond the end customer to encompass various distribution channels. For example, Seiko has gained access to every possible type of distribution channel for watches, and through its product line stretching and proliferation, it has sought to absorb as much shelf space as possible.

     Strategic encirclement has allowed the Japanese to throw their U.S. competitors on the defensive. The U.S. firms now find themselves as the prey, whereas previously many of them were in the role of attacker. The U.S. firms are experiencing difficulty in fashioning successful strategic responses. The result is that many U.S. firms exited from the marketplace when they found themselves encircled by the Japanese.

Conditions Facilitating an Encirclement Strategy

A number of conditions facilitate the employment and likely success of an encirclement strategy. Many of these conditions were present as the Japanese sought encirclement around the U.S. enemy.

Encirclement is highly feasible when the aggressor has superior resources *and* is willing to commit them for an extended period of time to achieve market dominance. It is not sufficient to possess only superior financial resources. Access to distribution channels is an important resource. So too is R&D and product development capacity: Encirclement is much easier if the aggressor can continuously stretch, proliferate, and improve its product line. The number and management of a sales force can be a significant resource.

Special emphasis should be placed on the aggressor's willingness to commit long-term resources in the pursuit of encirclement. And Japanese firms have shown this willingness. Much also depends on whether the entrenched competitors are willing to make a long-term commitment to defending their market. If existing competitors are not expected to compete on all fronts, then the encirclement strategy is more likely to succeed.

The U.S. competitors, unfortunately, did not "signal" a strong commitment to their markets. Many were unwilling to build new plants, update existing manufacturing technology, renew their supply contracts, and meet distribution channel demands. Many U.S. firms decided it was not worth mounting a major retaliation in these product-markets. One by one, many U.S. industries went from simply being "impacted" industries to becoming "lost" industries. The enemy encircled these industries and there was no way out.

Risks in Strategic Encirclement

Encirclement of a competitive position takes substantial resources and organizational commitment. Also, it does not happen overnight. A major risk in an encirclement strategy is, therefore, that eventually winning the terrain may not be worth the war. The battleground may have changed so that the winner is left with a stagnant—or worse, declining—product-market. Thus an encirclement strategy that is purely focused on defeating competitors and does not pay requisite attention to what is happening in the broader marketplace (e.g., technology developments, changes in customers' tastes) is fraught with danger.

BYPASS STRATEGY

Competitive market battles are typically depicted as taking place in well-defined arenas. The antagonists confront each other in some particular product-market—e.g., the market for high-priced digital watches. The implicit imagery is of combatants engaging in hand-to-hand combat. Frontal and encirclement strategies involve competing against particular competitors in specific market arenas. Even in the case of flanking strategies, the thrust is competition against specific competitors, although it takes place in markets where the competition is either weakly present or not present at all. However, the threat of the competition coming into the market is always present and is, of course, a threat that frequently materializes.

But if our strategic lens is exclusively focused on these direct forms of competitive confrontation, we miss a potentially powerful type of strategy, which we will call the *bypass attack*. This strategy derives its name from the initiating firm's desire not to directly confront a competitor in a particular product-market. The bypass is the most indirect of assault strategies and avoids moving against the enemy in the current period.

Types of Bypass Strategy

The bypass hinges on a much broader view of competition than does a battle with competitor A for market B. It means bypassing the competition and pursuing markets where it is not present. Three types of bypass strategy are possible: (1) develop new products—i.e., satisfy customer needs that are unserved by any competitor; (2) diversify into unrelated products; and (3) diversify into new geographical markets for existing products.

Develop new products. Instead of only fighting the competition with the current products, companies can attempt to leapfrog the competition with new products. Japanese firms historically did not use the leapfrog method, being content to copy and improve existing products. In recent years, however, Japanese firms have revealed a capacity to develop substantial product modifications and even whole new products. Most notably, they have procured the development and elaboration of new camera features (autofocusing, etc.), digital watch features, and entirely new products such as video recorders and compact disc players.

Diversify into unrelated products. Japanese firms have shown an increasing readiness to venture away from single-industry businesses into new arenas. For example, Sony has entered into the restaurant business and the construction business, among its recent ventures.

Diversify into new geographical markets. The Japanese have not been content to restrict their targets to Japan and the United States, even though these are the two largest markets in the world. As the Japanese were infiltrating the U.S. market, they were simultaneously attacking markets outside the United States and their own domestic market. Nor did they slow down their efforts once they had gained a good foothold in these markets, but rather they continued to press for market domination.

Conditions Facilitating Bypass Attacks

Bypass attacks typically involve building on an existing market position. Thus a prerequisite for a bypass strategy is some established presence in the marketplace, a springboard from which to bypass competitors. However, the specific conditions facilitating each of the three bypass strategy types noted above may differ.

The development of new products is likely to require R&D and technology capability, in fact, a capability different from that underlying prevailing product-markets. Internally sourced diversification into unrelated products may also require extensive R&D and technology capability, or at least sufficient resources to acquire companies with the capabilities. Diversification into new geographical markets for existing products may place a heavy premium on marketing capability.

A major motivating force in each of the bypass strategy types is frequently congestion in the competitive arena: A large number of competitors fighting in the same product-market may spur some firms to try to bypass the fight. However, the different bypass options reflect varying degrees of bypassing the competitive battle. Bypass via new product development involves moving the battle to a new product level within the same product-market area. Movement into digital and electronic watches bypasses mechanical watches, but the company is still fighting for position within the "watch industry" and probably against the same competitors. Movement to a new geographical market, on the other hand, is intended to bypass existing competitors completely or, at a minimum, to take the fight to a product-market segment where competitors are much less established. Japanese firms encountered their U.S. competitors at their weakest in foreign markets, if at all. Finally, movement into unrelated products is an attempt to avoid the fight altogether.

A good illustration of bypass strategy is the marketing strategy of Fuji Photo Film Co. Fuji, in realizing that it did not have enough strength to directly challenge Kodak, avoided all direct confrontation. Fuji captured a small but profitable market niche by selling film that fit Kodak's standard camera. It attacked weaker competitors such as 3M, which made private-label film for K-Mart and Sears. It also attacked Agfa, which had a weak position in the United States. In its market development strategy, Fuji diversified into developing countries where Kodak's presence was less intense in order to build up sales volumes and improve its marketing skills for challenging Kodak at a later time.

Risks in Bypass Strategy

Two major risks attach to bypass strategy. The strategy may exceed the skills and knowledge base of the firm. To the extent that the firm's skill and knowledge base is lacking, its strategy is at risk. As so many firms have discovered, this is especially true of firms diversifying into unrelated products.

A second risk is that a bypass strategy, especially one based on diversification into unrelated markets or into new geographical markets, may entail conceding some existing product-market to competitors, at least in the short run. The avoidance or minimization of direct confrontation leaves the opponents free to roam the marketplace. The risk is that competitors may be able to use this opportunity to reinforce their base from which to attack the bypassing firm. If the strategy of the bypassing firm falters, it may be extremely vulnerable.

GUERRILLA STRATEGY

Flanking, frontal, encirclement, and bypass strategies are extensive, broad-based, and continual attacks on competitors. They represent large-scale and prolonged combat. The aim is outright defeat of the enemy. There is, however, another type of strategy that is much less ambitious in scope and purpose but nonetheless is often a highly successful gambit in both military warfare and the business arena—guerrilla strategy.

A guerrilla strategy consists of making small, intermittent attacks on different territories or positions of the opponent. The overriding aim is to harass and demoralize the opponent in order to eventually secure concessions. A guerrilla strategy tries to keep competitors off balance.

They have to continually guess as to where the next strike is likely to come from.

The military rationale underlying guerrilla strategy was pointedly stated by Liddell Hart:

> The more usual reason for adopting a strategy of limited aim is that of awaiting a change in the balance of force—a change often sought and achieved by draining the enemy's force, weakening him by pricks instead of risking blows. The essential condition of such a strategy is that the drain on him should be disproportionately greater than on oneself. The object may be sought by raiding his supplies; by local attacks which annihilate or inflict disproportionate loss on parts of his force; by bringing him into unprofitable attacks; by causing an excessively wide distribution of his force; and not least, by exhausting his moral and physical energy.

Guerrilla Behavior: Two Types

A surprising amount of Japanese competitive behavior can be couched in guerrillalike terms. This behavior is manifest in their initial entry positioning, continuing efforts to acquire market penetration, and even in their attempts to encircle and bypass the competition. The Japanese seem to have followed two types of guerrillalike behavior: market-focused and non-market-focused attacks.

Market-focused attacks are most guerrillalike: Attack the competitors simultaneously in multiple places, often effecting quick retreats. The Japanese manifested this behavior in their efforts to build position in many markets. They would run special promotions, often in conjunction with the retail trade. They would reduce prices in selective geographical areas. They would frequently bring intense pressure to bear on specific distribution channels and, sometimes, on individual retail outlets in order to have more of their products displayed or to receive other preferences. We are familiar with one such outburst of pressure in which a specific retail outlet was informed by a Japanese supplier that unless the store expended more effort in promoting and selling its wide product line, it would withdraw its franchise with the store and give it to a neighboring outlet.

Non-market-focused attacks have also been well honed and frequently practiced by the Japanese. Japanese firms have often raided their U.S. competitors for key management personnel. In some cases, the raids have involved capturing complete firms in the form of acquiring either competitors or distribution channels. The Japanese have often taken over the distributors who initially distributed their products and, in the process, taught them much about the pecularities and details of the business in the United States.

Japanese non-market-focused guerrilla activity may be much more extensive than evidenced in the above examples. Much of the market and competitor intelligence activities of Japanese firms reflect guerrillalike traits. This is represented at one extreme in the covert and illegal efforts of Hitachi to gain access to highly secret IBM data. At the other extreme are the Japanese intelligence gatherers incessantly photographing everything in sight at trade shows. A real hit-and-run gambit in between these extremes is the Japanese penchant for "touring" U.S. factories and other facilities, a behavior that U.S. firms have increasingly emulated.

Conditions Facilitating a Guerrilla Attack

A guerrilla strategy is more likely to be appropriate if the firm is smaller, in terms of market position and resource base, than the firm(s) it wishes to attack. The strategy is appropriate if it will cause a disproportionate drain on the other firm's resources and the aggressor firm is building toward a broader and more-sustained competitive challenge. These conditions have typified much of the guerrillalike strategic behavior of the Japanese.

These conditions have generally prevailed in the Japanese use of guerrilla strategy. The Japanese most tenaciously use guerrilla strategy when they are struggling to establish market position. At this point, of course, they also have a much smaller presence in the market than their U.S. competitors, as evidenced by their competitive pricing and promotional practices. In recent years, many large Japanese firms have shied away from guerrilla strategy once they have established a significant market position.

Japanese guerrilla attacks have frequently caused a disproportionate drain on the resources of U.S. firms. They have caused U.S. firms to commit more resources to competing in the marketplace. Price cuts, promotional outbursts, and raids on sales forces and distribution channels require a competitive response. As a result, profitability of U.S. firms was often lower than it would otherwise have been.

In the case of the Japanese, perhaps, the most critical condition was that guerrilla strategy was viewed as another rung on the ladder to acquiring a stronger and more sustained competitive position. It is doubtful if it was ever regarded by the Japanese as an end in itself. It was just one more step on the road to market dominance.

Risks in Guerrilla Strategy

The major risk in a guerrilla strategy is that it may provoke a major backlash or retaliation by the targeted competitors, an onslaught that the firm may not be able to withstand. Provocation without the resource base to deal with its competitive consequences is foolhardy. Thus, guerrilla attacks without careful assessment of competitors' responses and the firm's own resources and capabilities may invite irreparable damage.

Another risk is that a guerrilla strategy may produce very low returns with the resources required to effect it. This may be especially true of major market-focused actions. As a consequence, the purposes of the strategy must always be carefully assessed. For example, the returns may be in the form of "damage" to competitors rather than immediate profits to the initiating firm.

STRATEGIC FLEXIBILITY

Much of what has been said may convey the impression that the Japanese develop a long-term "grand strategy" to enter, penetrate, and dominate the U.S. and/or world market and that their year-to-year strategy unfolds unambiguously from their grand plan. This presumes that the Japanese *know* what broad strategy to follow, and the sequence of strategic or competitive moves they should employ. The evidence suggests that this is not actually what happens.

It is one thing to follow a strategy built on product development (i.e., line stretching, proliferation, and improvement) and market development (i.e., segmentation, sequencing, and development). It is another to develop a strategic and tactical blueprint: a step-by-step sequence of actions to be implemented in order to penetrate and dominate a market. Such a blueprint would have to include the right products to introduce, the types of product improvements required, the items to be added to the product line, the sequence of market segments to enter, and the pricing, advertising, and promoting of the products over time.

Strategy and marketing textbooks typically exhort management to consider these issues carefully in choosing a strategy. Indeed, management should try to do this. Yet there is also a need to raise and debate these questions continually as a strategy is being implemented. The company must be flexible enough to change either the broad contours of the strategy or its details as circumstances unfold. It is this latter capability that has been so well mastered by so many Japanese firms.

Strategic flexibility has a number of characteristics. It consists of incremental competitive moves. These are frequently done on a trial-and-error basis. The firm seeks to discover what strategy works best. Learning by doing is the Japanese firm's operating motto.

The purpose underlying trial-and-error strategy is to learn as much as possible about the environment within which the firm is competing. The firm wants to learn about the market (e.g., What do customers want and appreciate?); about competitors (e.g., What strategies are competitors pursuing? Why are they successful? How can they be defeated?); and about distributors (e.g., What incentives do they respond to? Is it possible to develop new channels of distribution?).

The goal of this strategy is not to acquire enough market, competitive, and environmental knowledge to finally determine a grand strategy. The goal, instead, is to keep learning and adapting strategy to the changing environment.

Three conditions greatly favor strategic flexibility. First is the firm's uncertainty about its environment. When firms are uncertain about customer responses to their product offerings, on what basis customers buy, how competitors may react, and so forth, strategic flexibility makes sense. It allows the firm to learn from its own actions and those of others. In the case of the Japanese, much of their uncertainty was born of ignorance—lack of knowledge of the U.S. marketplace.

Second, strategic flexibility also makes sense in a turbulent environment, that is, when there is a high degree of customer and competitive change: customers switching from one product to another, competitors changing their strategies. Of course, a turbulent environment contributes to a firm's uncertainty.

Third, lack of resources may give rise to the need for strategic flexibility. A firm may seek to avoid committing its scarce resources until it is confident that its core strategy has a high probability of success.

We would argue that the notion of strategic flexibility lies at the heart of almost every Japanese infiltration of the world marketplace. The opportunity identification process described in Chapter 4 provides a broad strategic thrust and market direction for Japan both as a whole and in specific industries. It does not indicate the nature of the product-market strategies that will succeed in individual countries. Although MITI provided much direction for the development of the Japanese automobile industry, when Toyota entered the U.S. marketplace, it knew little about the U.S. automobile industry, what product characteristics were appropriate, or how to market its products. Toyota's capability to learn about the market, step by step, and develop its strategy so that it would be flexible enough to meet market conditions, are the factors that underlie its success.

Honda's initial efforts to penetrate the California market reveal a similar experience. Honda had trouble lining up distributors, and when it did, it did not understand the nature of many motorcycle distributors— they were motorbike enthusiasts first and only distributors second. Furthermore, Honda's motorcycles were ill suited to the requirements of the U.S. market. During the first few years, Honda's small motorcycles incurred many clutch and mechanical problems due to the way Americans treated their motorcycles. These problems were eventually solved by Honda's research and development people, but it was only after they had received many complaints about the durability and reliability of their products.

Both Toyota and Honda had a broad understanding of what they wanted to do in the U.S. market: enter in a market niche where U.S. competitors were particularly vulnerable, slowly develop a distribution system with particular emphasis on providing the distributors with as much incentive as possible to carry and sell their product line and improve and stretch their product line as they penetrated the market. However, the details of their competitive strategy only emerged as they entered and learned about the market. The details of their competitive approaches changed from year to year—and sometimes more quickly. They were always trying new tactics, keeping those that worked and discarding those that did not.

STRATEGIC INCREMENTALISM VS. STRATEGIC LEAPS

Two types of broad strategy thrusts seem to underlie the foregoing strategy types: strategic incrementalism and strategic leaps. Both are evident among Japanese and U.S. firms.

Historically, the Japanese have depended much more on strategic incrementalism than on strategic leaps. Strategic incrementalism can be succinctly depicted by the following: (1) concentrate resources on fairly well defined product-markets, (2) seek consistent improvement in market penetration, (3) gradually develop superior competitive advantages, and (4) commit the organization to a long-time horizon in the pursuit of its goals. The essence of strategic incrementalism is to do what the organization does well, but to continue to improve on it. The enemy ultimately feels as if it is slowly being nibbled to death rather than being run over all at once by a runaway steamroller.

Most Japanese firms—at least until the mid-1970s—relied on

"strategic incrementalism" to make their gains. Strategic changes were not the outputs of years of major investment. Instead the Japanese relied on cumulative improvements in product line stretching, proliferation, and improvement to push forward.

Strategic incrementalism is appropriate when a firm (1) lacks the resource base of its competitors (e.g., capital, sales force, technology, etc.); (2) confronts competitors who are well established in the market (e.g., brand names, trade support); and (3) faces a market that is rapidly growing. Under those conditions, a firm's strategy is likely to exhibit a cumulation of minor or modest product changes and market focus shifts rather than major strategic changes or leaps. The firm is not likely to initiate major new strategic thrusts—new to both the firm and the industry—until it has established a toehold in the market, learned extensively about competitors and customers, and developed the resource base and requisite skills to create and sustain aggressive moves. Thus almost all Japanese firms for some time after they entered the U.S. market maintained a low strategic profile by not calling attention to themselves by creating "strategic waves."

Incrementalism is a distinct strategic mentality that favors trial-and-error learning and a predisposition to action. It is the "try-it-fix-it" orientation noted by Peters and Waterman in their *In Search of Excellence*. It does not wait around for the "big bang" inherent in a dependency on strategic leaps. It grows out of a willingness to creep up on competitors gradually rather than blow them out of the water in one swoop. It is predicated on a commitment to "staying the course"; minor and even major setbacks will not lead to withdrawal.

Strategic incrementalism, which involves continuous moves, requires swift communication flows and frequent interaction among decision makers with different functional and other responsibilities. It is more likely to be successful if the organization's decision-making structure and processes allow the opportunity for much of its impetus to be "bottom-up" driven rather than "top-down" imposed. Those "in the trenches," those closest to the action in the marketplace, those with customer knowledge, serve as catalysts for strategic action.

Strategic incrementalism may appear to function as a risk-avoidance gambit—in contrast to strategic leaps where the firm gambles on a dramatic research breakthrough, major new-product feature, or a new distribution channel. However, this risk-avoidance approach runs the danger of some other competitor successfully consummating a strategic leap and thus creating a greater distance between the leader and the follower.

AN EXAMPLE OF CONFRONTATION STRATEGIES: THE TELEVISION RECEIVER INDUSTRY

The five strategies discussed above could be illustrated in the context of almost any industry the Japanese have penetrated in the United States in the past thirty years. We will now do so in the case of television receivers. This industry was founded and dominated by U.S. firms in the post–World War II era. During this period, this projected to the world U.S. industrial leadership, technological ingenuity, and commercial entrepreneurship. In the 1950s, television sets became one of the major consumer industries. With the exception of the automobile, perhaps no industry has so dramatically affected consumer life styles.

By the end of the 1950s, black-and-white television receivers were a mature market segment. Over 80 percent of U.S. households had at least one television set. A majority of these households had replaced their sets at least once. The large console sets had been overtaken by portable and table-top sets in the mid-1950s. Portables and table tops constituted the replacement market almost exclusively. In the later 1950s, the screen sizes of television sets were predominantly 17″ and 21″. During 1959–61, 19″ and 21″ screen sizes replaced the 17″ and 21″ in popularity. All the sets sold in the United States were the products of U.S. firms.

The Japanese Entry: Flanking

The first Japanese television sets were imported into the United States in 1961. Their entry and early strategy was almost prototypically flanking. Their strategy aimed at avoiding confrontation with U.S. firms. The size of the sets was much smaller than that of U.S. models. Sony, the first firm to enter the United States, initially entered with an 8″ battery-operated, fully transistorized set for $280. Approximately eight thousand of these sets were sold in 1961. Three Japanese firms were exporting television sets to the United States in 1962, and ten firms were doing so by 1963. Almost all of their sets were in the under-12″ screen range.

Not only did the Japanese TV sets flank U.S. firms in terms of product size, they also did so in the way the sets were marketed. Japanese firms sold under retailers' private labels or under U.S. manufacturers' labels. Japanese names were not therefore promoted as direct competition to U.S. brand names. Sony, as well as most other Japanese firms, used an exclusive distribution strategy through a few large and respectable stores. Thus, in the first few years, it did not try to confront U.S. firms in all its distribution channels. Given the smaller set sizes, Japanese sets were in a significantly lower price range than the U.S. competition. However, Sony sets were considerably more expensive than other Japanese sets, had higher dealer margins, and were not discounted.

Entering the Color Market

The U.S. color market began to take off in 1960. By mid-1963, all major U.S. television manufacturers were selling color sets. In 1964, the first Japanese color sets appeared in the United States. The initial Japanese strategy was basically the same flanking strategy they had employed in the black-and-white market. A very small number of Japanese color sets began to appear in the United States in 1964–65. The sets generally were much smaller than those of U.S. firms. The Japanese continued to use selective distribution systems. With the exception of Sony, the other makers were sold under the name of U.S. distributors or manufacturers.

The Logic of the Flanking Strategy

The logic of the Japanese flanking strategy is strikingly clear. The Japanese initially exported to the United States the sets they actually sold in Japan. Fortunately, their sets filled an unserved market niche. More fortunately, they arrived when the growth of the color market was beginning to explode. Thus the Japanese presence did not constitute a zero-sum game for U.S. manufacturers. Consequently, in the early years of the Japanese presence, U.S. firms did not directly retaliate. The Japanese did not have the resources to wage a frontal attack, nor did they possess the knowledge of the U.S. marketplace to do so. The Japanese had little choice but to adopt a flanking strategy when they entered the U.S. television receiver market in the early 1960s.

The U.S. Response

Flanking strategies are much more likely to succeed when the competition does not retaliate. The U.S. firms did not launch significant counterattacks against the Japanese until the latter half of the 1960s. The U.S. firms did not consider the bottom end of the television receiver market (i.e., below-16" screen sizes) as a market segment with much potential. They still pushed larger models (16" and above) throughout the early 1960s because they offered much larger profits than the smaller sets.

In 1965–66, U.S. firms began to address the Japanese challenge. Late in 1965, General Electric introduced a 10-inch color television receiver. Other U.S. manufacturers followed suit in the late 1960s with models smaller than 16 inches.

In the early 1960s, however, a number of key trends were emerging that further favored the Japanese. The composition of market demand was changing. The television market was no longer simply a first-set market. The second-set market was rapidly emerging. The latter segment was predominantly smaller portables. By 1963, the second-set market comprised approximately 25 percent of the total black-and-white market. These were precisely the types of products the Japanese supplied.

Also, it is clear that the color market preoccupied U.S. firms in the early 1960s. Although they continued to manufacture and aggressively market black-and-white television sets, U.S. firms vociferously proclaimed that "the future is color." This considerably lessened their incentive to tool up and compete intensely in the smaller end of the black-and-white market.

From Flanking to Frontal Strategy

The transition from a flanking to a frontal strategy Is hard to specify with precision: It gradually evolves over a period of time. However, there are usually a number of indicators that the strategy is becoming more and more frontal in scope and intensity and less and less flanking. Many such indicators were clearly in evidence in the mid-to-late 1960s, that the Japanese were no longer content with their role as "flankers" but rather were intent on taking the battle more directly and aggressively to U.S. firms.

Evidence of transition to a frontal strategy first appeared with regard to the products themselves. From 1964–65 on, Japanese firms were nudging closer and closer to the mainstay end of the U.S. producers' business, the 19"-plus-size television sets. They were gradually moving into that part of the battlefield that U.S. firms had staked out and dominated. In 1964 and 1965, they were selling sets in the 12"–16" screen sizes. Indeed, they dominated this market segment. A few manufacturers even sold 19" sets in 1965. In 1966, the first 19" Japanese color sets were shipped to the U.S. market. By the late 1960s, the Japanese were selling

19" sets and above. They were edging ever closer to attaining parity with U.S. set sizes.

The frontal onslaught on U.S. competitors went beyond simply challenging them in terms of types of products sold. A major component of the frontal attack involved the Japanese pitting their own brand names against the well-established household names of U.S. manufacturers. In 1966, Toshiba, Hitachi, and Panasonic sold their newly introduced 19" color sets under their own brand names. By 1970, all Japanese producers were selling some sets under their own labels, though the private-label/own-label proportions varied significantly across firms.

Distribution changes represented another major element in Japan's drive to go head-to-head against U.S. firms. In many respects, distribution management provided a much sterner test of Japanese marketing capability than product change or movement to their own labels. It involved movement toward Japanese control and management of the distribution channel and a major step in eliminating dependence on U.S.-owned and -controlled distribution elements. Around 1964, Japanese firms showed the first signs of taking charge of their U.S. distribution. A number of firms began to establish their own sales offices. Previously, they had contracted with local importers. Many of these contracts were not renewed during the mid-1960s. This effort was considerably aided by the Japan External Trade Relations Organization (JETRO), a division of MITI, which prepared thorough studies of all aspects of conducting business in the United States.

Encirclement Strategy

Flanking and frontal attacks dominated the Japanese drive to penetrate the U.S. television receiver market during the 1960s. By the late 1960s, however, the evidence was clear that the Japanese were driving toward encirclement. By 1970, almost all the Japanese firms were selling sets in the 19" and 21" screen sizes, the most popular set sizes. In the early to middle 1970s, most Japanese firms continued moving up the scale of screen size sold. In 1973, Japanese firms began to ship 19" color table models, three years after this size had been introduced by U.S. firms. By 1975–76, Japanese producers were selling almost all the screen sizes that U.S. firms offered.

The drive toward encirclement was also taking place within the distribution channels. The Japanese firms were proliferating and pushing their products through the channels. This form of encirclement was in part caused by the fact that the number of U.S. firms producing television sets actually fell below the number of Japanese firms doing so toward the end of the 1970s. Thus, when the consumer walked into a retail store, he or she was confronted with more Japanese than U.S. television sets.

It is important to note that U.S. manufacturers, spearheaded by Zenith, claim that Japanese success in the television receiver market was largely attributable to "dumping." These charges were upheld in an investigation conducted by the U.S. International Tariff Commission. Without doubt, the Japanese used aggressive pricing as a spearhead to frontally assault and encircle U.S. manufacturers in the U.S. market.

Bypass Strategy

As with the other strategy types, a bypass attack necessitates a careful delineation of product-markets and the position of the enemy within them. However, the thrust of a bypass attack is to avoid direct confrontation with the competition. Bypass strategy was a key element in the Japanese attack on the U.S. position in the global television receiver industry.

The Japanese adopted a bypass strategy vis-a-vis U.S. competition from the earliest days of their efforts to penetrate the world marketplace. They sought to penetrate geographical markets where the United States did not have a presence. Since U.S. firms paid such little attention to the export market, it was, of course, easy for the Japanese to bypass them. However, as the Japanese successfully penetrated the U.S. market, they simultaneously pushed their bypass effort in foreign markets. Thus, at the same time that Japanese firms were moving steadfastly toward winning the war in the U.S. marketplace, they were also doing so in Asia, South America, and Europe.

Their bypass attack, however, was not limited to penetration of foreign markets. They also bypassed U.S. firms through product diversification. Toward the later part of the 1970s, the Japanese successfully commercialized the videotape recorder (which is an attachment to the television set to record television programs). Thus they went beyond simply competing in the well-established television market to creating a new but related product-market.

The videotape recorder product-diversification-oriented bypass strategy was, of course, based on technology development. The Japanese themselves developed the technology underlying video recorders. Yet as early as 1969, the Japanese had significantly bypassed the U.S. competition in terms of TV product technology. In that year, Hitachi became the first firm to convert its entire line to 100 percent solid-state design. In the following year, all major Japanese firms converted to 100 percent solid state. This quick incorporation of solid-state technology by Japanese firms has been called "the turning point in the technological advancement of the Japanese over the American industry." In 1970, Motorola was the only firm with a 100 percent solid-state set. Motorola had actually developed the technology in 1966 but did not pursue it as vigorously as the Japanese. However, even with the success of the Japanese sets, the U.S. manufacturers did not quickly respond. RCA and Zenith did not produce 100 percent solid-state sets until 1973–74, and many of the smaller firms did not follow suit until 1974 or 1975. Solid state represented a major leap forward from previous technology. It helped create greater reliability, lessened service requirements, and reduced energy consumption. Sales of Japanese sets took a major upward swing as a consequence. Moreover, solid-state technology was less labor intensive than the previous vacuum-tube sets. It also facilitated considerable energy conservation in television set usage, and it allowed further automation of the production process and resulting productivity gains.

Guerrilla Strategy

It is not too farfetched to suggest that elements of guerrilla strategy are evident in the Japanese invasion of the U.S. television receiver market. Although they may not have been intended as guerrillalike strategy, these actions often had guerrillalike consequences.

In the early and middle 1960s, the Japanese played price and promotional games in order to win distribution channel favors and get publicity for their products. Although they were not yet competing head-to-head against U.S. firms, the price changes and related promotional outbursts made it more difficult for U.S. firms to respond. Frequently, the object of these attacks was specific channels or retail outlets in order to obtain greater "push" for their products. Similar tactics were also used even after the Japanese had succeeded in gaining a large slice of the U.S. market.

Also, as they moved toward building their own distribution systems and sales forces, Japanese firms often raided U.S. establishments, in part or in whole. As related by some longtime industry participants, Japanese television manufacturers would have had a much more difficult time than they did in gaining a market presence if they had not been able to raid U.S. manufacturers, distributors, sales forces, and advertising agencies for much of their personnel. They "bought" people who had relevant experience and who, of course, knew the U.S. marketplace, though not necessarily the television market.

Strategic Flexibility and Incrementalism

Much of the description of the Japanese penetration of the U.S. television receiver market starting in the 1960s illustrates a pattern of strategic flexibility. The Japanese learned as they went: They knew little about the U.S. marketplace when they first entered. With the exception of Sony, Japanese firms were dependent on U.S. organizations for the distribution and promotion of their products. Such was the level of dependence that the U.S. consumer did not even know that he or she was purchasing a Japanese-made television set.

The strategies of Japanese firms were marked by continued incremental changes in the first half of the 1960s. These firms gradually extended and upscaled their product line, they sequentially penetrated the distribution channels, and they added to their promotional efforts. Moreover, they continued to enhance the quality of their product and the variety of products they offered within each popular screen size. They gradually rolled out their market development activities, moving from private labels to their own labels, from distribution through others to self-distribution, and from narrow to broad market and retail coverage. They also became much more flexible in their use of the weapons within the marketing mix.

The incremental nature of the Japanese strategy is reflected in their performance. The Japanese did not overwhelm the U.S. marketplace with instant success. It took the Japanese five years before they sold one million black-and-white sets in one year, and in that year (1966) they accounted for less than 20 percent of the black-and-white market. Going into 1970, they had captured 40 percent of the market. Approximately similar results were obtained in the color market.

LESSONS AND IMPLICATIONS

This chapter points out several lessons about appropriate attack strategies under different company size and resource circumstances:

- Companies wishing to enter a foreign market but lacking the resources of the dominant producers should search for a flanking strategy. They should look for a market segment that is not being served or served well and should proceed to gain a foothold. If the total market is growing, the dominant producers will probably pay little attention to the intruder until it is too late.

- Companies might consider waging a frontal attack when their resources are strong in relation to competitors, when they can foresee eventually developing a competitive advantage, and when they can convince distributors to carry their product and customers to try it. Frontal attacks can be pure or price-based or R&D-based.

- Companies might consider launching an encirclement attack when they possess superior resources in relation to competitors and are willing to commit them for an extended period of time.

- Companies might consider a bypass strategy and avoid attacking their opponents when their resources and current products possess no advantage over the opponents. These companies should operate in geographical areas that are neglected by the dominant producers and wait for the day when their resources or technological advantages permit a more direct attack on the dominant producers.

- Companies might consider directing occasional guerrilla attacks when their resources are weak but when they can gain concessions or advantages by harassing the opponents and keeping them off balance.

- Companies should avoid following a "grand plan" frozen in time and instead adopt a pattern of strategic flexibility and incrementalism. As the market and competition change, the successful firm will reconsider and revise its core strategies.

chapter 8

Maintenance Strategies: Defending Market Leadership

Japan now dominates many product-markets in the United States and the rest of the world. Its export prowess in most industries seems to continue unabated. However, a historical perspective on the ebb and flow of economic leadership in the world marketplace indicates that Japan could go the way of Great Britain and even the United States in the past two decades and lose its dominant leadership position. Great Britain and the United States reached their world economic zenith as a result of favorable political and economic forces but began to lose leadership once new forces and conditions developed. Although Japan is beginning to experience some challenges to its dominance, it has not yet shown signs of running out of steam. On the contrary, Japan seems intent on protecting its leadership in current industries and moving into the forefront of emerging industries and into a leadership position in still other industries.

THREATS TO JAPAN'S DOMINANCE

Japan's success has provoked responses from other countries. They are no longer willing to allow Japan to go unchallenged. Three outside challenges to Japan's dominance can be identified: (1) an anti-Japanese syndrome has evolved in several developed countries; (2) the United States and the European countries have begun to fine-tune their response to the Japanese challenge; and (3) some Far East nations have begun to compete effectively with the Japanese. A fourth threat to Japan's dominance is occurring within Japan itself in the form of important economic and social changes.

The Anti-Japanese Syndrome

Japan's success has brought it into conflict with both developed and underdeveloped countries. Japan has increasingly been criticized by other nations because of its trade policies at home and abroad. Major hostility toward Japan has emerged in the United States and Europe because of Japan's remarkable market penetration. Further fuel was added to these fires when Japan weathered the 1980–83 recession much better than Europe and the United States; it did not suffer double-digit inflation, and its unemployment rate remained comparatively low. The viewpoint that Japan's success has been at the expense of other countries has become increasingly prevalent in Europe and the United States.

Unlike criticisms during the early 1970s which tended to make an issue of Japan's trade surplus, the focus in recent years has tended to revolve around specific commodities such as automobiles, motorcycles, television sets, and semiconductors. Japanese success in these industries has triggered a mood of protectionism against Japanese products. Threats of the imposition of import quotas led Japanese auto manufacturers to assume voluntary restrictions on their exports to the United States. In the case of television, the United States and Japan entered into an orderly marketing agreement: In effect, Japan accepted an upper limit on the number of television sets it could ship to the United States. The U.S. automobile and television industries heavily lobbied the U.S. government to take some kind of protectionist action against the Japanese. Harley Davidson, whose position in the U.S. motorcycle market has been annihilated by the Japanese, has pursued the same course over the past year. One reason for the continuing discussion of import quotas and voluntary quotas by the administration, Congress, and various industries is a desire to retaliate against Japan's covert and overt protection of its home market.

The Counterresponses

Japan's success has made believers out of U.S. and European firms. They no longer treat the Japanese with the skepticism and disdain that was so rampant for most of the 1960s. More importantly, respect for Japanese capability is being transformed into action: Many U.S. and European firms in various industries invaded by the Japanese have begun to counterattack the Japanese.

The U.S. and European firms no longer give the Japanese a free hand in major product-market sectors. Few "provided opportunities" are likely to be accorded the Japanese in the 1980s. The U.S. semiconductor industry provides a good example of a group of U.S. firms—Motorola, Intel, and Texas Instruments—that have committed themselves to "going to war" against the Japanese. Motorola, for example, pursued a strategy similar to the Japanese strategy by choosing a more conservative design for its 64K chip rather than complicated new designs and aggressively priced them. This helped Motorola, which had a 50 percent market share with its 16K chip, to capture a 20 percent market share of the 64K chip market.

In response to the Japanese victory in the 16K market, U.S. firms have adopted longer-term-oriented R&D, production, and marketing strategies. A collective R&D effort, in conjunction with a number of universities, has been initiated by a number of U.S. firms. They have also spent large sums building highly automated manufacturing plants—a major key to success in the precision and quality-oriented semiconductor business—in order to avoid the product scarcity that plagued the industry in its early years. Another element in the U.S. counteroffensive has been a commitment to reestablish an American reputation for quality. Texas Instruments' emphasis on semiconductor product quality helped it double its market share and achieve an estimated second place in the world market by about mid-1982.

Xerox's counteroffensive in the copier market provides another good example. After the once-mighty Xerox had seen its market share fall to about 45 percent, it reformulated its strategies and restructured its organization to fight back against the Japanese, especially in small and medium-sized copiers. To meet the Japanese head on, Xerox brought to market a new line of copiers, slashed prices by an average of 27 percent on many of its models, and added additional market channels to reach the small-business customers it had previously ignored. It has also sent teams of engineers and managers to study Japanese methods of quality control, engineering, and procurement practices as part of its effort to cut manufacturing costs.

Even the U.S. automobile industry has focused a good deal of its attention on counterattacking the Japanese. American automobile manufacturers had little choice but to overcome their reluctance to produce small, more-fuel-efficient, and less-profitable automobiles. The U.S. producers now market a wide range of compacts and subcompacts. Although a belated effort, its obvious intent is to give Japanese and other foreign producers a competitive battle in these auto market segments. They could no longer afford to give the Japanese "a free ride" in the most buoyant segments of the market.

In cameras, after losing substantial market shares to the Japanese producers, the German producers launched several counteroffensives to regain their market shares. Rollei-Werke Francke & Heidecke, the leading German producer, launched a massive reorganization and expansion program in R&D to create a new range of products. It also contracted with a large number of distributors in its primary markets (the U.S., the U.K., Germany, Switzerland, and France) to carry its products. Finally, it moved its production overseas (Singapore, etc.) where skilled labor was much cheaper.

The "New Japanese"

Competition against Japan is emanating from sources other than the developed West. The newly industrialized countries of Asia, especially South Korea, Taiwan, Singapore, and Hong Kong, as well as other developing countries such as Mexico and Brazil, are becoming Japan's tough competitors in many industries. Indeed, the above-mentioned Asian countries are frequently referred to as the "New Japanese."

As Japan's labor cost per hour dramatically increased, the "New Japanese" with their much lower cost structure were able to compete very effectively against Japan in industries where technology development was not the decisive factor. In many industry segments where Japan's competitive advantage has faded, these "little Japans" have stepped into the breach. For example, textiles and electronic watches now gush forth from Hong Kong, color TV sets from Taiwan, and ships and automobiles from South Korea.

These countries, especially Taiwan and South Korea, also seem to have fashioned significant segments of their institutional infrastructure along the lines of the Japanese model. They have vigorously established protectionist programs, allowing most domestic industries to develop behind high tariff walls until they become viable and competitive. Government agencies that are similar to JETRO of Japan have been established to promote exports—for example, Korea's KOTRA (the Korean Organization for Trade Advancement) and Taiwan's CETDC (the China Export Trade Development Council).

Change within Japan

Japan's capacity to maintain its position in many industries is also being influenced by changes within Japan itself. Japan, like so many countries before it, may well be a victim of its own economic success. The social and economic conditions that facilitated the emergence and development of the Japanese economic juggernaut have been altered so much by its success that the new conditions may make it difficult for the juggernaut to continue at anything like its previous pace in most industries.

Dramatic social and economic change has taken place in Japan. It is most clearly seen in economic statistics. Japanese wage rates have increased dramatically and are now approximately at the U.S. level. They are now about 50 percent higher than in the United Kingdom and about 15 to 20 percent lower than in West Germany. Clearly, Japan is no longer a source of cheap labor. Although productivity is still rising more rapidly in Japan than in other developed countries, the rate of increase has slowed and is now considerably less than it was in the 1960s. Japan's saving rate, while still the highest in the world, is now a full third below the levels of the 1970s, resulting in a slowing down of the rate of capital formation.

Continued economic growth and development is also impacting social customs and mores and political processes. Some segments of Japan's people have begun to pay greater attention to leisure and consumption. Labor is seeking a shorter work week. More Japanese people want to enjoy what they have produced. Sociopolitical interest groups are more vociferous in their demands: Japanese farmers have marched in the streets and large antinuclear demonstrations have occurred.

MARKET MAINTENANCE STRATEGIES

The dominant position of many Japanese firms in so many product-markets and the aforementioned threats to their dominance indicate that they will increasingly play the role of prey rather than predator. Japanese firms will increasingly face attacks from national governments, individual firms, and groups of firms. To penetrate and dominate product-markets is certainly a tough task; maintaining that dominance can be just as tough. At a minimum, the Japanese ability to fend off the retaliatory responses of the U.S., European, and other competitors will prove the sternest test yet of their strategic and marketing capability.

As Japanese firms have moved toward product-market dominance, they have had to shift from market entry and penetration strategies to market maintenance and protection strategies. The core of much of their maintenance strategies involves doing more of what won them the markets—product development and market development.

We will discuss six market maintenance strategies—position defense, mobile defense, preemptive defense, counteroffensive defense, flank-position defense, and strategic withdrawal—most of which have been employed by the Japanese.

Position Defense: The Fortified Front Lines

Faced with challenges from other Asian and third-world countries as well as the retaliatory strategies of U.S. and European corporations, the Japanese recognize that they cannot stand still. They know that competitive superiority is fleeting; unless they dedicate resources to moving the battlefield and to creating new competitive advantages, they themselves will be surpassed by others.

Whether in military warfare or business competition, a driving impulse is to defend one's present position, to hold one's front on the battlefield, to retain one's current product-markets. This traditional concept of defense is closely tied to a psychology of fortification. The French Maginot line, the German Siegfried line, and most recently the Israeli Barlev line on the Suez are all twentieth-century versions of the "fort" of the Middle Ages. Like almost all the great forts of history, these extensive, supposedly impregnable, fortified front lines all failed in the hour of peril. A static fortlike defense, like a frontal attack, is one of the riskiest strategies in military theory.

A position defense is also a highly risky gambit in competitive business strategy. A pure position defense presumes little change in the

Maintenance (Defense) Strategies

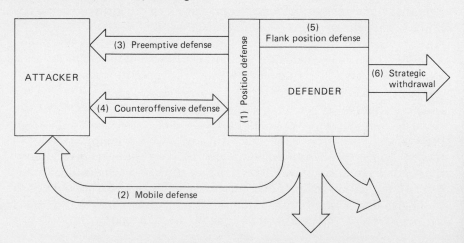

product-market or, more broadly, the industry. The firm sees its product as invincible. The market is expected to go on absorbing the product. Exclusive dependence on a position defense effectively means that a business is a sitting target for competition: The firm is forgoing other defensive and offensive strategies to compete in the marketplace. A position defense is ultimately destined for failure, since the defender will eventually find itself protecting a shrinking product-market. Unless a firm moves its "fort" in line with product and market evolution, a position defense can only result in outdated products and lost markets.

Japanese firms seem to understand very well that a strong fortified front line may bestow a competitive advantage but that if it remains stationary it invites competitive retaliation and will ultimately result in competitive inferiority. In the main, they have not relied on a fortified front line. Rather they have employed offensive and defensive strategies to continually move their "front"—i.e., their position in the marketplace. They do not rest on their laurels. Product improvement, line extension, and proliferation continue unabated. Not only do Japanese firms gradually take on more U.S. firms in head-to-head competition, they are increasingly moving past the positions of U.S. firms: in offensive terms, bypass attacks; in defensive terms, engaging in mobile and preemptive defenses. Also, as we will discuss shortly, the Japanese are not loath to engage in counteroffensive moves where they feel they have to directly defend themselves against the attacks of the U.S. firms.

In short, Japanese firms seem committed to avoiding the competitive sins inherent in "market myopia." Their passion for product development, and, more recently, market development, means that they themselves and not their competitors make their products obsolete. Clearly, as Japanese firms come under increasing attack from U.S. and other foreign firms, it will be foolhardy for them to rely on a static defense, devoting all their resources to building fortifications around their current product offerings.

Mobile Defense

Much of the West's concern, if not preoccupation, with Japan's penetration and domination of many world markets reflects Japan's commitment and dedication to not only preserving but enhancing its market leadership position. Japan is not just defending its current product-market positions; it is moving the battleground to new product-markets. Furthermore, Japanese firms move to new product-market arenas not so much through normal brand proliferation and product line extensions as through innovative activity on two fronts, namely, market broadening and market diversification. Over time, these moves entrench them in new product-market positions and generate strategic depth, which enables them to weather continual attacks and to launch retaliatory strikes.

It should be noted that market broadening and diversification are the defense-in-depth solutions advanced by Theodore Levitt in his widely acclaimed article "Marketing Myopia." Levitt argues that a company must shift its focus from the current product to the underlying generic need and get involved in R&D across the whole range of technology associated with that need. For example, a firm manufacturing motorcycles might see itself in the business of providing efficient transportation—there may be other realizable opportunities within this generic need, such as designing bicycles, small automobiles, and small vans. The firm's product and manufacturing technologies and expertise may be applicable to a wide variety of vehicles other than motorcycles. A mobile defense involves shifting to these product-market opportunities to better position the firm in the broader (than motorcycle) marketplace.

Technology Provides the Impetus. At the heart of Japan's mobile defense lies technology. It is a natural outgrowth of the continual technological progress made by Japan, from the low-level technologies of the 1950s and 1960s to the much-higher-level technologies of the 1970s to the knowledge-intensive industries of the 1980s. The aforementioned "vision of the 1980s" exhorts Japanese businesspeople to build a "technology-based" nation by 1990. Semiconductors, computers, robots, medical electronics, machine tools, and aircraft are indicative of the new emerging heartland of Japan's industrial juggernaut.

Propelled by this technology drive, the Japanese are stretching their product-market domain in two related ways: extending or broadening present product-markets and diversifying into new product-market territories. In almost every industry in which they have a large share of the world market, the Japanese are extending and broadening the scope of their product offerings and opening up new, unserved market needs. For example, in consumer electronics, they have moved from manufacturing television receivers to selling videodiscs and tape recorders, from radios to Sony "Walkmans," and from stereo systems to the most-advanced audio sound systems.

A mobile defense in the form of market diversification is also evident in the strategic thrusts of some firms in older Japanese industries such as steel, textiles, and shipbuilding. Mitsubishi Heavy Industries, Kawasaki Heavy Industries, and Fuji Heavy Industries, for example, are getting into aircraft building. They will be competing with Boeing for the next generation of commercial jetliners. Even the number-two automaker, Nissan Motor, has entered into a broad agreement with Martin-

Marietta of the United States to obtain basic technology for the development of aerospace and defense-related equipment and may be contemplating a leap into commercial aircraft production.

However, the Japanese are not just enlarging their grip on industries in which they have been competing for the past few decades. They have rapidly moved into a number of industries in the past few years, certainly since the mid-1970s. Computers, semiconductors, many segments of machine tools, and telecommunications are good examples. Robotics, biotechnology including new drugs and foods, and new materials such as ceramic and carbon fibers and optical fibers are examples of industries or industry segments where they are in the forefront of technology and market development.

> Japanese companies in the textile industry have started diversifying into the pharmaceutical and biotechnological industries. Toray, Japan's largest synthetic fibre producer, has committed its resources to the development of the anti-cancer drug beta-type interferon, which is expected to have a very high potential growth in the future. Teijin, Japan's largest polyester maker, has already moved into the prosperous pharmaceutical area by manufacturing Venilon, a drug for treating severe infections and also developing monoclonal antibodies for fighting cancer with Hybritech in the U.S., and cooperating with Biogen on an anti-hemophilia drug.

Investment in R&D. A dominant, highly noticeable feature of industries and individual firms leading the push toward product-market broadening and diversification is their level of investment in R&D. The Japanese companies have increased their R&D efforts, especially in such high-technology industries as electronics, with the objective of developing more sophisticated products. Hitachi, for example, increased its R&D outlays to 128 billion yen, or 3.8 percent of sales as of March 1981, from only 36.2 billion yen nine years earlier. Japan's industries as a whole boosted R&D expenditure by more than 300 percent in the 1970s. And this trend toward higher R&D allocation is expected to broaden throughout the 1980s, since Japan has already set upon a policy of sharp increase in R&D spending to 3 percent of GNP in 1990 from 2.2 percent currently, with the government's share of the R&D bill to rise from 27 to 40 percent.

Preemptive Defense

Strategically, the essence of a preemptive defense is to identify strengths within current product-markets and build on them. This involves intensifying current competitive advantages and/or developing new ones. In either case, the presumption is the same: The enemy is not retreating or standing still. The only way one can stay ahead of the enemy is to do what one does better and to continue to do new and better things. Only in this way is one likely to foreclose windows of opportunity for the enemy or, at a minimum, make it tougher for the enemy to exploit potential strategic windows.

The Japanese are maintaining—and improving—their position in almost all the product-markets they are in by doing more of the same, that is, using all the offensive strategies described in the preceding two chapters. They continue the product and market development strategies that allow them to flank, frontally attack, encircle, and bypass the enemy. The intent is to retain the initiative in existing product-markets broadly defined and keep the enemy on the defensive.

In the automobile industry, for example, Japanese manufacturers are continuing to push the product and market development strategies that have given them 30 percent of the U.S. auto market. Product improvement, line stretching, and proliferation abound. The Japanese are at the forefront of introducing electronic technology into their autos. Nissan's Cedric/Gloria series contained microprocessor controls for everything from fuel injection ignition timing to idling speed and air fuel ratios. Nissan is also working on a control computer to control all these functions. Toyota has already successfully introduced the electronic monitoring and control of engine functions in the development of its new passenger car. Isuzu Motors has received much acclaim for its small-car diesel engines. The Japanese also beat the U.S. manufacturers to the punch in the introduction of front-wheel drive autos. Honda's complete line was front-wheel drive by 1980. Japanese autos are moving further and further upscale and competing frontally with an ever-increasing slice of the product lines of U.S. manufacturing.

In motorcycles, Japanese makers now compete intensely against each other. They now have numerous models covering the whole product range from lightweight 50 cc.'s to 750 cc.'s and beyond. Their motorcycles now embody such sophisticated new refinements as electronic fuel injection, turbochargers, and remote control air suspension.

Managing the Marketing Mix.　　In addition to the product and market development strategies, the Japanese have also intensified and extended their efforts to manage the weapons in the marketing mix. The intent of these efforts is to preempt competitors' moves; to avoid leaving open windows of marketing opportunity and thereby lessening the range of marketing retaliatory responses open to competitors. The intensification of these efforts is also remarkably clear.

In many market segments where they already have a major or dominant position, such as automobiles, motorcycles, watches, and copiers, they have already strengthened their distribution network by adding more dealers.

Advertising and promotional efforts have also been significantly augmented in response to counterattacks from U.S. and other firms. Canon has devoted nearly $40 million in advertising to back its product lines over the next four years.

Counteroffensive Defense

Of course, a defensive option is always to attack the enemy directly. The defender mobilizes its resources and counterattacks the aggressor (the defensive counterpart of the aggressive frontal attack). A counteroffensive can take three forms: meet the attacker head on, maneuver against the flank of the attacker, or launch a "pincer" movement to cut off the attacking formations at the base of their operation. As U.S. firms began to respond in earnest to the Japanese challenge, Japanese firms demonstrated their capacity and willingness to use all three counteroffensive moves.

The strategy of Japanese firms in the 16K and 64K RAM chip market illustrates all three forms of counteroffensive defensive strategies. The U.S. firms successfully developed and marketed 16K RAM chips in the 1970s. In the late 1970s, Japan launched a massive frontal attack on the U.S. 16K RAM chip market, quickly capturing over 40 percent of this market. Disturbed by the surprising ease with which the Japanese so quickly penetrated their market, U.S. firms moved in haste to develop the next generation of chips, the 64K RAM. However, they were again beaten to the punch by the Japanese, who were already selling commercial quantities by the time U.S. firms were shipping prototypes toward the end of 1980. In effect, the Japanese took their U.S. counterparts head on before the latter got to the market (a preemptive defensive move).

In essence, a large part of the Japanese counteroffensive was aimed at a flank left exposed by U.S. firms. Here, we conceive of a "flank" as a segment of the product's attributes or the market's perceptions of the product. The U.S. firms, in large measure driven by technologists and engineers, sought a technically sophisticated design that would incorporate the most-advanced circuitry. The Japanese, on the other hand, successfully forged a "brute force product" that many U.S. executives charged was largely developed from U.S. design work. In the words of one U.S. executive, "We were trying to be too elegant, and maybe too smart. And we let the market window disappear on us."

As U.S. firms began to enter the market, the Japanese defended themselves in pincerlike fashion. They dramatically reduced prices. Many U.S. executives charged that the Japanese were selling at prices that could not produce profits, that is, they were selling below cost. In any case, the results were clear: Many U.S. firms were forced out of the business, either withdrawing or being taken over by larger firms.

Flank-Position Defense

Defensive moves must take into account where the enemy is likely to attack. Normally the enemy will attack an unprotected flank of the dominant firm. A flank-position defense, therefore, consists in the firm fortifying its flanks so as to discourage attack.

Since the early 1970s, Japanese companies have faced mounting competitive challenges from foreign competitors, especially from such newly industrialized countries as South Korea, Taiwan, and Singapore, which surpassed the Japanese in terms of cost advantage. Japan's rising production costs opened opportunity gaps rapidly captured by these countries to build up worldwide market shares at the expense of Japanese companies. Unless Japanese companies close this flank, sooner or later Japanese global market shares will be eroded by these competitors. As a result, the Japanese have started committing their resources to improved productivity to forestall their declining cost advantage.

While Japan has always heavily emphasized manufacturing's role in generating product quality, reliability, functionality, and lower price—all major competitive advantages—in the past few years it has made major strides in upscaling the technological sophistication of its manufacturing processes to boost productivity. *Mechatronics* (technologies that combine electronics and mechanized engineering) is the name frequently given to this broad movement. Mechatronics has been introduced in the production process of a large number of Japanese assembly-line industries, such as electronical and transportation equipment, precision machinery, watches, and cameras. Many Japanese firms have focused their strategies on cost reduction to strengthen their cost competitiveness. Nippon Steel, for example, developed a program of continued cost reduction by organizing a companywide campaign to reduce cost. Production processes were improved to reduce labor requirements. Substantial investments were made in energy-efficient, labor-saving facilities that included continuous casters, blast-furnaces, and new equipment combining intermittent operations into continuous operations. It upgraded the quality of its products as well as developed new products to maintain its competitive position throughout the world.

While mobile and preemptive defenses will typically consume many more resources, a flank-position defense is not a free lunch. A flanking position is of little value if it is so lightly held that an enemy could overwhelm it and march past virtually unmolested. If defending a flank is deemed necessary, resources must be committed, as seen in the Japanese defensive strategies. Any resources directed toward the defense may very well be wasted if the enemy easily surmounts the half-hearted defense.

Strategic Withdrawal: The Hedgehog Defense

The adoption of any one of the above five defensive strategies does not presume that a firm needs to defend all the segments of its current position. It is possible, and frequently desirable, to narrow the scope of one's position, that is, to engage in a hedgehog pattern of withdrawal along the front line, be it in terms of product withdrawal, market withdrawal, or some combination.

The strategic rationale underlying the hedgehog defense is to allow the firm to concentrate its forces either to defend itself better or to allow for a focused counterattack. It implies that the firm does not have the resources for a broad fortified defense. Frequently, the hedgehog defense is a pivotal cornerstone in launching a major defensive or offensive campaign.

DEFENSIVE STRATEGIES: THE CASE OF THE TELEVISION RECEIVER INDUSTRY

We will use the television receiver industry to illustrate the maintenance strategies of the Japanese firms. We will outline the defensive strategies they have employed not only to protect but to expand their position.

The road to glory for the Japanese in the U.S. television receiver industry was not paved with instant success. In their first ten years in the United States, the Japanese managed to gain only a 10 percent market share. During the late 1960s, U.S. firms began to compete aggressively against the Japanese. No longer were the Japanese beneficiaries of "provided opportunity." They would have to earn their market gains. Consequently, as the Japanese gained market presence, they had to defend it; they had to employ defensive as well as offensive strategies.

Position Defense

The Japanese chose not to practice position defense. They did not simply "dig in" and rest on their laurels. They pursued continuous product and market development, building on their market prominence and technological leadership.

Mobile Defense

The Japanese have significantly moved their front forward; indeed, they have moved the front of the entire industry forward. In 1977–78, through technology innovation, they broadened and diversified beyond the narrow television receiver product-market into video cassette recorders (and tapes). In the 1980s, they have further miniaturized the television receiver. The Japanese now produce "pocket-sized" receivers, and they have even built television sets in watches. They have also broadened their market for the television receiver by giving heavy emphasis to foreign markets other than the United States.

Their successful entry into video cassette recorders (VCRs) is extremely significant in the battle between U.S. and Japanese firms. Sony initially developed the VCR. Matsushita quickly followed suit. These two Japanese firms were in a hot race to get their product to the market before a countertechnology, videodisc, was fully developed by RCA and North American Philips/USA. The latter two firms were reported to have spent an estimated $150 million in developing their system. In February 1977, Sony signed an agreement with Zenith to allow the latter to market the Sony "Betamax" VCR under the Zenith name. A little later, RCA signed to market Matsushita's video recorder.

These moves were significant for a number of reasons. First, they gave the Japanese a major leg up on the U.S. competition in getting to the market first in the emerging technology war between the VCR and videodisc systems. Second, the Japanese tied up the two dominant U.S. firms, RCA and Zenith, as distributors for their products in the U.S. market. Third, although the Sony and Matsushita systems were quite different (e.g., the cassettes for the two systems were not interchangeable), their introduction prior to the videodisc system allowed the Japanese to gain an initial burst of consumer loyalty and confidence.

As a consequence, the two dominant U.S. producers, RCA and Zenith, now found themselves distributing the first major new products in the industry for two Japanese firms. RCA pressed on in its efforts to develop and commercialize videodiscs. It finally introduced the product in 1978. However, RCA was never able to compete effectively against the more versatile VCRs. The product was ultimately withdrawn in 1984 with losses of about $400 million.

The Japanese did not limit their mobility in the marketplace to issues of competitive behavior. Their mobile defense is also evident in their manufacturing strategy. In the late 1960s and early 1970s, many U.S. firms (with the notable exception of Zenith) began to move significant portions of their television receiver manufacturing operations offshore—to such places as Mexico and the Far East—in search of lower labor costs. A frequently espoused rationale was the need for cost competitiveness to combat what was depicted as the superior cost position of the Japanese. At the same time, however, the Japanese were also beginning to go offshore—to the United States. Sony, the first firm to do so, began manufacturing operations in 1971. Over the course of the 1970s, Sony was followed by almost all the major Japanese participants in the U.S. market. Eight Japanese firms now produce television sets in the United States. One major reason for the Japanese moving manufacturing operations to the United States was their desire to avoid being barred from the U.S. market if import controls were imposed. As early as 1968, some U.S. firms had sought such controls to bar Japanese television sets or at least limit their importation on the grounds that they were being "dumped" in the United States.

Preemptive Strategy

The Japanese defensive strategy in the television receiver product-market is highly preemptive in that the Japanese firms kept refining their products and attacking new market segments. Particularly evident in the mid-1970s was an intense Japanese effort to gain market share through preemptive pricing attacks in the color television market. Through their lower prices, Japanese firms also wooed away a large slice of the private-label business, which the large retail chains had been giving to U.S. firms. One result of this effort was an increase in Japan's market share from 11 percent in 1975 to almost 30 percent in the color segment in 1976. Another result, of course, was that U.S. firms and labor unions charged the Japanese with "dumping," a charge that was upheld a number of times in court during the 1970s.

Counteroffensive Strategy

Increasingly during the 1970s and into the 1980s, the Japanese found themselves confronted with aggressive U.S. counterattacks on their position. Almost every time, the Japanese have engaged in a counteroffensive. Their commitment to aggressive price competition represented the frontal attack component in their counteroffensive strategy. They also met U.S. firms head on in promotional programs and in incentives to the distribution channels.

A classic counteroffensive strategy is the pincer movement, that is, destroying the enemy's base of operations. In the competitive business arena, this translates into taking over in one form or another the operations of competitors. In 1974, Matshushita acquired Motorola's television receiver business; in 1975, Sanyo took over Warwick's business.

Flank-Position Defense

As the Japanese have gained position in the television receiver industry during the 1980s, they have methodically protected all their flanks in the industry. They have sealed off all possible opportunities for U.S. firms to attack segments of their position. The U.S. firms have not been the beneficiaries of provided opportunities. They have had to create opportunities, as Zenith quite successfully did with the introduction of its large-screen projector television set in the late 1970s.

The Japanese seem to have taken to heart the motto that "The best defense is a good offense." They have continued to extend their product line in both price directions. They have also continued to extend and solidify their distribution channel coverage. Moreover, as they develop and exploit new related product-market opportunities (in the form of VCRs), they do not let up on their efforts to extend and sustain their core business—television sets.

Strategic Withdrawal

Individual Japanese firms have not engaged in much strategic withdrawal in the television receiver industry. They still continue to attack the television set "market" aggressively and defend their position within it.

In summary, there are now more Japanese than U.S. firms producing and selling television sets in the United States. Many U.S. firms have accused the Japanese of dumping and pricing. As evidenced in multiple studies by the ITC (International Trade Commission), there is a substantial element of truth in the accusations. No doubt these practices have helped the Japanese garner market share. However, they do not fully explain Japanese success. The Japanese have not stood still on the product, market, or technology fronts. They have used a variety of strategies to defend their position. They have not presumed that competitors—or customers—are standing still.

DEFENSIVE STRATEGIES EMPLOYED BY THE JAPANESE GOVERNMENT

A dominant theme running through this book is the widespread, encompassing, and aggressive role of the Japanese government in shaping Japan's economic miracle. While it is sometimes difficult to disaggregate the relationships between industries and government in Japan, it is clear that Japan's government through its actions and nonactions has spurred many industries toward worldwide preeminence and is now facilitating the retention of that position. In other words, it is also instructive to examine the role of the Japanese government from the perspective of maintenance strategies.

The Japanese government has avoided a position defense or fortified front line in fostering and sustaining the country's economic miracle. It has not dug its heels in and tried to fight it out with other countries in extant product-markets or industries. The Japanese government has long recognized that to stand still invites the enemy to attack, and to continue doing as it has done allows the enemy time to prepare and launch not only a frontal attack but perhaps an encirclement or bypass attack. The following describes some defensive strategies undertaken by the Japanese government to maintain Japan's global market shares.

Mobile Defense

A mobile defense is much better at capturing the thrust of many of the efforts of the Japanese governmental infrastructure to avoid having the nation's industries caught from behind or surpassed by foreign competitors. The continued targeting of specific industries can be seen as an effort by the Japanese government to channel resources into areas where market broadening and diversification might not take place as quickly (if at all) if the nation were to be solely dependent on the efforts of the private sector.

The veritable plethora of governmental initiatives in recent years to move Japan's position forward in many industries and to open up or create new industries revolves around Japan's commitment to become a technology-driven nation. Japan, as a nation, has dedicated itself to extending its present industrial structure and prominence into a knowledge- or technology-based nation. Japan is now intent on moving the competitive battleground from the staid territories of the 1960s and 1970s—automobiles, watches, copiers, etc.—to the high-stakes territories of the 1980s and 1990s—computers, semiconductors, electronic components, biotechnology, and fiber optics. Whoever wins the wars in these new terrains will have placed the losers at a significant strategic disadvantage; catching up in these industries and gaining position for offensive strategies (e.g., leapfrogging to the next generation of products) will be much more difficult than it was in the dominant industries of the 1960s and 1970s. It will require much more sophisticated knowledge and technical expertise; the discontinuities or "leaps" will be much closer to differences in kind than differences in degree.

Preemptive Defense

A preemptive defense is also evident in the Japanese government's strategic moves in the attempts to maintain Japan's worldwide market shares in its aging industries. During the 1970s, various Japanese industries, including textiles, steel, and shipbuilding, faced difficulties due to increased exports from other developing countries as well as the nearly saturated world demand. In textiles, for example, exports from newly industrialized countries (South Korea, Taiwan, etc.) had been increasing their worldwide market shares at Japan's expense. Steel, which had steadily followed a path of high growth for over twenty years, faced a turning point where Japanese steel production sharply declined as the world market for steel reached saturation. Shipbuilding, which had contributed to Japan's economic successes during the early stage of its industrialization, faced growing difficulties requiring some shipbuilding plants to be closed down and new capacity to be frozen. However, the Japanese government has not withdrawn its support from the industries that propelled it to economic prominence in the past three decades. While these industries do not need the infrastructural supports that sustained them in their early phases, the Japanese government still supports these industries in many ways.

Countries clearly face the hard choices inherent in moving resources from declining to prospering sectors of the economy. While Western ideology would argue that such adjustments should be left to the free play of market forces, Japan has "intervened" in the process. It now tries to manage its declining industries—those industries where it has lost its competitive edge. It thus tries to effect a "strategic withdrawal" from these industries.

Eight industries have been designated as being in decline: aluminum, cardboard, cotton and wool spinning, electric-furnace steel, ferrasilicon (a steel alloy), fertilizers, shipbuilding, and synthetic fibers. Assistance to these industries, orchestrated by MITI, has taken many forms. The Depressed Industries Law, passed in 1978, gives financial assistance to declining industries and exempts them in some cases from Japan's Antimonopoly law. These industries have also been allowed to form long-term cartels (not all of them have done so) and thereby eliminate some of their excess capacity.

In textiles, for example, the Textile Industry Rationalization Agency buys obsolete equipment and provides loans through government and private channels to Japanese producers in order to improve their production operations or diversify their business into other profitable fields.

Flank-Position Defense

In retrospect, it may seem surprising but the Japanese government has long exercised a flank-position defense. It has vigorously defended (protected) its home market from the inception of its attack on the world marketplace. Indeed, this defensive strategy was a key undergirding element of its offensive strategies to exploit export opportunities.

Particularly instructive of the Japanese commitment to protecting and establishing their home base as a springboard for their export onslaught is the long list of rebukes suffered by U.S. and European firms trying to enter and penetrate the Japanese marketplace. For example, Zenith's efforts to market TV sets in Japan in the early 1960s ran into a sequence of roadblocks created by the Japanese authorities. MITI, for example, denied permission for export dollars to the major trading companies enlisted by Zenith to help it get its products into Japan. Also, MITI brought extensive pressure to bear on the trade and distribution system not to promote and sell Zenith's product line.

FACILITATING MAINTENANCE STRATEGIES: OFFSHORE MANUFACTURE AND JOINT VENTURE

How well an army or a company performs in the heat of battle is, of course, strongly influenced by its state of preparedness in going into battle. Many of the elements of preparedness that facilitate competitive success may not be readily visible to the external observer. Two such factors greatly assist Japanese maintenance strategies: (1) manufacturing their products offshore and (2) entering into joint ventures with foreign firms.

Manufacturing Abroad

Changing conditions in both Japan and the rest of the world, especially in Europe and the United States, have made it much more preferable for Japan to manufacture many products abroad rather than at home. Many of the early advantages for producing domestically, such as relatively low labor costs, an undervalued yen, and low transportation costs, no longer apply. Moreover, a rising tide of protectionist sentiment and actual tariff and quota barriers further impelled Japanese firms to set up manufacturing facilities overseas. Investment in foreign manufacturing facilities serves a number of purposes. It allows the Japanese to manufacture close to their markets. It allows them to incorporate the latest manufacturing technology processes into their production facilities. It facilitates customizing products for individual markets. Those factors together should lead to products that are more appropriate for their markets and are of higher quality and lower cost.

Another purpose of these investments is, of course, to help ensure access to foreign markets. It is the principal means for circumventing actual tariffs and quotas or the threat of them. Thus, in 1977, when Japan was compelled to enter into an orderly marketing agreement for the delivery of television sets to the United States, the agreement did not apply to television sets being produced by Japanese manufacturers in their U.S. facilities.

Although Japan has been active in direct foreign investment since the early 1950s, it was only in the late 1960s and early 1970s that Japanese overseas investment really began to take off. In 1968, Japan's direct foreign investment reached $557 million, doubling the preceding year's figure of $275 million. What is noteworthy is that part of this sudden upsurge was due to an increase in investment in the United States and in European Economic Community (E.E.C.) countries. However, this investment was heavily concentrated in commercial and service sectors, such as branches, sales and service offices, and warehouses.

In the 1970s, and especially in the late 1970s and 1980s, Japanese investment in manufacturing facilities in the United States and E.E.C. countries has dramatically increased, as shown in the next chapter.

Joint Ventures

Since the mid-1970s, a decided trend toward joint ventures between Japanese and U.S. firms has emerged. These joint ventures take a variety of forms. A number of such agreements revolve around jointly manufacturing products. The General Motors–Toyota agreement to manufacture automobiles in a vacant GM plant in California has recently received widespread publicity. Chrysler had previously entered into a similar agreement with Mitsubishi Motors. These two companies have also committed themselves to manufacturing a small truck to be marketed in the United States. In the electronics field, Mitsubishi Electric Corporation has negotiated a joint venture with Westinghouse Electric Corporation to manufacture semiconductors in the United States.

Another form of joint venture involves Japanese firms supplying the product and U.S. firms providing the marketing, distribution, sales, and service capability. General Electric and Matsushita formed such a joint venture which allowed the latter firm to enter the infant videodisc market in the United States.

In European markets, Japanese companies have skirted around E.E.C. trade barriers by setting up joint ventures with E.E.C. companies. Three Japanese heavy-engineering firms—Mitsubishi Heavy Industries, Kawasaki, and IHI—are working closely with Rolls-Royce, the British aeroengine manufacturer, to develop one of its new jet engines. Honda developed a joint venture with British Leyland to produce the first Triumph Acclaim car under license from Honda and also considered a joint development of a lightweight frame for an 80 cc. motorcycle with Peugeot-Citroen.

Joint ventures serve many of the same purposes for the Japanese as investing in their own foreign manufacturing operations. They gain access to markets, they can adapt products to individual markets, they can build in the latest technology developments, they lessen Japan's balance-of-payments "problems," and they help with some of the anti-Japanese sentiments. In addition, some specific benefits accrue to the Japanese from joint ventures which aid their market penetration and maintenance efforts.

Joint ventures provide Japanese firms with a degree of market access that they would otherwise have extreme difficulty attaining. In distribution-oriented joint ventures, the Japanese quickly acquire substantial market coverage. And they avoid the costly and laborious efforts involved in developing distribution and service capabilities. Mitsubishi automobiles would not be experiencing their market success if they had not gained access to existing dealerships, in this case, Chrysler's distribution system.

Manufacturing-oriented joint ventures allow the Japanese to bring products to the market that their own resource base would probably not otherwise allow. At a minimum, given their finite resource base, joint ventures allow Japanese firms to participate in a broader product offering, thus extending their market coverage.

Joint ventures may also serve to lessen potential competition for the Japanese. This would certainly seem to be the case in the short run. The U.S. and European firms that enter into distribution joint ventures with Japanese firms may not have much incentive to develop competitive products. The same may also be true of U.S. and European firms that enter into manufacturing joint ventures. They may not have the resources or the incentive to develop competitive or superior products.

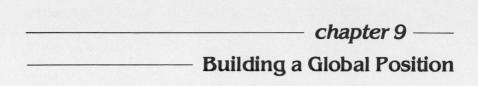

chapter 9 ——

Building a Global Position

THE GLOBAL MARKETERS

One of the salient characteristics of Japanese-style marketing is the ability to view the entire world as a potential market. Japanese firms put stress on foreign sales and aggressively seek ways to expand their overseas markets. This global perspective prevails not only among the well-known leading Japanese firms but also among small and medium-sized manufacturers which are, in fact, the spearheads of Japanese exports.

In contrast, the United States has been such a large and prosperous market that many American firms have never sought to go beyond it. Although the United States is still the leading country in international business, this foreign activity is limited only to certain groups of multinational corporations. A national drive to go worldwide comparable with that of Japan does not exist. The great majority of U.S. firms concentrate their sales in the United States. Until recently, they have been content to serve the home market and have had little incentive to go abroad.

The United States' domestic fixation permitted globally oriented countries like Japan and West Germany to penetrate and control various industries around the world. The Japanese, in particular, have emerged today as the quintessential global marketers. As Japan's economic power grows, Japanese companies seem to expand and cover the global markets as rapidly as did the leading U.S. global enterprises in past decades.

173

This chapter will examine the nature of the Japanese strategic global marketing that contributes to the impressive successes of Japanese global enterprises. Two major strategic components of Japanese global marketing are investigated—the Japanese global market expansion path and the development of a global marketing network.

THE JAPANESE GLOBAL MARKET EXPANSION PATH

The order in which foreign markets are entered has to be thought through carefully. In general, Japanese business firms followed one of three global expansion paths:

    I. Japan $\rightarrow$ Developing Countries $\rightarrow$ Developed Countries
   II. Japan $\rightarrow$ Developed Countries $\rightarrow$ Developing Countries
  III. Developed Countries $\rightarrow$ Japan $\rightarrow$ Developing Countries

Global Market Expansion Path: Type I

The most prevalent expansion path among Japanese firms consisted of moving from Japan to developing countries to developed countries, respectively. This occurred in steel, automobiles, petrochemicals, consumer electronics, home appliances, watches, and cameras. This expansion path consisted of the following steps.

Step 1: Domestic market as home base.   Initially, most Japanese firms rely on building up their home market first. They seek to make products that will replace the ones imported from the West. To make these products, they often import U.S. or European technology, either copying the technology or licensing it. For example, transistors, silicon planers, and integrated circuits were American innovations but were quickly adopted by Japanese firms. Large blast furnaces, LD converters, and strip mills in the iron and steel industry were introduced from advanced Western countries. In consumer electronics, the Japanese licensed processes for manufacturing monochrome and color TV from U.S. producers, mostly from RCA. The Japanese computer industry, which today is the leading rival of IBM, got its patents from IBM in return for granting permission to

IBM to manufacture in Japan. In integrated circuits, the Japanese received patents from Texas Instruments, and this laid the groundwork for the growth of electronic specialist companies like NEC, Fujitsu, and Hitachi. In the auto industry, the Japanese automakers, with the exception of Toyota, acquired their production technology through the knockdown assembly of foreign automobiles such as Ford and GM. In the camera field, the Japanese have borrowed their lens technology from the Germans.

Having acquired the necessary technology, Japanese firms built products for the home market. These firms were assisted and protected by the government through such means as import restrictions, import duties, and foreign investment restrictions. Many Japanese firms carried on keen competition among themselves and against foreign brands. They sought to expand their domestic market share in order to gain economies of scale. Because foreign firms faced barriers to entry and did not devote enough resources to the Japanese market, one after the other lost its market position while the Japanese took over control of almost the whole domestic market. Their increased market share brought down their manufacturing costs and created a competitive advantage. The following are some examples showing the efforts of Japanese firms to build up their home market base.

> *Watch Industry.* Japan was once a major importer of both cheap and expensive watches, especially from Swiss watchmakers. Japanese watchmakers began to focus on the cheap watch sector in Japan and won control largely due to the lack of response from foreign brands. Once they had controlled the low-end market, the Japanese began challenging the Swiss brands by invading the medium and higher-end market. They relied on a "push" and "pull" strategy. The Japanese strengthened their distribution network, brought sales outlets under their control, organized retail outlets throughout the nation, and gave high margins to facilitate selling efforts. Product lines were expanded and supported by heavy advertising and sales promotion programs. Meanwhile the Swiss watchmakers concentrated only on advertising and failed to initiate any effective steps to counter Japan's aggressiveness. As a result, Seiko, Citizen, and the other Japanese watch companies expanded their market share and almost controlled the whole Japanese watch market, with only the small sector of very expensive products left to the Swiss.

> *Steel Industry.* In the early postwar period, the Japanese steel industry was small and backward in terms of technology. As a result of government support and guidance, huge investments were made by Japanese producers in order to raise their productive capacity and catch up with foreign productivity. The first wave of investments was

made by the three top Japanese makers, Yawata, Fuji, and Nippon Kokan. Between 1950 and 1953, this raised production capacity by 4 million tons. In 1956, the second wave of huge investment took place through the support of the government. Six Japanese makers were involved—Yawata, Fuji, Nippon Kokan, Kawasaki Steel, Sumitomo, and Kobe. This involved an investment of about 300 billion yen to increase production capacity and introduce new technology into the production process. The growing market demand induced still a third wave of investment during the 1960s. These intense investment waves, combined with the keen intracompetition among the Japanese makers to introduce the latest technology and enlarge the size of their capacity, brought about an accelerated jump of productivity during the 1964–73 period. The Japanese makers managed to reduce their labor-hours per ton substantially below those of their American counterparts. Their blast furnaces had an average size of 1.67 million tons against the Americans' 723,000 tons. Their production process was more fully automated and energy saving. This buildup of strength among Japanese steelmakers not only helped them dominate the Japanese market but also provided a mighty competitive edge in steel exporting.

Step 2: Developing countries as springboards. As Japanese firms added more production capacity, this expanded capacity led to saturation in certain markets at home. Many Japanese firms began to consider overseas markets as outlets for the excessive production. The major target aimed at by most Japanese companies was the developing countries, especially Southeast Asia and Latin America, since these countries had less competition and could be used as a base for building volume and sharpening marketing capabilities before moving into highly developed nations like the United States.

In the mid-1950s, about two-thirds of Japan's exports were channeled to these developing countries. The major portion of Japanese exports to less-developed countries were products of heavy, capital-intensive, and high-technology industries, while most of the light and labor-intensive products such as textiles were exported to developed nations. The Japanese cleverly selected less-developed countries for highly technical products because they were mainly facing less-competitive manufacturers. They realized that neither the quality of their high-technology products nor their marketing capabilities were ready to compete against competitors in well-developed countries. They used the developing countries to get rid of surplus production and as a base for product and marketing experiments. Although Japanese consumer electronics, electric appliances, motorcycles, automobiles, and watches that were exported to developing countries were not up to Western standards, their prices were lower and consequently were more in line with the lower purchasing power of these nations. Japanese firms used these countries as a proving ground before moving into more-advanced markets.

Step 3: Aiming toward the U.S. market.   With the marketing experience gained in overseas markets and the cost improvement from volume sold to less-developed countries as well as the continuous improvement of product quality, Japan's penetration into markets in advanced countries was ready to take place. Beginning in the 1960s, targeted countries for Japanese exports began to shift from less-developed countries to the highly developed countries, especially the United States. The U.S. market, traditionally the destination of Japanese textiles, pottery, fish, and so forth, became the market for Japan's most-advanced industries, especially for consumer electronics, steel, automobiles, motorcycles, machinery, and instruments. This market penetration also spread rapidly into European countries during the 1970s. In 1954, only 30 percent of Japanese exports were sold in developed countries in North America and Europe, but this number increased to nearly 50 percent by the end of the 1970s. In the same period, exports to developing countries in Asia and Latin America dropped from nearly 60 percent to 42 percent.

The U.S. market attracted the Japanese companies because of its size and high purchasing power. In addition, once its products had been accepted here, the reputation and experience gained made it easier to achieve acceptance in other Western countries. The Japanese focused on specific geographical areas and market segments ignored by U.S. producers in order to gain product and customer knowledge from which to build brand acceptance and capture market share. Once they had gained a foothold, they began to add new products and enter new channels. By the 1970s, nearly 50 percent of Japanese exports were directed to developed countries, of which more than 30 percent were sent to the United States. Details of the marketing strategies employed by Japanese firms in entering and penetrating the U.S. markets have already been discussed in the previous chapters.

Step 4: Entering the European markets.   The European markets have long posed a special challenge to Japanese firms due to such existing national barriers as geographical distances, and cultural and linguistic differences. However, once Japanese products have been accepted in the U.S. market, they can more easily be sold in European countries. The Japanese began to penetrate into Western European countries such as the United Kingdom, West Germany, Italy, and France. Between 1960 and 1979, Japanese exports to European countries increased from 13 percent to nearly 18 percent. Between 1977 and 1980 alone, Japanese exports to these countries almost doubled and reached $17.3 billion. A flood of imported cars, motorcycles, TVs, watches, cameras, and office equipment entered these countries. A decade ago, Europe imported very few Japanese automobiles. Today, Japanese automobiles enjoy a 10 to 12 percent market share in the United Kingdom and West Germany; a 20 percent market share in Switzerland, Austria, Belgium, and the Netherlands; and a 30 percent share in Denmark, Ireland, and Norway. In motorcycles, the Japanese brands dominate the European continent. In watches, Japanese brands such as Seiko and Citizen outsell the Swiss brands. In fine cameras, Germany was supreme two decades ago. But the Japanese took patient steps to improve their products and adapt them to European tastes and expectations. Today, German camera makers survive mainly in the very small expensive market segment while the Japanese dominate the rest of the market.

Nothing seems to stop the Japanese attack in Europe. Europe now absorbs 18 percent of Japanese exports and has become an important market for Japanese producers.

The Japanese successes in Europen markets are no longer based on their "cheap labor" or dumping, as frequently seen by European business leaders in the past. On the contrary, their current successes are the result of good planning and efficient execution of marketing strategies. The following are some samples of how the Japanese companies develop and execute marketing strategies in penetrating the Eruopean markets

> *Passenger cars.* The Japanese automobile-marketing strategies in Europe were largely based on the experiences and lessons gained from their invasion of the U.S. market. They decided not to challenge the European industry for the luxury car market but to compete against smaller-car producers such as Fiat, Renault, and Volkswagen. They have a major competitive advantage in this market segment in terms of price and product quality. The next step was to decide which country in the European community should be entered first. Although France, the United Kingdom, Italy, and Germany were the largest European markets, these countries were not likely to open their doors to Japanese exports. Besides, the countries had their own producers which the Japanese had to fight with on their home front. As a result, the Japanese used a "peripheral" attack. First, they started exporting to small nonproducer countries which left them more opportunities to enter, such as Switzerland, Finland, Norway, Portugal, and the Benelux countries. Once their exports had begun to soar, the next step was to target the most valuable and easiest to enter among France, Italy, the United Kingdom, and Germany. The United Kingdom was chosen because it was the weakest major car-producing country with a relatively open economy compared with the others. With the Japanese competitive price and high quality that could not be matched by British producers,

Japanese exports grew rapidly in the United Kingdom by the mid-1970s. The United Kingdom became a major beachhead for the Japanese to launch further attacks on other nearby countries. The Japanese had also decided to develop intensive manufacturing bases in Europe to compensate for the rising cost of shipping and tariffs that might offset their price advantage. Manufacturing plans were first established in Ireland, which was a more open economy and was intended to serve as the Japanese manufacturing base for developing a larger industry for sales to Germany, France, and Italy. By this strategic move, Japanese cars have continued to flood into the European community. Germany, in particular, became a major market for Japanese cars and their sales increased from under 3 percent in 1977 to 11 percent in 1980. France and Italy not only have to face Japanese competition on their home fronts but also have to face losing their market shares in other countries to the Japanese.

Watches. Seiko provides an excellent example of the Japanese penetration into the European watch industry. Seiko relied heavily on extensive marketing research. The company had sent its sales representatives to conduct market research studies aimed at evaluating the company's ability to compete against local manufacturers long before it started entering European markets. Local retail jewelers, as well as watch repairers, were contacted and asked for opinions about and reactions to Seiko's brand. Once the company was satisfied that Seiko's brand had a future in the market, the next step was to develop an entry strategy.

Seiko made its first move by selecting countries where high potential demand existed and distribution channels were accessible. Although it was difficult to find good distributors to carry Seiko's products because Swiss brands were well-established in European countries, Seiko finally found its first good distributors in Sweden. "Penn Specialten," which was the large leading chain store dealing with only quality stationary products, was selected by Seiko to carry its products because it could help improve Seiko's image and carry out distribution functions through its extensive distribution network. With Seiko's competitive price and high-quality products supported by a strong distribution network, Seiko achieved substantial sales in Sweden. From this base, Seiko made its second strong entry into Greece, which served as a beachhead for penetrating other larger European markets such as the United Kingdom, France, and Germany, where competitors from well-established Swiss brands were entrenched. In these markets, Seiko had to surmount the prevailing "shoddy-Japanese-goods" syndrome and had to convince consumers that Seiko's quality could match that of Swiss brands. To achieve this goal, Seiko started building up its image by heavy investment for the timekeeper's honors in many sports events held in Europe. For example, Seiko took the honor from Swiss makers at the 1965 World Amateur Wrestling Championship in England, the 27th Balkan Games, and the 9th European Athletic Championships held in

Athens, with the purpose of publicizing its brand name as a precision product to European consumers. Supported by these investments, Seiko began to crack the U.K. market by focusing on the youth segment that was not committed to Swiss brands. In the United Kingdom, Seiko first sold its products through the mail-order houses and later through jewelers and watch dealers that were lining up to carry Seiko's products after its brand name became well known. In a short period of time after the first entry into the U.K. market, Seiko's sales began to dominate this market and Seiko rapidly expanded into other European countries. By relying on the same strategies previously used in the U.S. and other U.K. markets, Seiko increased its sales from four thousand to six hundred thousand units within a decade. Today nothing seems to be able to stop Seiko's growth in European countries.

Construction and farm machinery.   Although the most prevalent Japanese market expansion path is the movement from home market to less-developed countries, to the United States, and finally to European countries, respectively, the expansion path from the United States to European countries might be reversed in some Japanese industries. The global expansion path of Komatsu, the leading Japanese construction machinery and farm machinery producer, is a good example.

Komatsu first entered into this industry in 1921 when its products were no match for imported machinery, especially the products of Caterpillar, the world's leading producer. However, Komatsu continued to boost its spending on engineering, manufacturing facilities, and designing of new product lines with its grandiose ambition to compete not only in Japan but on a global scale. Komatsu's global expansion started in less-developed countries, especially in Asia and Africa. After winning market shares in these markets, Komatsu began focusing on developed countries as the next target. Instead of exporting its products to the United States, Komatsu first entered European markets and saved the U.S. markets for the last. Komatsu wished to avoid head-on competition with Caterpillar in Caterpillar's home market. Komatsu realized that it had to win European markets so that these markets could serve as its strong base for launching a final attack on the U.S. markets. Besides, if Komatsu could sell well in Europe, its products would be a lot easier to sell to U.S. customers.

Accordingly, Komatsu started penetrating several European countries by lining up good local distributors. To strengthen its marketing functions, Komatsu established a wholly owned subsidiary in Belgium as a parts depot, training center, and technical assistance base to serve its distributors in other European countries. Only five years after its intensive market development in Europe, Komatsu successfully gained strong market shares in Europe and began to look at the United States. In the United States, Komatsu focused its marketing efforts on selling lightweight farm machinery that was not well covered by American manufacturers who placed more emphasis on heavy construction machinery and equipment. Being denied access to established distributors in the United States, Komatsu's selling approach was to line up those over-the-road construction equipment dealers in rural areas of the Sun Belt to sell its products to U.S. farmers in rural areas that needed smaller farm equipment. Komatsu set its prices very competitively to attract customers and provided its dealers with high incentives to sell its products. In less than a decade, Komatsu was able to gain substantial market shares in the United States and emerged as Caterpillar's major challenger, not only in the United States but also on a global scale.

Global Market Expansion Path: Type II

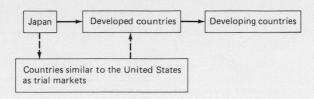

The type II Japanese expansion path is found in high-technological-content industries such as computers and semiconductors. After the Japanese had secured their home market for these products, their next targets were developed countries such as the United States. Developing countries, on the other hand, had market demands that were too small or nonexistent for these products. Later, when developing countries' demands started to grow, the Japanese did not hesitate to make strong inroads into these markets. Let us take a look at the Japanese computer industry as an example.

Computer production in Japan was begun in 1958 by six major companies: NEC, Fujitsu, Hitachi, Toshiba, Mitsubishi Electric, and Oki Electric Industry. At that time, their technology was much less advanced than IBM's. Japan allowed IBM to establish a wholly owned subsidiary in Japan in exchange for IBM's granting patent rights to Japanese makers. Once technology had been acquired, the Japanese started producing the products. Fujitsu chose to develop large mainframe computers that were plug-compatible with IBM while NEC and Mitsubishi focused on smaller-size computers. To gain market share in their home market, the Japanese companies aimed their guns at IBM. They fought IBM with a vigorous price-cutting policy. They were assisted by the Japanese government in several ways. MITI sponsored a "buy Japan" policy. The

Japan Development Bank and private banks provided strong financing at low interest rates. Government agencies, universities, and industrial monopolies like NTT (Japanese telecommunications industry) placed computer orders with the Japanese companies. Thus IBM was not simply competing against Japanese computer manufacturers but against a powerful partnership that included government and banking interests. As a result, Japanese companies' home market share grew rapidly. Although IBM had the number-one global market share, it began losing its market share in Japan and eventually lost its leadership to Fujitsu. In the personal computer end of the market, NEC alone captured almost 40 percent of this market.

As their home market shares grew, the Japanese turned to overseas markets. Fujitsu started an aggressive selling campaign in Australia. The Australian market bore many similarities to the U.S. market and could be used as a testing ground. If the company failed, it would not hurt its chances in other markets; if it succeeded, it would be ready to compete in the United States. In the United States, however, the Japanese product could not compare with IBM's in terms of technology. But the Japanese relied on the key strategies of price and distribution to penetrate the U.S. marketplace. Prices were set 10 to 20 percent lower than comparable IBM machine prices. The Japanese relied on American manufacturers or distributors to move their products: Fujitsu sold its products through Amdahl's network; Hitachi, through Intel's; and so forth. These same strategies were employed to penetrate European markets as well. Fujitsu, for example, made an agreement with Germany's Siemens HG and sold its computer under the Siemens brandname in eleven European countries.

As the Japanese penetrated the developed countries, computer demand started to grow in developing countries, particularly Hong Kong, Brazil, and Taiwan. In these countries, Japan used price cuts as the key strategy. In Hong Kong, for example, Hitachi offered discounts from 50 to 60 percent below IBM's list price to banks and government agencies. This marketing approach also worked well in Brazil. In Southeast Asia, each Japanese computer firm targeted a different country. In Thailand, only NEC worked hard to chip away IBM's 80 percent market share by selling through Datamat Ltd., the sole distributor in Thailand. Hitachi and NEC concentrated on Singapore and Hong Kong while Fujitsu targeted the Philippines market by selling through Facom Computers Philippines. The Japanese sought to build a strong market position in these developing countries so that they would be there to take advantage of the high rate of economic development expected in these countries.

Global Market Expansion Path: Type III

Developed countries as targeted markets → Japan's market → Developing countries

Although most Japanese exports went through the previous expansion sequences, there were exceptions. Japan developed some products to sell in developed countries instead of the home market. These were products for which home market demand was still not developed or was too small to serve. The products included videotape recorders (VTRs), color TVs, and sewing machines.

Videotape recorders represented a technological breakthrough. They were exported to the United States and to other developed countries instead of being sold in Japan because of the huge size of the foreign market. VTRs were later supplied to the Japanese market once the demand began growing.

Color TV had become very popular in the United States by 1964, whereas there was inadequate demand in Japan. The Japanese makers decided to produce color TV for the U.S. market, but almost five years passed before the Japanese market would demand it.

Sewing machines are another example. The Japanese makers produced the zigzag sewing machine and exported it to the United States almost four years before the Japanese market began to demand the zigzag model.

DEVELOPING A GLOBAL MARKETING NETWORK

The Japanese ascendancy in global markets could not have been achieved without a highly developed global market network. It took the Japanese almost three decades to develop a strong and efficient global marketing network. Japanese firms passed through several stages in the process of becoming internationalized. Let us take a closer look at these stages.

Stage I: Trading Companies as Spearheads

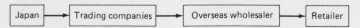

Japan → Trading companies → Overseas wholesaler → Retailer

Most Japanese firms started their export activities by utilizing the large Japanese trading companies. These trading companies were familiar with the social atmosphere, business customs, legal procedures, and language of the host countries. They could spread out the risks associated with changes in price, fluctuations of exchange rate, changes in tariffs and customs, and so forth. The great diversity of commodities they carried and geographical areas in which they traded provided a hedge against risk. These trading companies also kept distribution costs low. Much of the distribution cost of a firm consists of the cost of market information collection and transportation. Hence the trading companies were able to effect economies through their scale of operation and experience. Furthermore, they were able to advise their clients about new product and market opportunities, and new merchandising approaches.

Stage II: Seeking a Better Alternative

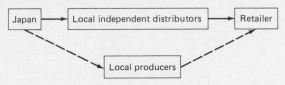

Other Japanese firms started their export activities by directly searching out and signing up local distributors, instead of using trading companies on the one hand or setting up their own sales branches on the other hand. For example, Seiko sold its watches in the United States by signing up exclusive regional distributors. Most of these distributors were already in the wholesale jewelry business and were able to provide immediate access to jewelers as well as capital sources. Seiko employed this strategy because it needed distributors who had enough capital to carry a large inventory and who had a certain standing in the jewelry community.

Still other Japanese firms entered the U.S. market by using producers that had well-established sales channels and market expertise. In copying machines, for example, Ricoh first sold its machines in the United States through the Savin Corporation. After attaining competitiveness and marketing know-how, Ricoh began to sell on its own.

Stage III: Establishing a Local Sales Company

As Japanese companies gained a foothold in the United States, many of them started to replace their current arrangements with trading companies or local distributors or local companies with their own overseas sales branches and distribution networks. This approach enabled them to gain managerial experience and to strengthen their brand reputation by directly controlling local advertising, promotion, and after-sales service in each market-country.

For example, Toyota and Nissan have established their overseas sales companies and successfully developed their dealer networks in local markets around the world. Nihon Gakki, a highly diversified Japanese manufacturer selling under the Yamaha brand, established the Yamaha International Company in the United States in 1959 and then successfully developed a dealer network.

Stage IV: Local Production in Developing Countries

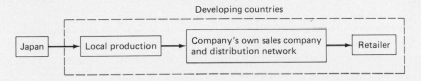

Beginning in the late 1960s, several changes in world economics and politics occurred and strongly affected Japanese firms. Two were particularly important. First, Japan's home market was becoming deprotected as a result of pressure from foreign governments. Second, the reevaluation of the yen currency resulted in Japan's loss of its cost competitive edge in the world market. These abrupt changes forced Japanese firms to seek a way to regain their competitive edge. One solution was to invest directly in factories and companies in less-developed countries to exploit the local cheap labor and raw material used in production. By 1971, the number of manufacturing subsidiaries of large Japanese firms in Asia and Latin America was around 42 percent of the total. Japanese manufacturers in the fields of textiles, steel, chemicals, electrical equipment, and automobiles set up local manufacturing units in such countries as Thailand, Singapore, and Malaysia. Their objective was to exploit the abundant cheap labor and raw material and also defend their market position in these countries from the increasing trade protectionism that was occurring. The products made in these countries not only served the local demand but were also exported to other countries. Nippon Electric, for example, exported from its plants in Mexico to Panama; Nissan built a manufacturing plant in Mexico and exported trucks to other Latin American countries such as Nicaragua and Costa Rica. It established a plant in Malaysia to manufacture standard components and exported them to subsidiaries in Thailand, Singapore, and Indonesia for assembling.

Stage V: Local Production in Developed Countries

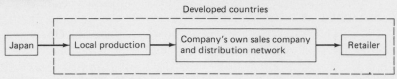

Developed countries

| Japan | → | Local production | → | Company's own sales company and distribution network | → | Retailer |

After completing the preceding four stages, the Japanese firms began to consider establishing local production in the developed countries, especially in the United States, which was viewed as the most attractive market for volume creation due to its size and high standard of living. Until the late 1960s, Japanese firms had enjoyed a strong competitive edge in the developed countries in a variety of industries. However, their competitive edge began to erode. During the 1970s, the Japanese began to face strong pressure from trade protectionists in developed countries that they had successfully penetrated. In the United States, the trade protectionists called for import restrictions on Japan. Japanese firms responded by undertaking direct investments in U.S. plants and facilities. By this step they hoped to quiet the increasing voices of U.S. firms—particularly those making automobiles and electronic products—that called for strict limitation of Japanese exports. To invest in the United States and other developed nations would enable them to jump these barriers and to strengthen their market position.

The Japanese began to establish local production by either acquiring companies or starting factories from scratch. By 1980, the Japanese operated seventy plants in machinery manufacturing, forty-four plants in electronic products (radio, TV, semiconductors, etc.), and eight plants in precision instruments in the United States.

In consumer electronics, Sony was the first Japanese firm to start producing in the United States by establishing its own plant in San Diego. Later, Matsushita acquired Motorola's color TV plant in Illinois; Sanyo acquired Warwick's color TV plant in Arkansas; Mitsubishi Electric and Toshiba were latecomers and undertook local production in California and Tennessee, respectively. Toshiba located its plant in Tennessee to produce large-scale integrated circuits (LSIs) and integrated circuits (ICs) to increase local procurement, and it imported new printed circuit boards equipped with new LSI devices from the Toshiba parent company in Japan.

In automobiles, Nissan undertook a huge feasibility study and afterward established an auto plant in Tennessee, followed by Honda opening an auto plant in Ohio. In Europe, Nissan is contemplating opening an assembly plant in Britain that will produce two hundred thousand cars per year.

Another good example is the zipper fasteners industry. YKK (Yoshida Kogyo), the leading Japanese zipper maker, has established its wholly owned manufacturing plants and sales subsidiaries in virtually every country it enters. It begins with a modest investment in a manufacturing plant and relies on initial imports of raw material. Once market shares in each country start growing, manufacturing plants are expanded. In Europe, for example, YKK established its first factory in Holland and then developed a network of six manufacturing plants in different European countries. Through local manufacturing, each manufacturing plant and sales subsidiary is able to concentrate on only the consumers of that country and adapt its products to serve their specific needs.

Stage VI: Toward a Global Market

To become a global marketer, one further step is required. The company must establish plants around the world and decide which plants should manufacture which products for which markets to obtain the lowest costs of production and distribution. Today a number of Japanese firms, especially in automobiles and consumer electronics, have already reached this stage. They are able to distinguish between those production functions that can best be left in Japan and those that can advantageously be located abroad.

Initially, each overseas subsidiary served only its local market and had no direct tie with subsidiaries in other countries. Beginning in the 1970s, the forging of close multinational links in production began to occur. It was realized that multinational production planning would enable each subsidiary to benefit from economies of scale and capitalize on factor cost differences in various countries.

Generally, subsidiary manufacturing firms in particular countries make products to serve local demand and export the surplus to other countries as well as to Japan. For example, Pioneer exports its electronic products from a plant in Belgium to France; and Honda exports products from its motorcycle assembly subsidiary in Belgium to other Common Market countries. In addition, subsidiary manufacturing firms located in low-cost countries export components to the subsidiaries in other countries. The role of manufacturing firms in Japan is to produce high-technology components and products, export them to subsidiaries in developing countries and in some developed countries, and send management staffs to subsidiaries all over the world for managerial training, planning, and control.

STRATEGIC GLOBAL MARKETING: LESSONS FROM THE JAPANESE CONSUMER ELECTRONICS INDUSTRY

Consumer Electronics as a Target Industry

We will now examine in some depth how Japan achieved global dominance in one of the major industries, consumer electronics. The Japa-

Global Marketing Network

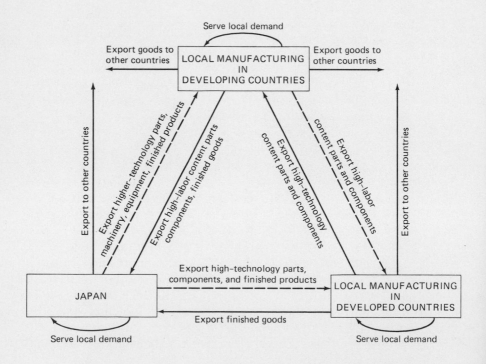

nese targeted the consumer electronics industry for several reasons:

1. The consumer electronics industry is based on a few technological breakthroughs and is able to lead to the development of a broad range of consumer products, namely, radios, phonographs, tape recorders, TVs, videotape recorders, and so forth. The worldwide market potential for these products is huge. The Japanese can penetrate any one of those product-markets and use it as a platform to expand to other product-markets that are based on similar technology.

2. Consumer electronic products rely on technology, highly skilled labor, and productivity and have a low requirement for natural resources. The Japanese assessed the technology content of consumer electronics in the 1950s and knew they could catch up with the West. The high value added by this industry matched the Japanese economic development policy that shifted its interest to higher value added and heavy industries.

3. The U.S. companies, as the major producers of electronic products in the late 1950s, were more interested in industrial electronics than in consumer electronics. Furthermore, import restrictions against imported electronic products in the 1950s period were weak, thus providing the opportunity for the Japanese to enter and compete in global markets much more easily than in other types of industries.

As early as 1957, the Japanese policy makers identified the electronics industry as a priority sector for development, passing into law what was appropriately called "Extraordinary Measures for the Promotion of the Electronics Industry."

Building up Competitiveness
at the Home Base

Realizing the need to keep up with the superior technology of foreign producers, especially the U.S. firms, the Japanese began to search for the necessary technology, mostly from U.S. producers, in the early 1950s. The Japanese government provided grants and long-term low interest loans to stimulate acquisition of foreign technology and underwrite R&D, set import quotas, and put restrictions on import and currency exchange licenses in order to encourage the development of an internationally competitive consumer electronics sector. Once their products had become highly competitive, the Japanese began to enter overseas markets with carefully planned strategies.

The first strategic move of the Japanese global market expansion path was to penetrate nonproducer countries, such as less-developed countries where market competition was not intense. The Japanese spent a number of years patiently developing their export markets in Southeast Asia, Latin America, and the Far Eastern countries. The Asian countries, in particular, have served as Japan's major outlets for consumer electronic products for decades without significant competition from U.S. or European electronic producers. Japanese brand names such as Sony, Sanyo, Toshiba, Hitachi, and National (Panasonic) rapidly replaced American and European brand names. In the late 1960s, the Japanese began establishing local manufacturing firms in such Asian countries as Korea, Taiwan, and Singapore to exploit the cheap labor and raw material as well as to avoid the uprising protectionism in those countries. Once their products sold well in Asian countries, the next stage was to export to Latin America and the Middle East. In these regions the Japanese have also expanded their manufacturing plants in several countries. At least five Japanese firms have now entered the Brazilian color TV market, compared with two European producers, Philips and Telephunken. Although American brands such as Philco and GE also appear in countries such as Brazil, they have already lost their leadership position to the Japanese because of insufficient willingness to invest in these areas when compared with the Japanese. The products manufactured in these developing countries have been exported to other countries as well as back to Japan. Matsushita, for example, began establishing plants in Korea, Taiwan, and Malaysia to manufacture parts and components for subsidiaries in other countries as well as for export to the parent company in Japan.

Invasion of the U.S. market.   The Japanese consumer electronic producers started advancing methodically into the U.S. market in the late 1950s. The first strategic step in approaching this market was to carefully research the market, products, distribution, and so on, in order to detect the major openings.

The "holes" in the market could be attributed to the strategies chosen by U.S. firms. The U.S. firms emphasized higher-value products with more "step-up" features for which profit margins were higher. These strategies created opportunity gaps for the Japanese to exploit. In addition, major U.S. producers tended to promote brand names via extensive national advertising and did not emphasize private-label markets. These private-label markets were served by weaker firms that were usually divisions of stronger firms but did not have high corporate priority. The poorly served private-label segment of the market constituted an opening for the Japanese. The private-label mass merchandisers provided a mass-entry point into distribution. The competitive behavior of U.S. merchandisers further widened the opportunity for the Japanese. In the TV market, the 1964 color TV price war caused a profit squeeze among U.S. firms. RCA's maintenance of high color-tube prices to other U.S. manufacturers encouraged U.S. companies, notably Sears, to buy lower-priced sets from the Japanese. These circumstances provided the Japanese firms with opportunities to establish themselves in the U.S. market.

Market Entry and Penetration Strategies

Not surprisingly, the Japanese never ignored such opportunities. They started making strategic moves into U.S. markets by addressing the markets not effectively served by domestic manufacturers. They focused on a few high-volume potential products with high quality and stripped-down sizes and features, used aggressive pricing, and marketed them through traditional and nontraditional outlets as well as private-label merchandisers that helped them overcome the transportation, servicing, distribution, and brand recognition disadvantages facing them.

After capturing each target segment, the Japanese put heavy emphasis on product innovation by offering the market a new, high-quality product at a lower price. The Japanese employed channel integration strategies, moving upstream into semiconductor industries to make the components that entered into consumer electronic products. Hitachi, Matsushita, Toshiba, and so forth, gradually turned themselves into major semiconductor suppliers and spent substantial sums to build semiconductor plants and equipment. They also invested heavily in semiconductor R&D in the hope of achieving leadership in this market. With this heavy spending, as well as the competition among the subsidiary or subcontract semiconductor producers to offer the parent company innovations of semiconductor products with higher quality and lower prices, the Japanese consumer electronic producers were able to develop innovative products with prices lower than U.S. producers.

In addition, the Japanese also invested heavily in R&D, much of it related to semiconductors in the hope that it would be the leader in a new product market.

Strategic Steps of Market Domination:
Product-Market Evolution

After attaining leadership in a certain market, the Japanese would move into another related product-market. Their first success took place in the radio market. After dominating that market, they moved successively into tape recorders, TVs, and video equipment. Step by step, market by market, they finally controlled the whole consumer electronics industry. Let us look at this process more closely.

Radio. The Japanese started their mass production of radios with small, high-performance MT tubes in 1952 and began to market the first mass-produced transistor radios in 1955. In 1957, the Japanese exported about one hundred thousand small, three-transistor radios to the United States, priced at $14, when U.S. firms were marketing six-transistor radios for $60. The products were viewed as toys and were ignored by U.S. firms. Instead of establishing their own distribution network, the Japanese distributed their products through such nontraditional re- tailers as catalog outlets, discount chains, drugstores, and mass merchandisers.

As their radios gained a foothold, they lowered the price to less than $5, and their export volume rose to over 100 million in 1962. The Japanese then began marketing six-transistor radios with a price ranging from $9 to $19 and began adding product features. The product lines were extended to include portable multifunction radios, costing up to $250. Through these strategies, the Japanese began controlling the radio market in 1963.

Tape recorders. As they gained control of the radio market, the Japa- nese took steps to move into the tape recorder industry, using strategies similar to those used in the radio market. They began by exporting fifty thousand units of tape recorders in 1960 with a price of $13 each, compared with the average price of $100 for a U.S. product. As a result of this aggressive pricing policy, the Japanese exported over 2 million units in 1963. After 1963, the Japanese expanded their product line, still keeping prices low. By the late 1960s, they dominated the tape recorder market. In 1970, they exported $318 million worth of tape players to the U.S. market while U.S. firms as a whole sold only $38 million.

Monochrome TVs. In 1952, the Japanese obtained licenses from U.S. firms (primarily RCA) and began TV production that same year. The Japanese employed transistor technology to create product innovations and process efficiency in monochrome TVs, and they began to export twenty thousand TV units to the United States in 1961, concentrating on small-screen, few-features, low-priced sets, since these sectors were a low priority for U.S. producers. The products were distributed through large-volume retailers, often under private label. The exports increased to 155,000 units in 1962. In 1963, all monochrome TV sets under 11″ bought in the U.S. were Japanese made, mostly transistorized. Next, the Japanese began broadening the product line by producing 12″ and 16″ monochrome TVs with more features. By 1966, they had captured 15 percent of the monochrome TV market. Each year they increased their market share and finally dominated the market by 1970.

Color TVs. In 1960, the Japanese obtained a license from RCA to produce color TVs and began marketing them in Japan the same year. In 1964, the Japanese entered the U.S. market, exporting 14" sets priced at $370 and 17" sets priced at $430, both cheaper than the competitors' sets. In 1965, the color TV price war in the U.S. market forced U.S. retailers and mass merchandisers to seek lower-priced lines of color TVs. Sears introduced a 16" color set made from Japanese components, selling for $300. The Japanese grabbed this opportunity to build up their market position.

Japan's penetration of the U.S. color TV market repeated its strategy in marketing monochrome TVs. To develop a high volume, Japan entered again at the low-priced, small-set end of the market while U.S. producers concentrated on the larger, higher-priced, high-margin console business. The Japanese employed a one-step distribution system from manufacturers to retailers to export their products as an economical method of serving a relatively small number of high-volume accounts. Mass merchandisers working with the Japanese had extensive warehouses and facilities that eliminated the need for a second step in the distribution chain. In addition, the Japanese promoted their product by heavy spending in advertising and by employing dealer push strategies to support their brand. These strategies contributed to a great expansion of their market share from 1967 to 1970, which created scale economies leading to lower costs and sufficient earnings to allow them to expand further.

Facilitated by government grants for solid-state R&D, the Japanese moved into commercial development and the incorporation of solid-state technology into color TVs, giving them an edge in the new technology. The scale economies resulting from the expansion of both monochrome and color TVs provided earnings for the Japanese to invest in developing a high-technology production system that was more automated and used equipment that was cost efficient and quality enhancing. Through this competitive edge, the Japanese successfully expanded their market share. By the early 1970s, most U.S. producers began to lose money and were forced to merge or be taken over. At this point, the Japanese began to acquire and/or build plants and facilities in the United States, beginning with Sony in 1971. By 1976, Japanese sets accounted for more than 30 percent of the color TV sets sold in the United States. They continued to improve their products and they moved into consoles and 25" screens. As their products became widely accepted, the Japanese raised the price to gain a higher profit from the market.

From the color TV market, the Japanese expanded into the videotape market and, more recently, into the videodisc market. Today Japanese makers dominate the U.S. video market and account for 90 to 95 percent of the total output for the world market. Within less than three decades, the Japanese have become the dominant producers of consumer electronics in the United States and the world.

Japanese Strategies in Europe

The tremendous successes in the U.S. market provided the Japanese companies with a strong base for further expansion into Europe. The Japanese first entered European markets in the early 1960s by focusing their marketing efforts on major countries such as Germany, the United Kingdom, and France. The company's wholly owned sales subsidiaries were established to handle marketing functions. For example, Mitsubishi organized its distribution network in Europe by establishing sales subsidiaries in West Germany and later on in nearby countries such as France, Belgium, and Italy. After almost a decade of patiently developing a European distribution network, the Japanese saw their sales on radio, TV, and tape recorder items take off in 1969. When Japan's color TV had begun dominating the U.S. market during the mid-1970s, Japanese exports of color TV began flooding into Europe. From a negligible level of market penetration in 1974, Japanese exports were able to account for 6 percent of Western Europe's color TV markets by the end of 1970. These European countries are now facing a new generation of products succeeding color TV, such as videotape recorders and videodiscs, whose sales are rapidly growing.

The penetration of Japanese exports resulted in the proliferation of protectionism in most European countries, especially in the United Kingdom and France. Japan then shifted its pattern of trade from simply exporting to manufacturing in local markets. In the United Kingdom, for example, there are at least six Japanese producers that manufacture their products locally. At this stage, the majority of Japanese producers are now genuine global marketers with manufacturing plants located in every area of the world as part of a clear strategy of internationalizing production and marketing in order to achieve maximum national utilization of labor and capital around the world.

Hitachi, for example, has a factory assembling TV sets in the United States using chassis imported from subsidiary firms located in Taiwan and Singapore, both of which have cheap labor. The tube is made by GE's U.S. plant and other components are either local or Canadian. The only thing imported from Japan is management.

BUILT-IN ADVANTAGES OF GLOBAL MARKETING

Japanese firms today are no longer merely exporting firms but are multinational firms playing for high stakes in the global game of international businesses. They locate plants and facilities around the world. Japanese exports now consist of goods produced not only in Japan but also in their overseas factories. Global marketing has greatly benefited Japan and is the key to its trade success. Some of these major benefits gained from global marketing are summarized below.

Advantage from Experience Curve Effect and Economies of Scale

Research has shown that for many industries, each time the accumulated experience of manufacturing a product doubles, the real unit cost declines at a fairly constant rate. Japan has benefited from this experience curve effect as well as from the normal economies of scale made possible by its global marketing strategy. This has enabled Japanese firms to reduce their prices and set them lower than those of their nonglobal competitors.

     The Japanese motorcycle industry provides a good example. In this kind of industry, price relative to competitors is an important determinant of market share. Even a very sophisticated machine cannot carry a premium of more than 30 to 40 percent over the competitor's product. The price set by the competitor with the least-expensive product in a given class puts an upper limit on how much the most-expensive product in that class could sell for. Because of the vast scale of the global markets in which Japanese motorcycles are sold, Japanese producers can sell their motorcycles at substantially lower prices than their competition and still be profitable.

Advantage from Decentralized Production System

The dispersion of Japanese markets, plants, and facilities throughout the world has enabled Japan to achieve the lowest production costs because many of these countries have cheaper labor or lower-cost raw materials. By establishing decentralized regional production and distribution centers, Japanese firms have reduced their production and transportation costs. This global strategy has helped Japanese firms maintain their competitiveness in the world market even in the face of increasing competition and trade protectionism.

ADVANTAGE FROM PROFIT TRANSFER

A third benefit of global marketing is Japan's ability to transfer profit from successful markets to smaller fledgling markets. Japanese firms have frequently used their profits from one market to finance their expensive inroads into new markets. For example, Japan earned a great deal in its home market by keeping prices high and keeping foreign competition low. Zenith claimed that it could sell its TV sets in Japan for less than Japanese sets were selling for, but it was blocked by invisible trade barriers. It also claimed that Japanese TV manufacturers priced their TVs in the U.S. lower than in Japan—an act known as *dumping*. This pattern meant that Japan was using its profits in certain markets to subsidize its attacks elsewhere.

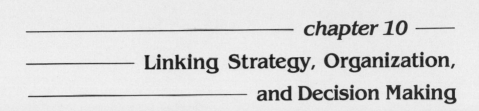

chapter 10
Linking Strategy, Organization,
and Decision Making

The success of a business firm will be greatly influenced by the fundamental ways in which it goes about formulating its strategy, structuring its organization, and handling its decision making. Each company will carry on these processes in its own unique way as a result of its history, culture, people, and resources. At the same time, the business firms within a particular country may exhibit some common patterns of handling these processes. We believe that Japanese patterns of strategy thinking, organization design, and decision making have contributed greatly to Japan's competitive success in global markets. We also believe that U.S. and European firms can draw several important lessons from studying these patterns.

This chapter will examine the main components underlying the Japanese pattern of management.

STRATEGIC MENTALITY

Much of Japan's commercial success lies in what we will call the strategic "mind-set" of Japanese firms. The beliefs, values, and goals that drive Japanese strategic behavior are fundamentally different in essence and orientation from those found historically in U.S. firms.

Japan's natural environment, history, and culture have conditioned a fiercely competitive and achievement-oriented spirit in the

**The Major Components of Japanese Strategy, Organizational
Structure, and Decision Making**

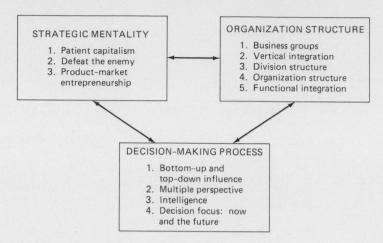

Japanese character. Japan has been subject to harsh environmental conditions (earthquakes, typhoons, and monsoons) as well as poor natural resources, both creating an aggressive, survival-oriented spirit. Japan has also been the scene of many wars. The drawn-out battles among the Japanese themselves to unite their nation, the battles against China, Korea, and Russia, and finally Japan's unfortunate engagement in World War II have kept alive for generations a sense of the art of warfare. Culturally, one of Japan's major classes of earlier times—the Samurai—dedicated themselves to perfecting their skills in the martial arts. Many Japanese young people study such martial arts as Kendō, Judō, Karate, and Shō Rinji Mempō, where they learn the best means of attack and defense. The game of "GO," originated by the Chinese and perfected by the Japanese, provides a mental training in principles of indirect attack and encirclement as well as the need for opportunistic planning.

The Japanese started with a sense of cultural inferiority to the Chinese from whom had they borrowed so much. In the past few centuries, they have suffered from a sense of material inferiority in relation to the West. This has generated a strong will to catch up with and surpass other countries. Japanese ambitiousness is also fueled by an ancient belief in their spiritual superiority over other people. All of these have nurtured a spirit of competitiveness not only toward foreigners but even between different Japanese groups within Japan itself.

The mentality underlying Japanese competitive behavior is captured in the following three elements:

1. The desirability of a long-term orientation
2. The importance of targeting competitors for defeat as well as wooing customers
3. The definition of product and market development as the key to strategic success

Patient Capitalism: A Long-Term Focus

U.S. business firms have been criticized for their preoccupation with short-run profitability, which often leads them to forgo needed investments in product and market development for the sake of reporting higher current profits. The short-run preoccupation of U.S. management is the result of many factors, including the pressure of stockholders and Wall Street financial analysts who judge company management performance by current profit levels, the payment of management bonuses based on current profit performance, the high interest rates that result in the high discounting of far-off profits, and so on.

In contrast, Japanese firms take a longer-term view in making product and market investments. Japanese firms are bent on winning a longer-term position in world markets, not milking their position for short-run benefits. The Japanese are the very model of patient capitalists. Pursuing a flanking strategy over a number of years eventually allows them to adopt the aggressive, combative tactics inherent in frontal attacks. Many Japanese firms have been willing to incur substantial losses as the price they must pay for later successes. For example, it took at least five years for Sony's considerable investment in its own selling, distribution, and service organization as well as in its own manufacturing arm in the United States to show a profit. The proclivity of many Japanese firms to invest much time and money in bringing their engineers, product designers, and market planners to the United States to learn U.S. customs, tastes, and market conditions could only be justified by their plans to enter this market for the long haul.

The patience and determination of these Japanese firms is exemplified in their continuing to invest large sums of money in the face of poor financial and market returns. NEC, for example, has been in the semiconductor business for two decades but has only turned a profit in the past few years. Even during the profitless years, NEC continued to invest heavily in R&D. In contrast, some wealthy American companies such as GE, Westinghouse, and RCA grew impatient with the slow payoff in their semiconductor businesses and each withdrew from the industry. Others, such as Motorola and Texas Instruments, exhibited more of the characteristics of patient capitalists and reaped rewards later.

The same Japanese patience and perseverance is evident in other Japanese companies that are still waiting to turn a profit in the U.S. marketplace. Suntory International, one of the world's largest whiskey manufacturers, has spent nearly a decade trying to establish a market presence in the United States but has to date achieved minimal success. Shiseido, one of the largest Japanese cosmetics manufacturers, has tried to penetrate the U.S. market since 1968 but also with minimal success. It has devoted its time and energies to learning the U.S. market and developing its own distribution networks. Today Shiseido owns a manufacturing plant in New Jersey and sells its products through its distribution network at prices lower than those of market leaders like Estée Lauder and Clinique.

Over the past few decades, most of Japan's profitability results (such as return on sales and return on investment) have been lower than those of U.S. firms across many industries, but the Japanese have continued to amass market growth and penetration. These trends have been especially manifest in the electronics industry. In a study conducted by Shimizu, most of the leading electronics companies such as Matsushita, Nihon Kohden, Hitachi, Sharp, Sanyo, Pioneer, Fujitsu, and Nippon Electric have identified sales growth and market share expansion as their primary objectives. On the other hand, short-run capital gains and dividends, which are so important in the "objective function" of American firms, were accorded the least importance by the Japanese firms surveyed.

Defeat the Enemy

Japanese firms seem driven by a conception of markets as battlefields. They are propelled by a will-to-win, which views competitors as an enemy to be defeated. "Live and let live" is not a noticeable theme in the reflections of Japanese corporate leaders or in their actions.

The Japanese way of marketing seems to move from normal marketing competition as usually practiced by American companies to marketing warfare. A key ingredient for success in marketing warfare is the establishment of competition-centered strategies and not just customer-centered strategies. It is the commitment to competing and winning that shapes and drives the strategic behavior (flanking, frontal, and bypass attacks, etc.) discussed in previous chapters. "Going to war" over a market and doing whatever it takes to win over the long run motivates the aggressive battle plans so evident in many Japanese strategies since the late 1960s.

A conception of markets as battlefields suggests that military principles may well underlie the offensive and defensive strategies adopted by the Japanese. A flanking strategy is succinctly captured in the following two military principles: "An army may be likened to water, for just as flowing water avoids the heights and hastens to the lowlands, so an army avoids strength and strikes weakness"; and "To be certain to take what you attack is to attack a place the enemy doesn't attack." Clearly, Japanese firms employed these principles in invading the U.S. markets. They avoided the dominant firms in well-established product-markets and identified and gradually attacked weak points in the broader product-market that were not likely to be contested or defended by the dominant firms.

Product-Market versus Financial Entrepreneurialism

The third central tenet of the Japanese strategic mentality is that ultimate business success flows from product and market development and not from financial dealing and trading. The Japanese believe that the firms that outperform others in the product-market battlefield win not only the competitive war but ultimately the financial spoils.

This element is evidenced in the market entry, penetration, and maintenance strategies used by the Japanese. As they penetrated the U.S. marketplace, they did not rest on their laurels. They continuously improved and proliferated their product lines and extended their market reach. Japan's institutional efforts to identify and nurture opportunities have been continuous in the post–World War II period. Japan recognized early that unless it developed product, market, and technological entrepreneurialism it would be destined to be a follower rather than a leader in the global competitive battlefield.

ORGANIZATION STRUCTURE

All companies have an organizational structure, and U.S. management theory has heavily emphasized its formal elements: a hierarchy of authority and reporting relationships, a manageable span of control, and the creation and integration of task-related or functional subunits such as departments and divisions. Here we will describe the main structural elements found in Japanese companies. We will first discuss the macrolevel (groups of business entities) and then the microlevel (structure within individual firms).

Macro-organization Structure:
The Business Groups

Business organizations in Japan have historically derived a lot of strength from being members of larger groups called Zaibatsu and, later, Keiretsu. Each group member may have further vertical links with suppliers to its own industry. These groups and linkages are examined below.

The Zaibatsu or business group originated in the sixteenth and seventeenth centuries and exerted dominance over Japan's industrial and commercial activities until the end of World War II. Although the U.S. forces succeeded in dismantling these mammoth industrial groups as part of their efforts to impose sweeping democratization of Japan's economic, political, and social systems, the dissolution did not work out as planned. In particular, the emergence of communism as a rival threat to the West, marked by dramatic fears of possible Communist dominance in Asia (precipitated by the Communist takeover on Mainland China and by the outbreak of the Korean hostilities) led the United States to reevaluate its hopes and plans for the recovery of the Japanese economic system and the restructuring of Japanese institutions. A rising tide of sentiment within the U.S. occupation authorities saw Japan as a capitalist bulwark against communism in Asia. Thus, quick economic recovery was deemed essential, and the Zaibatsu structure was seen as providing an organizational framework that could quickly contribute to initiating and sustaining economic rehabilitation. Accordingly, the Zaibatsu dissolution program was virtually abandoned in 1949, and the Zaibatsu structure we see today in Japan began to unfold.

However, the prewar "Zaibatsu" were not exactly duplicated. What emerged were the postwar conglomerate groups that subdivided into two major and powerful groups:

1. The Keiretsu, or so-called modern Zaibatsu, and
2. The industrially linked groups (the so-called Konzern, since they are similar to the original German industrial conglomerates, the Konzern).

The Keiretsu, or modern Zaibatsu, can be subdivided into two groups:

1. The direct descendents of the old Zaibatsu. This group includes Mitsubishi, Mitsui, and Sumitomo groups.

2. The bank-centered conglomerate groups, which are the product of the merger of smaller Zaibatsu and groups of enterprises organized by large banks and large industrial corporations. This segment includes the Fuyo, Sanwa, and Dai-ichi groups.

The modern Zaibatsu consists of a core bank, a general trading company (or sogo shosha), and a number of manufacturing firms. This group is thus linked by a common financial bond, with a bank or a set of banks serving as the financial center. Each group has its own financial, marketing, and manufacturing arms.

SOME IMPORTANT JAPANESE BUSINESS GROUPS

GROUP	CORE BANK	GENERAL TRADING CO.	MANUFACTURING FIRMS (some examples)
Mitsui	Mitsui Bank	Mitsui & Co.	— Toray Industry (textiles) — Mitsui Toatsu; Mitsui Petrochemical Industry (chemicals) — Tokyo Shibaura Electric (electric machinery) — Mitsui Shipbuilding and Engineering (transportation equipment, etc.)
Mitsubishi	Mitsubishi Bank	Mitsubishi Corp.	— Mitsubishi Rayon (textiles) — Mitsubishi Chemical Industries: Mitsubishi Petrochemical Mitsubishi Gas (chemicals) — Mitsubishi Electric (electric machinery) — Mitsubishi Heavy Industries (transportation)
Sumitomo	Sumitomo Bank	Sumitomo Shoji	— Sumitomo Chemical (chemicals) — Sumitomo Metal Industries (steel) — Sumitomo Building & Machinery (machinery) — Sumitomo Electric Industries: Nippon Electric Co. (electric machinery)

SOME IMPORTANT JAPANESE BUSINESS GROUPS (Continued)

GROUP	CORE BANK	GENERAL TRADING CO.	MANUFACTURING FIRMS (some examples)
Sanwa	Sanwa Bank	Nissho-Iwai Co.	— Teijin (textiles) — Ube Industries; Sekisui Chemical; Hitachi Chemical (chemicals) — Kobi Steel (steel) — Hitachi Manufacturing; Sharp (electric machinery) — Daihatsu; Hitachi Shipbuilding & Engineering (transportation)
Fuyo	Fuji Bank	Marubeni Corp.	— Nippon Kokan (steel) — Kubota Tekko (machinery) — Oki Electric; Hitachi Manufacturing (electric machinery) — Nissan motor (transportation) — Canon Camera (cameras)
Dai-ichi Kangyo	Dai-ichi Kangyo Bank	C. Itoh & Co.	— Kawasaki Steel (steel) — Asahi Denka; Shiseido (chemicals) — Fuji Electric; Fumitsu; Fujitsu Facom; Fujitsu Electric Industries (electric) — Kawasaki Heavy Industries; Fuji Diesel (transportation, etc.)

The Konzern, or industrially linked groups, on the other hand consist of a large corporation that may be viewed as the hub of a system of subcontracting or supplier relationships. This kind of conglomerate group is peculiarly a product of the post–World War II era. Well-known examples include the Matsushita group, the Toshiba-IHI group, the Toyota group, the Nippon Steel group, and the Honda group.

The difference between these Konzern groups and the Keiretsu groups is that the former are less dependent on financial institutions for their funds. They generate much more of their own finances through profitable operations, something at which most of these groups were remarkably adept during the 1970s.

At the same time, there are considerable linkages between these industrially linked groups and the modern Zaibatsu through stock purchases, loans, and investments. For example, Sumitomo Bank is linked with Mazda and the Matsushita groups, Mitsui is linked with the Toyota and Toshiba groups, and Mitsubishi is linked with the Honda group.

Impact on strategic marketing. These conglomerate structures have been integrally related to how Japanese firms have approached the international marketplace and to how they make strategy and marketing-related decisions. The history of the Japanese invasion of the world marketplace is, in part, the story of the evolution of these conglomerate groups.

In the case of the modern Zaibatsu (Keiretsu), the General Trading Company (GTC) was the spearhead of its early onslaught on foreign markets. Indeed, the GTCs were originally established for marketing activities: identifying possible markets, gathering intelligence on these markets, appraising the strengths and weaknesses of competitors, and so forth. The GTCs have evolved into a worldwide intelligence network system, providing a flow of data and information into and out of Japan that far surpasses that of any other country.

The GTCs are typically structured into worldwide product divisions characterized by a country-product matrix system. Each division thus has indepth knowledge and experience in particular product areas and countries. GTC personnel specialize in specific product groups, with particular emphasis on a particular country or group of countries. The concentration of the marketing function in the GTCs has led to a highly organized and efficient marketing machine dedicated to the exploitation of the world marketplace.

The industrially linked groups (Konzern), because of their indirect links to the modern Zaibatsu (Keiretsu) and the absence of their own overseas marketing operations, also began their export drives through the GTC. However, their dependence on and utilization of the GTCs have varied considerably. For example, steel manufacturing firms have been very heavy users of GTCs while electronic companies have been very light users.

A structure for international emphasis. As international sales became more important to Japanese manufacturing firms, the GTCs became increasingly inadequate to serve these manufacturers' exporting needs. GTCs could not devote the resources and attention to the myriad of functions required to build a strong presence in overseas markets. GTCs were ill equipped to perform required functions such as in-depth market, customer, and product analysis, new-product development planning, distribution system development, and customer service activities. Thus Japanese manufacturing firms found it essential to establish their own overseas management structure. A number of firms initially established an "export division," and part of its charge was to work closely with the relevant GTC(s). In general, export divisions were divided into subdivisions focusing on particular groups of countries or regions.

Eventually export divisions increasingly became insufficient for the tasks involved in penetrating foreign markets. Manufacturing firms in automobiles, consumer electronics, and electrical appliances whose success depended on establishing strong relationships with customers, distribution channels, and retailers, and the provision of speedy service, began to realize the necessity of having an organizational subunit dedicated to addressing these marketing needs. Consequently, Japanese firms began to establish a sales subsidiary within the rubric of their "export divisions." These sales subsidiaries began to perform many of the tasks associated with product and market development, such as assessing market opportunities, analyzing investment projects, evaluating market and customers' preferences, searching for local distributors, developing retailer relationships, and fostering contacts with local governments.

Microlevel Structure: Individual Firms

The internal structuring of individual firms in Japan also contributes to effective strategic marketing. Five structure-related elements will be discussed: vertical integration, product-market division structure, hierarchical structure, functional integration, and project structure (teams).

Vertical integration. Many of the marketing strengths of Japanese firms (e.g., aggressive pricing, high quality, fast and stable delivery, after-sales service, etc.) could not have been achieved were it not for their high degree of vertical integration. Vertical integration is inherent in the industrially linked conglomerate structure. The large firms at the core of this structural entity subcontract for the supply of components with small companies in order to derive the benefits of lower costs, committed supply, and lower overhead.

Automobiles, electronics, and watches are Japanese industries characterized by a high degree of vertical integration. In consumer electronics, for example, most firms had in-house sources of components, developed in close collaboration with end-use requirements. By contrast, no U.S. consumer electronics firm had established integrated planning of supply or product design, even in firms with semiconductor or television-tube capacity. Also, in the semiconductor and computer industries, all major Japanese manufacturers were highly vertically integrated, whereas such integration was rare in U.S. firms.

Product-market division structure. As in an earlier era in the United States, the most prevailing organizational form in Japan was functional departmentalization. Only a few firms, such as Toshiba and Matsushita, adopted a divisional structure built around a product-market orientation. However, the rapid expansion of product lines in the past decade has caused a substantial shift from a functional to a divisional form of organizational structure. According to one source, nearly 40 percent of large Japanese firms and around 30 percent of medium-sized firms have moved to a product-market divisional form.

Japanese firms adopted a divisional structure for reasons similar to those that spurred U.S. firms in the same direction: the need to decentralize decision making, to focus efforts on product and market development, to enhance flexibility and adaptability to the environment, and, more generally, to infuse an entrepreneurial spirit into their organization.

Internal organization structure. Many observers have commented on the lack of emphasis on formalized, rigid, and standardized organizational structures in Japanese firms in comparison with their U.S. counterparts. In U.S. firms, organization structure in the form of an organization chart with concrete and well-publicized authority and reporting relationships, clear-cut descriptions of responsibilities, and well-specified tasks are typically the norm. Formalization and standardization are presumed to lay the groundwork for organizational efficiency—i.e., they help to get things done.

In contrast, Japanese firms typically do not commit themselves to any rigid hierarchical structure or organization chart. Many Japanese firms, when asked, cannot produce organization charts or written job descriptions. For them, organization structure (i.e., how organizational members report and relate to each other) should be fluid and flexible and designed and adapted continuously to serve and facilitate the formulation and implementation of programs of action.

From an organization structure perspective, the evolution of the Japanese firms' approach to establishing a marketing organization is illuminating. Not until the mid-1970s did many Japanese firms profess to have a "marketing department." Some Japanese firms still do not lay claim to a marketing function or department. Rather, they have tended to have a sales department that performed many of the activities frequently subsumed within the "marketing departments" of U.S. firms.

Functional integration. The openness and fluidity in structural arrangement is reflected in a high degree of functional integration in Japanese firms—much more so than is the norm in U.S. firms. Many managers have been "career pathed" through several of these functional areas—instead of largely within one. The formal and informal aspects of the structuring of Japanese firms facilitate and support interaction among the functional areas (i.e., marketing, manufacturing, engineering, R&D, finance, human resources). In this respect, marketing decisions are the product or consequence of the inputs of not just "marketing" people but of other functional units as well. We will elaborate this theme when we consider the Japanese decision-making process.

Project teams.   The fluid and flexible structuring of Japanese firms and their pursuit of functional integration manifest themselves in the propensity for using project teams. These ad hoc teams serve as the mechanism for generating and fusing relationships and insights across functional and specialist areas and between different levels in the organizational hierarchy. The tasks assigned to teams are varied and many. In one firm, project teams work on product-market development during periods of high market growth. In another firm, project teams work on cost reduction programs, especially during periods of economic difficulties. Project teams are selectively used: One source has estimated that the average number of teams per firm is little more than four, with an average of forty members participating in each team. Another source has suggested that approximately three-fourths of all Japanese firms employ project teams as a dominant means of achieving organizational integration.

DECISION-MAKING PROCESS

Japanese decision-making styles are influenced by their strategic mentality and organization structure, and vice versa. Here we describe a number of characteristics of Japanese decision-making style.

Bottom-Up and Top-Down Influences

Many students of decision making in Japanese firms have concluded that a "bottom-up" rather than a "top-down" process dominates the Japanese style of decision making and that the bottom-up style of influence is more pervasive than it is in U.S. firms. The much-touted "ringi system" has often been proclaimed as the distinguishing feature of how Japanese firms make decisions.

Today, strategic decision processes in Japanese firms are varied, with strict application of the ringi system being more the exception than the rule. Like U.S. firms, the most important or strategic decisions are made by top management. Information and alternatives flow upward, but the locus of evaluation and choice clearly resides among the higher echelons. An important point to note here is that a bottom-up oriented decision process does not necessarily imply that strategic decisions are made at lower levels of the organization. Decision options and recommendations may be funneled to the higher levels in the hierarchy (i.e., lower levels play a major role in shaping decisions or choices), but it remains the prerogative of the top management to decide (i.e., to make choices, commit resources, and establish precedents).

An issue that has received much attention recently is the extent to which middle and lower levels of management should take the initiative in strategic decision making. Japanese firms have frequently been cited as models of how middle management should be the driving force in strategy making. Unfortunately, such a blanket statement betrays a lack of understanding of critical differences across Japanese firms.

In general, we can categorize Japanese firms into two groups regarding the participating role of middle and lower management levels in the making of strategic decisions. The predominant category is those companies in which middle-level management plays a positive and substantial role in initiating and formulating company strategy. In these firms, the operating presumption is that marketing decisions and their implementation are primarily the prerogative of middle and lower management levels. Top management's role is largely that of providing a sense of strategic direction. And much of the direction of the firm's strategic thrust as chosen by top management may well be based on the inputs of lower levels of management. For example, in one Japanese firm we have observed the following decision flow: When middle management in the foreign subsidiary finds that the firm is at a competitive disadvantage, they discuss and debate the issues among themselves. The output is a proposal to redress and improve the situation which is then forwarded to senior management. This is followed by a series of meetings between middle and senior management in which the proposals are critiqued and frequently modified before they receive the support and commitment of top management.

The second category consists of Japanese companies that are led by the founder, or "one-man" president as they are described in Japan. In these companies, middle- and lower-level management participation in strategy making is less important; the ringi system is present but much less visible. Matsushita, Mitsubishi, Toyota, Sony, and Honda are well-known examples in this group. In the Mitsubishi Electric Corporation, strategic decisions are "made" by a general committee or group of top management within each division, and the ringi system is used only occasionally. The founders of Honda, Sony, and Matsushita have been the dominant influences on decision making in their organization.

Although the decision-making role of top management is much larger and stronger in these founder-dominated firms, it would be a grave mistake to picture these firms as successful dictatorships. Far from it. All of these leaders and their senior management teams do not make decisions in a vacuum: They know how to use "bottom-up" participatory activities as a means of data gathering, idea testing, option development, and commitment creation. They recognize that their decisions will have to be implemented by middle- and lower-level management.

Multiple Perspectives

A fundamental axiom of management theory is that the way organizations are structured and the way they make decisions are intimately linked. This linkage is clearly seen in Japanese firms. Perhaps its most significant manifestation is the apparent capacity of Japanese firms to bring multiple perspectives to bear on decision making.

The new-product planning process in one Japanese automobile firm is illustrative. The product development process involves marketing, engineering, production, quality control, R&D, and human resources. Sales and marketing personnel develop the parameters of what might constitute a quality product with high appeal for a particular customer market. The engineering department then translates this product outline into a design with specifications that are only loosely designated and describe the critical functional characteristics that relate to other departments. Staffs from other departments then meet with the design engineers to work out the product development details. This decision process culminates in a design review where the detailed specifications are formalized. As the product is brought to fruition, cross-departmental meetings are held to keep all parties appraised of its development and to provide an opportunity for product-related issues to be identified and resolved.

The impact of functional integration on the decision process is also evidenced in a more general way in the procedures adopted by another Japanese firm. Every Wednesday, representatives from each functional area hold a meeting to review all phases and aspects of the firm's operations. The agenda is left partially open so that time is available to discuss issues that may surface during the meeting. One major output of this meeting is a variety of requests and directions that are channeled to lower-level representatives of all functional areas, who hold a similar meeting on Friday of each week. An obvious consequence of these meetings is that the functional areas are cognizant of each other's ideas, perspectives, interests, and information.

Intelligence

The Japanese penchant for data and information—market, competitive, and environmental intelligence—and the way they use intelligence in decision making tell us much about decision making in Japanese firms and, in many respects, how it differs from decision making in many U.S. firms. Simply stated, the Japanese are driven by an apparently unrelentless thirst for intelligence and an unrivaled assimilation capacity to make use of that intelligence.

Their strategic mentality and organization structure facilitate, reinforce, and reflect a vast organizational apparatus and commitment to massive data gathering, appraisal, and dissemination. A competitive mind-set predicated on the will and need to compete over the long haul demands information of many types as well as the willingness and flexibility to question, test, and challenge that intelligence. However, that mind-set must also be supported by an organization structure that allows and rewards data collection and evaluation.

The Japanese, as they pondered their entry into and penetration of the U.S. marketplace, may have had little choice but to turn their firms into "beehives of intelligence activity." They did not know the U.S. market, culture, or competition, and many of their initial setbacks and slow success reflected that ignorance. However, unlike many U.S. firms in foreign markets, as early as the 1950s the Japanese committed extensive time and resources to learning about the U.S. marketplace, its customs, tastes, and preferences, U.S. competitors, and the U.S. business environment. The Japanese themselves are fond of pointing out that a major reason why so many U.S. firms have not succeeded in Japan is that U.S. firms do not devote enough time and attention to learning what it takes to succeed in the Japanese marketplace.

Decision Focus: Now and the Future

An important factor in Japanese decision making is their capacity to retain a broad view of the current and future battlefields at the same time that they become absorbed in the details of managing current operations. They seem to have mastered much better than many U.S. firms the art of simultaneously managing today's businesses well and laying the groundwork for tomorrow's businesses. This is, in large part, a consequence of their strategic mentality.

Japanese firms are concerned with the futurity of present decisions as well as the present implications of future decisions. They assess the broad implications of current decisions and what needs to be done now to prepare for possible future decisions. Decision analysis thus involves considering the "broad mosaic" of the future as well as intensely appraising today's circumstances. Trade-offs between the present and the future are inevitable. A distinguishing feature of decision making in Japanese firms is that these trade-offs are pushed to the forefront for discussion and analysis. They are not willingly or unwittingly suppressed in favor of the present, as is so often the case in U.S. firms.

CONCLUSION

The strategies adopted by Japanese firms reflect their strategic mentality, organization structure, and decision processes within their organizations. Their strategy choices and the way they modify and adapt their strategies are not accidental; they are natural outgrowths of how Japanese organizations think and behave. This merely reflects what organization theorists and managers have long known: what happens within an organization influences and shapes the way that the organization relates to the outside world.

As discussed in this chapter, strategic mentality, organization structure, and decision-making processes can and do impact strategy formulation and implementation in Japanese firms. However, it is the interrelationship of these three factors that is crucial. They are highly complementary. This is evident in many ways.

For example, at the heart of the Japanese strategic mentality is commitment: commitment to succeed in the marketplace; commitment to strategy improvement. This commitment underlies their patient capitalism, perseverance in the face of little success, will-to-win and competition-centered strategies. It is the driving force behind their major strategy thrusts. The structuring of Japanese firms facilitates that commitment. Structure at the macrolevels and microlevels allows them to pursue that commitment and live with its implications: Their group structure makes capital acquisition comparatively easy because it facilitates raw material acquisition at one end and international marketing at the other; individual firm structuring allows coordination and integration in many forms—organized subcontracting, divisional linkages, and functional integration. Without these structural elements, commitment would be much more difficult to translate into successful strategies. Decision processes reinforce mentality and structure in the context of commitment. Multiple-level participation (ringi-system attributes) in strategic decision making, lower-level initiation of strategic decisions, and continuous appraisal of strategic options further create and sustain commitment to strategic initiatives and programs. Mentality, structure, and process each contribute to and reinforce strategic commitment.

A second example of the interrelationship of these three elements and their importance in understanding Japanese strategy making is in the context of information and intelligence gathering, analysis, dissemination, and use. The Japanese appetite for intelligence is legendary. In part, it is both a cause and a consequence of their strategic mentality. Market and competitive intelligence stimulates strategic thinking: It spurs questions that might otherwise remain unasked; it challenges answers that may be unquestioned. Furthermore the Japanese strategic mentality requires such intelligence: Product-market entrepreneurialism is rather difficult without it. Yet it is the structuring of Japanese firms that allows the intelligence to be collected; general trading companies, banks, and sales subsidiaries, among others, collect hives of data. And, of course, it is their decision process that assimilates and makes sense of this continual circulation of information. To do so, multiple perspectives and fluid decision processes are almost essential.

Another manifestation of the importance of the interrelationships of these three organizational attributes is their contribution to the capacity of Japanese firms to establish and nourish organizational competencies that are conducive to strategic success in the marketplace. Without the mentality, structure, and processes discussed in this chapter, product quality, cost control, attention to detail, and the many other competences associated with Japanese firms would be extremely difficult to realize. By comparison with U.S. firms, these are truly "distinctive competences." At a minimum, they are competences that U.S. firms have found difficult to establish.

The interrelationships between strategic mind-set, structure, and processes influence Japanese strategic behavior in very subtle but very powerful ways through their impact on the definition and measuring of strategic success. Success is not simply measured in financial (profitability) or sales growth terms. Rather, success is delineated in terms of product-market entrepreneurialism: producing the best products in the market, gaining position in the market, and, as a consequence, outperforming and outdistancing competitors. The structural dimensions greatly facilitate pursuit of this definition of success. The processes of decision making help ensure that this notion of strategic success remains vibrant in the organization.

In view of the current popularity of managing "organizational culture" as a means of building sustained strategic success, it is striking to note the importance of strategic mentality in *explaining* Japanese strategic behavior. Whether by chance or design, the Japanese found themselves with an organizational mentality that was highly conducive to strategic success in competitive battlefields dominated by U.S. firms. Their primary beliefs or values—long-run orientation, competition focus, and product-market entrepreneurialism—go a long way toward explaining the strategic behavior of Japanese firms described in this book.

One obvious implication here is that any organization that seeks competitive success needs to infuse itself with a strategic mentality or, more broadly, a strategic culture. For most U.S. firms, assumption of a strategic mentality along the lines developed above will require a major cultural shift. The current beliefs and values in many firms will have to be replaced: An operations-driven mind-set will need to succumb to a strategic mind-set. However, before an organization embarks on a mentality or cultural shift, three lessons derived from the Japanese experience should be borne in mind.

First, the desired culture must permeate the entire organization. It is not sufficient to modify the culture at the top or the bottom of the organization or in one or a few functional areas. It is relevant to note here the emphasis in recent years in the United States on the need for firms to develop a "marketing culture." Unfortunately, the thrust of this effort has often failed to embrace functional areas beyond marketing: R&D, manufacturing, finance, and human research functions have continued as before. One result, of course, has been heightened tensions between marketing and the other functional areas. Similarly, a strategic mentality must be embraced by all levels and functional entities within the organization.

Second, although culture is in large measure self-sustaining (individuals do not easily give up long-held values or beliefs), the truly *strategic* components of a culture will likely need occasional if not constant reinforcement. Even Japanese firms fall prey to inertia and complacency—both of which are frequently born of success. Product-market entrepreneurialism needs its champions; a long-run orientation needs to be pushed in the face of performance deviations; and dealing with new competitors or preempting their emergence needs forceful strategists. The need for strategic cultural reinforcement will be especially true of U.S. firms seeking to change from an operations to a strategic mind-set.

Third, many U.S. firms are currently discovering that cultural change does not happen overnight. It is a long, arduous, and frequently painful process. Moreover, to significantly impact strategy and strategy making, it must tackle how individuals think, how they relate to each other, and how they act—mentality, structure, and process. This is no easy task, yet it is unavoidable for many U.S. organizations if they wish to attain or regain competitiveness in the world marketplace.

PART III
MEETING THE NEW COMPETITION

---------- *chapter 11* ----------

---------- Responding

---------- to the New Competition

We have seen that Japan is not resting on its past successes but instead is aggressively pushing into such new markets as computers, aircraft, pharmaceuticals, trucks, tires, cosmetics, fashions, banking, and hoteling. In this new invasion wave, the Japanese are using marketing strategies similar to those employed in the past, as well as some new ones. The major question then becomes, *How can Western nations and companies meet Japan's continuous challenge and the increasing challenge coming from other nations in the Far East?* In this chapter, we consider the broad range of responses, from militant to innovative, that Western firms and their governments can adopt to respond to the New Competition.

FOUR POTENTIAL RESPONSE STRATEGIES

Response strategies for meeting the New Competition can be classified along two dimensions. The first is whether the *public* or *private* sector undertakes the response. The second is whether the response is *competitive* or *cooperative* in nature. By crossing these dimensions, we arrive at the four broad response categories that make up the Strategic Response Matrix. Each response category contains several possible strategies. The four response categories are examined below.

A Classification of Potential Strategic Responses to the Japanese Challenge

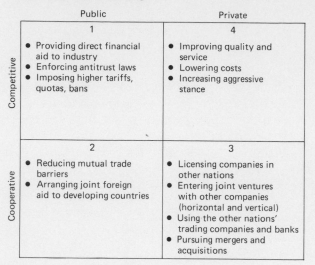

	Public	Private
Competitive	**1** • Providing direct financial aid to industry • Enforcing antitrust laws • Imposing higher tariffs, quotas, bans	**4** • Improving quality and service • Lowering costs • Increasing aggressive stance
Cooperative	**2** • Reducing mutual trade barriers • Arranging joint foreign aid to developing countries	**3** • Licensing companies in other nations • Entering joint ventures with other companies (horizontal and vertical) • Using the other nations' trading companies and banks • Pursuing mergers and acquisitions

Public-Competitive Responses

As the Japanese have increased their market penetration in various nations, these nations have typically responded by adopting defensive measures to discourage or limit further inroads. They have also adopted stimulative monetary and fiscal measures, such as lowering the interest rate, decreasing taxes, and providing direct aid to industry. A further line of defense has been to apply antitrust laws to prevent unfair competition in the form of dumping, below-standard engineering, unfair advertising, and so on. Governments have frequently moved to more restrictive measures by placing higher tariffs or taxes on importers, erecting invisible trade barriers, and imposing actual quotas or even bans on specific import categories. Thus the U.S. government has demonstrated its willingness to intervene on behalf of a single company (e.g., higher tariffs against motorcycles to protect Harley Davidson) or one industry (e.g., trigger pricing for steel import quotas for automobiles).

Such response strategies are understandable but short-sighted. At best, they slow down the trade invasion but do not correct the underlying problems of high wages not matched by sufficient productivity, uncompetitive product features and quality, and so on. The more restrictive measures raise costs to the consumers and hence are inflationary. The government's effort to help one industry (e.g., the steel producers) often hurts other industries (e.g., steel users such as automobile manufacturers and industrial construction). Furthermore, domestic companies that receive protection often fail to reform their operations and strategy. Protectionism, as a line of defense, is at best a temporary expedient, not a cure.

Public-Cooperative Responses

A very different type of response occurs when the government seeks to increase cooperation with its opponent, that is, to turn a zero-sum game into a positive-sum game. The United States, for example, has repeatedly pressed Japan to lower its trade barriers to permit U.S. penetration of Japanese domestic markets as the price for not raising further U.S. trade barriers against Japan. On another front, two governments can cooperate in making overseas loans to third nations to increase their business in these third nations. Two nations can also cooperate in scientific research, such as space missions, to bring technological benefits to both nations. In general, international cooperation can reduce some of the bad effects of excessive international conflicts over certain markets.

Private-Cooperative Responses

Cooperative responses can also take place between private companies, even in the context of normal competition. At least four types of private cooperative responses can be employed.

First, a U.S. company can offer to license its products or technology to a Japanese firm for use in Japan. Hart Schaffner & Marx has licensed men's clothing and Unimation has licensed robots in Japan. Typically, the agreement restricts the licensee to selling the goods in defined markets. The licensor in return receives a fee. Thus the licensor has turned a potential competitor into a cooperator. However, there is the risk that the licensee will eventually become the licensor's competitor. Or the licensee might sell the technology to a third party, who will export to the licensor's home market. According to some observers, the willingness of U.S. firms to license their technology to Japanese companies was a major factor in ultimately creating strong Japanese competitors.

Second, a firm can sponsor joint ventures with companies in other countries. There are two types of joint ventures that a firm could enter. The first type is horizontal cooperation wherein a firm collaborates with another firm that occupies a similar place in the production chain. Recent horizontal joint ventures between U.S. and Japanese firms include GM/Toyota, Caterpillar/Mitsubishi, and Deere/Yanmar. Each partner may be seeking a different advantage. A partner may gain freedom from import barriers (Toyota), an ability to study or contain a rival in its home market (Caterpillar vs. Komatsu), or a short-term addition to the product line (Deere).

The second type of joint venture is vertical cooperation wherein two firms at different levels of the production-marketing chain arrange to work together. Vertical joint ventures offer the opportunity to lower total costs or increase market penetration or both. Commonly, a Japanese manufacturer will team with a U.S. distributor or a U.S. manufacturer will team with a Japanese distributor. Some recently formed vertical joint ventures include IBM/Kanematsu Gosho (office automation equipment), Allied/Mitsui (electricity-conducting alloys), and Aramco/-Mitsubishi Rayon (plastic composites).

A third private-cooperative option is to utilize components of the other nation's infrastructure, such as its trading companies and banks. The Japanese trading companies, in particular, are willing to serve American clients. They provide an expertise in purchasing low-cost raw materials, exporting goods and services worldwide, arranging joint ventures with partners from Japan and other countries, and financing to a limited degree. Japanese commercial banks are also willing to lend money to American companies and support the companies with their information network and business ideas. It makes good sense for American firms—especially small to medium-sized companies that have limited in-house capabilities—to use the low-cost services of Japanese trading companies and banks.

Finally, U.S. firms may consider merging with, acquiring, or being acquired by Japanese firms. The multinational corporation of the future might be companies jointly owned by Japanese and American manufacturers.

Private-Competitive Responses

The fourth broad category of response is where U.S. and Western firms recognize the depth of the challenge of the New Competition and think through new creative competitive responses. Many firms failed to recognize the depth of the challenge until it was too late. They discovered that having technological leadership and ample financing and managerial resources was not enough. They discovered that they needed to offer better quality and service and lower costs. They needed to invest more deeply in plant modernization and managerial and worker retraining. Many U.S. companies today are finally working to define new strategies and new levels of aggressiveness.

EXAMPLES OF CURRENT RESPONSES BY U.S. FIRMS TO THE JAPANESE CHALLENGE

We have described four broad categories of response to the New Competition. In practice, a Western firm is likely to resort to a mix of responses, some competitive and some cooperative, some purely private and some calling for government assistance. Even firms within the same industry are likely to respond differently. Here we will illustrate the patterns of response that several major U.S. firms have taken to defend themselves. We will present seven examples drawn from the following three classes of companies:

> *Medium-tech companies:* Inland Steel, John Deere & Company
>
> *High-tech companies:* G. D. Searle, American Hospital Supply Corporation, U.S. banks
>
> *Companies supplying Japanese companies:* Illinois Tool Works, Signode Corporation

Medium-Tech Companies

Industries in the medium-tech category include both heavy manufacturing industries (steel, farm machinery, and autos) and consumer electronics industries (radios, televisions, and tape recorders). These industries were once considered high-technology industries. Relative to some new industries such as gene splicing, aerospace, and semiconductors, however, they have become medium technology. Specifically, the products of these industries have for the most part become medium technology. The production processes, by contrast, may actually be high technology (e.g., CAD/CAM, robots).

The Japanese have already hit American companies hard in several of these industries. They have captured a significant share of many product-markets. Many medium-tech U.S. companies are now several years behind the Japanese in terms of manufacturing and marketing capability. The challenge to American companies in these industries is to catch up with the Japanese and, it is hoped, move a few years ahead of them.

The U.S. companies have responded to the Japanese challenge by acting in different cells of the Strategic Response Matrix. Conventional wisdom is that they should concentrate in the microcompetitive

MEETING THE NEW COMPETITION

and macrocompetitive cells. It is clear, however, that U.S. firms have also begun to exploit options in the other two cells.

Case 1: Inland Steel. Inland Steel is currently operating primarily in two cells of the Strategic Response Matrix, the public-competitive and private-cooperative cells:

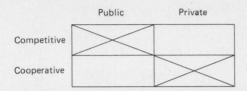

In the public-competitive cell, Inland Steel, along with other U.S. steel producers, has supported the adoption of several public measures to restrict steel imports. The adoption of tariffs, quotas, and antidumping measures has provided some relief to the firm in the past five years.

In the private-cooperative cell, Inland is improving its engineering and computer systems by retaining Nippon Steel Company as a consultant. Inland managers have toured the Nippon Steel plants and received guidance on JIT (just-in-time production) and TQC (the quality circle). Fortunately, the firm began a modernization program before the Japanese took over most of the market. Now Inland seems to be rapidly acquiring some of the techniques of low-cost production so that it could compete again in the market for high-value-added steels.

There is a touch of irony in the fact that Inland is in the private-cooperative cell seeking help from the Japanese. Fifteen years ago, Inland was giving help (not selling it, as the Japanese are doing now) to the embryonic Japanese steel manufacturers. Inland opened its factories to the Japanese and explained the details of its technology, order entries, inventory control, and operations management. Inland assumed that the Japanese steel companies would never be capable of competing with American companies. It is hardly surprising that the Japanese figured out how to surpass U.S. steel makers so decisively.

In the mid-1960s, when Inland awoke to the Japanese challenge, it put some effort in the private-competitive cell for a few years. The periods of cooperation fifteen years ago and today have been more normal than head-on competition with the Japanese. This is due to the long time Japan spent in isolation preparing its competitive attack and the speed with which it overwhelmed the U.S. steel industry in the late 1970s. Inland's movement through the cells over time is illustrated in the following matrix.

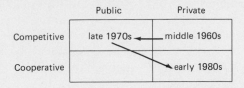

Case 2: John Deere & Company. John Deere is relying mainly on actions in the private domain to catch up with its Japanese competitors:

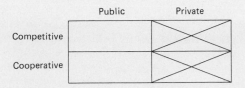

Deere is gaining on Kubota (its main competitor from Japan) and also worldwide. Some of its gain is the result of automating rapidly (raising the capital-to-labor ratio of the production process), sharpening the focus of its plants (so that each one does not try to make too many products), and increasing its use of a participative management system. But Deere still needs to learn how the Japanese produce at such low costs. For example, it needs to learn how to make low-horsepower tractors as inexpensively as Kubota does. Toward that end, Deere entered a joint venture with Yanmar, a Japanese firm making low-horsepower tractors. Deere sells the Yanmar machines in the United States. Unfortunately, this joint venture serves mainly to supplement the Deere product line rather than to transfer technology or process technology.

High-Tech Companies

The high-tech group includes both past industries targeted by the Japanese (e.g., semiconductors and office automation systems) and industries about to be targeted (e.g., pharmaceuticals, medical instruments, and aerospace). These industries contain a high degree of technological sophistication and the highest capital-to-labor ratios in the United States. America still has the lead in many of these product-markets, but it may lose that lead quickly. Much depends on the strength of Japan's targeting efforts and the vigor of America's strategic response.

Case 3: Pharmaceutical Industry. Although the Japanese currently import more pharmaceuticals ($1.17 billion) than they export ($0.41 billion), and although they currently license foreign drug manufacturers to manufacture and distribute their products abroad, a number of factors indicate that the Japanese could become a major competitor in overseas pharmaceutical markets.

First, the demand for pharmaceuticals in the Japanese market is likely to exceed by far the $20 billion spent in 1981. This high demand is the result of a cultural bias toward the use of medicinal drugs, a rapidly aging population, and the fact that almost all prescription drugs are covered by health insurance.

Second, important changes are occurring in the structure of the Japanese pharmaceutical industry. Currently there are 2,235 drug manufacturers in Japan. Although the forty largest firms average sales of between $100 million to $500 million (in a $19 billion market), the vast majority of these firms are very small operations that concentrate on providing low-cost imitation products. Only 9 percent of the firms in the Japanese drug industry employ more than one hundred workers. Within the past six years the Japanese government has passed a series of laws that (1) relax restrictions on foreign drug company investment in Japan and (2) provide for direct patent protection and brand pricing. With these two new provisions, a weeding out of a great number of small "copycat" manufacturers is inevitable.

Given these incentives, the major Japanese drug manufacturers will be willing to increase their R&D budgets. Already world leaders in the field of antibiotics, the Japanese parlay their own research as well as the scientific information they are receiving from foreign joint ventures into a competitive advantage in a wider number of drug areas.

By and large the relationship between Japanese and U.S. drug manufacturers has focused on the "private cooperative" quadrant. Virtually every major drug manufacturer in the world has a subsidiary in Japan and/or a joint venture or licensing agreement with a Japanese firm. And although 100 percent foreign ownership of pharmaceutical companies was finally permitted in Japan in 1975, foreign firms have generally maintained their licensing and joint venture agreements with Japanese companies.

Foreign firms have maintained their cooperative relationships with Japanese drug companies for two reasons: (1) a Japanese joint venture allows access to the second-largest pharmaceutical market in the world, and (2) licensing agreements allow U.S. firms to fill out their product lines and compete better against their domestic and non-Japanese international rivals. In return, the Japanese partner receives distribution help throughout the world and scientific information regarding the foreign products it distributes (50 percent of Japanese drug production is of products developed abroad).

Often the joint venture is a one-way street. G. D. Searle and Dainippon have a joint venture in which Dainippon receives the exclusive distribution rights in Japan for all Searle products. Dainippon controls product testing, quality control, and distribution. In addition, Dainippon receives the technology for those products that Searle wishes to sell in Japan. But Searle does not have a corresponding exclusive distributorship for Dainippon's products in the U.S. market.

The critical question is, How competitive could the Japanese be in pharmaceuticals? The answer is, Very competitive. First, one blockbuster drug can launch a firm (and perhaps ruin a competitor). Second, the Japanese would have no problem distributing their drugs if they decided to set up subsidiaries in the United States. The 434 major wholesalers who cover the U.S. market would be happy to distribute a "hot" new product.

The key competitive element really rests in the development of effective new products. In this area, the Japanese have already shown leadership in the field of antibiotics. With the expertise gained from their licensing agreements as well as with that generated as a result of the new Japanese patent and brand-pricing laws, the Japanese could develop a considerable competitive advantage in a number of drug groups.

Although the Japanese have the capability to enter the U.S. drug market in force, they have been reluctant to do so. The Japanese licensed Marion Labs (a small drug company) to manufacture and distribute Cardzim (an antihypertensive). Last year's sales of that product reached $100 million, a phenomenal success that led industry analysts to wonder why the Japanese did not buy Marion Labs rather than license their drug to the American company. Possible reasons may center on a fear of government regulations and a feeling that the timing is not right. Japanese firms could be waiting for more scientific breakthroughs, or they could be unwilling at this time to upset their joint-venture partners in Japan.

Ironically, the most potent tools U.S. firms have to compete against the Japanese are their cooperative joint ventures and licensing agreements. If we consider the penetration movements of the Japanese in other industries, Japanese firms in the pharmaceutical industry are now in the entering stage and U.S. companies have to prepare for this.

Case 4: American Hospital Supply Corporation (AHSC). Traditionally, foreign firms have enjoyed a fair degree of access to the Japanese health market. In large measure, this stems from the wholesale importation of Western hospital and health systems at the time of the Meiji

Restoration as well as the product superiority that the West has maintained over the years. As a consequence, most of the relationships between U.S. and Japanese firms in the laboratory and medical specialties fields have been in the realm of the private-cooperative. American Hospital Supply Corporation, Baxter Travenol, Abbott, and Johnson & Johnson all have joint ventures with Japanese firms for the manufacture and distribution of their products.

Given the current degree of market penetration by U.S. health-care companies in Japan, it would hardly seem possible for Japanese companies to reverse the situation. Yet the potential for a Japanese power gain seems high if we consider (1) the growth and attractiveness of the Japanese health-care market; (2) the resources that the Japanese could invest to develop their capabilities in this market; (3) the technological expertise of the Japanese in automation, computers, and consumer electronics; (4) the rapid technological pace of modern medicine where one breakthrough could render an entire line of medical products obsolete; and (5) the fragmented nature of the American market for these products.

Clearly, the Japanese are developing the capability to enter selected segments of the laboratory and medical specialties fields. Hitachi has devoted a considerable amount of R&D to the automation of lab instruments. Another Japanese firm has developed a fully automated (lowest-cost) filling line for a diagnostic reagent. There is nothing to prevent the Japanese from starting a company in the United States. In fact, the fragmented and regionalized nature of the U.S. laboratory and medical specialties market would facilitate this type of entry. Foreign firms can establish regional distribution systems by purchasing American firms. Green Cross (AHSC's joint-venture partner in Japan) has purchased Alpha Therapeutics in order to gain greater access to the U.S. market for liquid medical products. Likewise, the Swedish firm Pharmacia has made inroads into the U.S. medical instruments market.

Could the Japanese pose a threat to a corporation such as American Hospital Supply whose major strength lies in distribution? If the Japanese came into the United States with a new "wonder drug," AHSC would most likely serve as its distributor. Realistically, AHSC could face a threat on two levels. First, the Japanese could (depending on the nature of the product) try to develop their own distribution system. Second, in 1981 AHSC manufactured 27,000 of the 145,000 products it distributed, and these represented 56 percent of the corporation's gross profit. As AHSC moves toward manufacturing more of its product lines, particularly those in the high-tech, high-value-added laboratory and medical specialties areas, it may collide with the Japanese.

Case 5: Commercial Banking Industry. The U.S. commercial banks are responding to the Japanese challenge by taking action in all four cells of the Strategic Response Matrix:

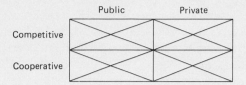

The U.S. banking industry has been very active in the public-competitive realm. Prior to the 1978 International Banking Act, foreign banks were exempt from reserve requirements and restrictions against branch and interstate banking. Freedom from these restrictions naturally gave a significant advantage to foreign banks. Consequently, the U.S. banking industry pressed hard for the passage of the 1978 legislation. Currently, foreign banks face exactly the same restrictions as U.S. banks.

The prosperity of the banking system is highly contingent on public-cooperative policies of the world's governments. Through domestic regulation of banks, moderate macroeconomic policies, restrained currency intervention, and support of the World Bank and International Monetary Fund, government policy influences the welfare of all banks. Cooperation among governments greatly increases the economic benefits of being an international banking institution.

There is some degree of private cooperation between U.S. and foreign banks. This cooperation takes the form of currency swaps, letters of credit, and international loan syndications. These arrangements play an important role in servicing the international needs of bank clients and in diversifying the bank's portfolio of loans. Given the importance of these interactions, there is little danger of competition growing out of bounds and threatening to destroy these elements of cooperation.

Yet U.S. banks are facing increasingly strong private competition, both inside and outside the United States. While U.S. banks have retrenched their international operations, Japanese and other banks have moved to fill the gap in other countries. In addition, foreign banks have dramatically increased their U.S. operations. The assets of U.S. offices of foreign banks increased from $15 billion in 1972 to $150 billion in 1979. More than 15 percent of the $259 billion of commercial and industrial loans made in the United States were made by the U.S. offices of foreign banks. The Japanese have been a major force in this expansion of foreign operations in the U.S. banking market. As the U.S. banks have retrenched their international operations, the Japanese have expanded their worldwide banking networks. This is in response to the movement of Japanese corporations abroad and also a function of having surplus funds to lend. The effect of these trends has been to increase the attractiveness of Japanese banks to multinational corporations. The fact that more American corporations are opening operations in Japan has enabled the Japanese banks to make significant inroads into the *Fortune 500* loan market. In addition, the recent influx of Japanese manufacturers into the U.S. market has provided a key base for the expansion of Japanese banks here. Finally, while the 1978 International Banking Act eliminated some of the advantages that foreign banks had enjoyed over their American competitors, the law may legitimize more fully the role of foreign banks in the United States. Foreign banks may now be federally chartered, use the services of the Federal Reserve, and participate in the FDIC program. Consequently, foreign banks in the United States may find it easier to boost their local dollar deposits and make loans without using the resources of the parent bank.

The U.S. banks believe that the domestic deposit base of the Japanese will limit their lending activities in this country. While the loan capacity of a branch bank is theoretically limited only by the capital of its parent, exchange rate exposure limits the amount of capital transferred from the parent bank. American banks believe that the costs of currency hedging would offset the cost of capital advantage (Japanese interest rates are regulated by the government and are lower than those in the U.S.) that Japanese banks currently enjoy.

What the U.S. banking industry may be failing to comprehend is that the Japanese can and do work in concert. Increasing amounts of low-cost Japanese capital could be lent internationally, with the entire Japanese banking industry maintaining a fairly closed position. Furthermore, as the number of Japanese firms in the United States increases, the Japanese may find it increasingly unnecessary to borrow from the parent bank or translate and repatriate dollars back to Japan.

U.S. Suppliers of Japanese Companies

Here we want to examine the responses of U.S. firms that directly supply Japanese companies. Two cases in particular—Illinois Tool Works and Signode Corporation—illustrate how the integration of both cooperative and competitive actions is important in dealing with the Japanese.

Case 6: Illinois Tool Works. Illinois Tool Works, Inc. (ITW), manufactures, among other things, a wide variety of custom-designed fasteners for use in the manufacture of automobiles. ITW has been able to soften the impact of the decline of the U.S. automobile industry through its joint venture in Japan that serves Japanese car manufacturers.

In both its U.S. and its Japanese operations, ITW possesses a number of distinct advantages. These advantages include (1) the company's technical expertise and patents on products, (2) its continued technological development of new products using different materials, and (3) the speed with which it can fill an order. These factors, in conjunction with the fragmented structure of the fastener industry and the importance of locating near one's customers, have given ITW a significant competitive advantage in the U.S. and Japanese markets.

Although ITW's business with the Japanese has been profitable and constant, two potential dangers must be avoided. First, ITW has to establish more control over its Japanese joint ventures. Although ITW is a 40 percent owner and provides technical product and engineering advice, the Japanese have taken great pains to restrict ITW to a "portfolio" role. The amount of information ITW receives from its joint-venture partner is almost nil. A second and related point is that ITW must establish secure business relations with the Japanese automobile and other manufacturing firms in the United States. Specifically, Honda and Nissan in the United States want to import parts (they already import all their steel) from Japan. Given the transportation costs and low value of mechanical fasteners, Japanese firms in the United States have put pressure on ITW's joint-venture partner to open a U.S.-based factory to supply them! The Japanese are attempting to put together the same close relationships with banks and suppliers that they enjoy in Japan.

ITW and other potential suppliers of the Japanese in the United States must address this threat on two levels. The first is to try to adapt somewhat to the Japanese manufacturing system—particularly in regard to lowering inventories—and shortening lead and delivery times. The second is to improve its management and control of any Japanese joint venture. This goal might be accomplished by stricter controls on product and process technology as well as deeper involvement in running the joint venture. The ITW case clearly shows that (1) some companies can take advantage of the presence of the Japanese in the United States as well as penetrate the Japanese home market (thus softening the loss from the decline of their historical U.S. customers); and (2) this opportunity is fleeting, and if adaptation is not forthcoming, is easily lost.

Case 7: Signode Corporation. What U.S. managers often fail to perceive is that Japan's economic development has been uneven in some areas. That uneven development has enabled some U.S. firms to sustain a considerable competitive advantage over their Japanese counterparts. Signode Corporation, for example, produces machines and materials for the mechanized "bundling" of various types of steel, bricks, lumber, and other bulk items. Signode's comparative advantage stems from its engineering expertise, the customized nature of its product (each "bundling" machine must be designed into the user's current production system), its production of both the metal strips used for bundling and the machines that do the bundling, its after-market operations, and its constant development of new applications for bundling. For all their mechanical skill, the Japanese have not been able to compete with Signode's custom-designed systems.

Signode faces little competition from the Japanese except for the sale of the steel-banding material. Even in this area, customers are discovering that the cheaper steel banding is unacceptably poor in quality. And since few companies make both banding machinery and banding metal, many banding strips on the market do not fit well with machines currently on the market. To maintain its competitive advantage, Signode needs to keep up its engineering skills and product development and carefully manage its Japanese joint venture.

Signode has licensed a Japanese steel company to manufacture the steel banding that it sells in Japan. In addition, Signode and another Japanese firm have begun to manufacture the bundling machines in Japan. Two points are of special interest. First, since customer contact is so essential to its product, Signode directly controls its distribution of banding machines and materials. Second, Signode has taken great pains to protect its technical expertise from potential competitors (including its joint-venture partner).

The lessons to be learned from the Signode case are significant. First, there are more market opportunities in Japan than popular mythology regarding Japan would suggest. Literature on the subject has stressed the extreme competence and resources of Japan's most successful international companies. Little has been said about the "other Japan," the undercapitalized, labor-intensive industries that MITI has not targeted. Even though protectionism will continue to pose certain constraints on the entry of American firms, the Japanese government has become increasingly flexible on the issue of protectionism if for no other reason than to avoid a counterattack on its successful export industries. In addition, Japanese firms are extremely anxious to improve their operations. Firms (such as Signode) that can show them how to do that are very welcome whatever their country of origin.

A successful operation in Japan can often serve as a springboard for entering Asian countries. Signode plans to undertake similar ventures in Taiwan, Malaysia, Mainland China, and South Korea. A second major point is that to protect its competitive advantage, a firm must manage its cooperative relationships carefully. A firm must draw a fine line between maintaining trust between partners and protecting the firm from future competition.

STEPS IN BECOMING MORE RESPONSIVE TO THE JAPANESE CHALLENGE

As shown in the above examples, U.S. corporations have used a mix of responses to cope with the Japanese challenge. As the decade of 1980 progresses, numerous signs point to an era of increasing Japanese threats to several more U.S. industries. To cope with this threat, counter-strategies at the level of cooperation, at either the public level or the private level, are not enough. The U.S. companies must learn to fight harder and smarter. There are some things that firms can do and must do immediately. There are other things that whole industries can do. The U.S. government can also contribute to industry's efforts to become more competitive. Here are several important steps that companies can take right away.

Step 1: Identify and Assess Competitive Advantage

U.S. firms must continually monitor and appraise structural change and competitive dynamics in those industries in which the new Competition is active. Japanese firms have caused major changes in the structure and competitive dynamics of almost all industries they have entered. The old ways of doing business will no longer generate success for U.S. firms.

Specifically, U.S. firms must determine what competitive advantages they possess in each line of business. They must also figure out how large these advantages are, the rate at which they are losing or gaining advantage, and what is required to sustain the advantages they possess and overcome their disadvantages. The attainment and maintenance of competitive advantage in the marketplace must become the overriding focus of U.S. firms' strategic efforts.

An Advantage-Time Plane is illustrated for a hypothetical firm. The figure shows current and estimated future competitive advantage for its two products, A and B. Note that the firm is losing its advantage in product A much faster than in product B. The firm's goal is to find ways to level out the slopes of the advantage lines or even make them slope upward from left to right. Otherwise, the firm will have to face shifting more of its resources into product B.

The Advantage-Time Plane

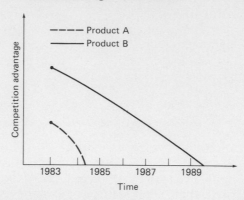

Step 2: Know All the Factors Affecting the Slope of the Firm's Advantage Line

Using the Advantage-Time Plane requires knowledge of the variables that affect the position and slope of the advantage line. These factors are both internal (e.g., the company's strategic response) and external. The external factors include the following:

- For Japan:
  —National portfolio management and targeting
  —Industry characteristics
  —Industrial groups
  —Company characteristics

- For the United States:
  —Government policy
  —The behavior of competitors
  —The behavior of other industries

The importance of other industries deserves clarification. In Japan, national portfolio management ensures that mature industries will help targeted industries grow quickly. The mature industries generate cash for investment and maintain high-employment levels so high-technology companies can automate. The high-technology firms contribute to mature industries in the area of process technology. Robotics and office automation, for instance, help mature industries reduce operating costs.

Industries also affect each other in other ways. As already noted, U.S. commercial banks and industrial suppliers are central to the success of both medium-technology and high-technology industries. The banks can help absorb risk and generate and circulate marketing intelligence.

They can agree to restructure overdue foreign loans (e.g., to Brazil), thereby enabling Brazil's highly subsidized steel industry to continue taking market share from U.S. steel manufacturers, which in turn eventually hurts American high-technology industries. Industrial suppliers are important in that they can help establish JIT production and TQC in the plants of their customers (e.g., John Deere & Co.).

Step 3: Know the Japanese Success Model

The next step is to understand Japan's success model thoroughly. American firms must realize that Japan's power stems from a combination of success factors related to Japan's sociocultural environment, government/business environment, competitive environment, and organizational environment. The U.S. managers must use this cognitive map to view the Japanese capabilities and weaknesses broadly.

Step 4: Realize the Breadth of the U.S. Firm's Options

The U.S. managers must keep the Strategic Response Matrix in mind and continually explore ideas and opportunities in each of the four cells. They must investigate ways of operating in different combinations of cells and moving through cells over time.

One very important point is that U.S. companies could try to influence Japan's choice of target industries. They could use market signaling to indicate their intention to maintain leadership in certain industries. By acting tough, by investing in the most modern plants and equipment, by maintaining or increasing product R&D, they signal their determination to retain global leadership in that industry. This may force the Japanese to reconsider their choice of that industry as a target industry.

Step 5: U.S. Companies Must Engage in Longer-Run Planning

The preference of U.S. stockholders for early returns on their investments acts as a constraint on the competitive capability of American corporations. Japanese companies, which are largely bank financed, do not have a similar constraint. Three things would enhance the ability of U.S. firms to take more risk and to persevere—in a word, *compete*. First, U.S. shareholders could change the performance measures from EPS, ROI, accrual-based net income, or stock prices to more appropriate indicators. Second, they could lengthen the time horizon they use in evaluating management. Quarterly earnings statements and even annual reports are simply too short term. And third, they could accept lower profits in the short run in the hope of gaining higher profits in the long run.

Step 6: Planning and Executing
Competitive Strategies

Knowing how to plan and execute competitive strategies is very important in competing against the Japanese. Unfortunately, many U.S. firms are not skilled in planning and implementing aggressive competitive action and thus allow the Japanese to aggressively penetrate their markets.

TYPES OF COMPETITIVE MARKETING
STRATEGIES

What are the competitive strategies available to U.S. and Western European firms to compete more effectively against the New Competition? We will discuss separately the strategic options available to smaller and larger firms.

Strategic Options for Small and Medium-
Sized U.S. Firms

Small and medium-sized U.S. firms find it hard to cope with the Japanese offensive. They have lower financial and marketing strength compared with their Japanese competitors. Therefore, their best counteroffensive is an indirect one. Their three best options are flank-position defense, flanking attacks, and guerrilla strategies.

Option 1: Flank-Position Defense. First, small and medium-sized American companies must correct any exposed flanks they have. They need to anticipate the corners that the Japanese might try to attack. The objective is to create a strong fortification in terms of the companies' current marketing mix policy that can withstand any possible attack by Japanese invasion.

As an example, a U.S. equipment manufacturer of a well-regarded medical diagnostic machine reasoned that the Japanese, should they attack, would make their machine smaller, cheaper, and with self-diagnostic capability. This led the U.S. company to work on a lower priced, more compact model, even though it would potentially cannibalize some of its larger machines sales.

At the same time, U.S. companies must analyze the attacker's potential weakness in manufacturing, finance, product line, pricing, distribution, promotion, and so forth, looking for a possible counterattack strategy. By preparing to counterattack at a point of the opponent's weakness, the firm has a good chance of holding its ground and stopping the Japanese advance.

Option 2: Flanking Attack. A key strategy for small and medium-sized U.S. companies is to rely on a flanking or indirect attack. American companies need to carefully conduct an intensive analysis of the Japanese competitors' strengths and weaknesses in their product-markets and avoid directly challenging their strengths. Marketing research must be conducted to identify Japanese weaknesses in product, price, distribution and promotion. As suggested by Johansson and Nonaka, intensive marketing research must identify not only weaknesses but also possible maneuvers that would exploit these weaknesses through a surprise attack.

Small and medium-sized companies should search for market segments whose needs are not being met by larger competitors.

Kotler has suggested that the chosen market segments should have the following characteristics: (1) the segment is of sufficient size and has growth potential; (2) the segment is of negligible interest to the stronger competitors; (3) the firm has the required skills and resources to serve this particular segment; and (4) the firm can defend itself against an attacking major competitor through the customer goodwill it has built up.

Once specific market segments have been identified, U.S. companies must focus their resources on these segments to capture strong market shares. The U.S. companies should concentrate on developing and improving their product functions, quality, services, and distributions rather than on price cutting that could possibly lead to stronger retaliation from their opponents. In those industries currently dominated by the Japanese, their domination implies a dispersion of their resources over many segments and marketing mix lines. They cannot defend all segments and have great strength in every single marketing element. Thus opportunity gaps are available for smaller U.S. companies to wage flanking attacks against larger Japanese competitors.

Option 3: Guerrilla Strategy.   In market segments where the Japanese are strong and opportunity gaps are few, U.S. firms can apply a guerrilla strategy by launching short, intermittent attacks. Small U.S. firms might launch a barrage of short-term price cuts and promotional bursts in random corners of Japan's weaker market segments. The key to this strategy is surprise, keeping the opponent uncertain about where and when the next attack will occur.

   Although large companies can launch a sustained major attack to take share from the opponent, smaller firms need to play out a smaller, carefully sequenced strategy. This forestalls any massive retaliation from the opponent. After several of these "guerrilla" attacks, at an appropriate time, a strong marketing attack may be launched to win leadership in that segment as a base for further expansion.

Strategic Options for Large U.S. Firms

Large companies with ample financial resources are in the best position to prevent major inroads from the Japanese. In addition to the previous-mentioned strategies, a large company can consider the following additional strategies.

Option 4: Encirclement Strategy.   A large firm can consider launching multiple offensives on several corners of the market dominated by the Japanese. As the Japanese disperse their troops to defend their corners, weak spots are created which the opponent can attack in the future. The attacker moves out from its own market base and launches attacks in an "encircling" manner. An effective approach is to bracket the Japanese brand through product line stretching. An alternative is to launch several brands with different attributes to surround the Japanese product. Product proliferation can be achieved through different design, functions, features, styles, and even images. The goal is to encircle the Japanese market territory and gradually regain market leadership.

Option 5: Bypass Strategy.   If the Japanese already are very strong, the company might "bypass" them and attack easier markets in order to broaden its resource base. The company might diversify into unrelated products and/or new geographical markets either domestically or internationally. At the international level, U.S. firms in the past were unwilling to devote their marketing efforts to penetrate international markets. This reluctance opened up the opportunity for the Japanese to establish their current global shares. The U.S. firms should not make this mistake again. Economies of scale resulting from market expansion will help reduce production costs and will in turn sharpen the company's pricing competitive edge. There are considerable opportunities remaining in international markets. Japanese products in many developing countries are lower in quality than U.S. products. For example, Thai consumers regard U.S. refrigerators as being better than Japanese, but unfortunately they are more expensive. The U.S. firms should construe this as an opportunity to export their high-quality products at a more affordable price to fill this quality gap.

Large U.S. firms that want to compete with the Japanese must pursue multinational global marketing—not just exporting. They must establish joint ventures and wholly owned marketing and production subsidiaries. They must consider locating production in newly industrialized countries such as South Korea, Thailand, Singapore, and Taiwan, where labor is cheaper. Efforts must be made to establish strong international market shares.

Even in Japan's home market, U.S. firms have a chance to expand. In the past, many U.S. firms failed to penetrate this market and blamed Japan's protectionism for the failure. The failure of General Foods in Japan is a good example. General Foods tried to penetrate the Japanese market without doing sufficient marketing research.

Other companies have been successful in penetrating the Japanese marketplace. Warner-Lambert—which sells Schick safety razor blades—provides a good example. Through its marketing research, Warner-Lambert foresaw how difficult it would be to gain distribution in Japan's marketplace on its own. The company decided to form a partnership with K. Hattori & Company, which has its own well-established distribution system for Seiko watches. Warner-Lambert relies on its partner's strength to penetrate the market. The result is that its market share in Japan is 70 percent compared with the largest U.S. producer, Gillette, whose share in Japan is only 10 percent.

Undertaking a strong push into Japan's market will contribute considerable benefit in strategic terms. The U.S. companies not only gain more market share in a very large market but also undermine the Japanese concentrated efforts overseas, thus weakening their marketing strength in overseas markets. This will provide a good opportunity for U.S. companies to regain their market position in either the U.S. or overseas markets.

Option 6: Innovation. A firm facing the Japanese challenge must give major attention to innovation. An innovation strategy is the most likely to perpetuate market leadership. The firm should refuse to be content with the way things are and should constantly seek new-product ideas, customer services, innovative distribution, and cost-cutting methods. By continuously creating new customer values, the firm actively discourages competitors from further invasion.

Option 7: Buying Market Share. The large company can follow the Japanese strategy of producing a high-quality product and selling it at a low price, absorbing losses for awhile. This strategy is most effective when the U.S. firms also strive for low-cost leadership by making strong investments in process R&D. If the particular Japanese invaders are not financed enough to sustain losses, their penetration in the industry will be limited.

Option 8: Head-on Counterattack. If the U.S. company has greater resources than its Japanese competitors, it might choose to launch a head-on attack. It would match every dimension of Japan's marketing strategies, product for product, price for price, advertising for advertising, and so forth. In fact, it might set lower prices and spend more on promotion. The head-on competition against the Japanese might be conducted through cooperation among U.S. firms. This cooperation might occur at the level of product development, promotion, pricing, or distribution, depending on what is permitted by the U.S. antitrust law. Joint programs in product and process R&D are especially promising. This is now occuring in semiconductors and computers. At least two joint research groups have been established: Micro Electronics and Computer Technology Corporation (MCC) and Semiconductor Research Corporation (SRC). The purpose of SRC is to develop a leapfrog product in memory chips that would aggressively reassert U.S. leadership in this technology. Meanwhile, major projects being conducted by MCC are aimed at studying artificial intelligence, new computer design, computer-aided design (CAD), and computer-aided manufacturing (CAM) tools for the production of tomorrow's very large scale integrated chips. Through this type of cooperation, it is hoped that U.S. firms will find a way to combat Japan's government-subsidized offensives in every industry.

Joint cooperation is not limited only to U.S. companies. It can also occur between U.S. and Japanese companies. The recent tie-ups in joint ventures between Western and Japanese firms (GM and Toyota) represent a good example. Through this kind of cooperation, the

Japanese companies have to carry part of the competitive fight among themselves. Joint cooperation between the U.S. companies and companies in newly industrialized countries such as South Korea, Taiwan, and Singapore is also a good choice. American companies can provide these countries with technology in return for utilizing their cheap labor and lower-cost resources that will help strengthen American competitiveness in facing the Japanese challenge.

EXAMPLES OF EXCELLENT COMPETITIVE RESPONSES BY U.S. FIRMS

Although many U.S. companies have coped with Japanese challenges by relying on public or cooperative strategies, some U.S. companies have fought back on "true" competitive terms and have successfully regained their market positions or, at least, slowed down the Japanese advance into their market territories. We will examine the responses of Motorola, Black & Decker, Xerox, and IBM.

Motorola

Motorola, one of America's high-tech equipment companies, is one of the more successful examples of U.S. competitive actions in response to the Japanese challenge. Motorola has become renowned for its private-competitive advertising campaign featuring full-page ads on the theme "Meeting Japan's Challenge." It has concentrated on product-markets in which it has a decisive technological lead (e.g., mobile pagers). It has improved its product quality in some cases to less than fifty defects per million units produced. And it has changed its management style through its Participative Management Program. This process has apparently achieved employee loyalty to a degree unusual in America.

 Motorola has also operated aggressively in the public-competitive cell. Through its publicity about the Japanese challenge and its congressional testimony, it has become a spokesperson for many American industries. Motorola has repeatedly urged the U.S. government to put pressure on the Japanese to adopt free-market principles. It has also argued for countervailing penalties against certain Japanese firms and for relief to U.S. companies hurt by these firms.

Motorola is also pursuing private-cooperative activities where feasible. The firm had operated a joint venture for distribution of its mobile pagers in Japan, but it now owns the venture fully. Motorola's strategy primarily is to operate in the two competitive cells until it can eliminate or at least reduce the need for its role in the public-competitive cell.

Black & Decker

Black & Decker, the U.S. machine tool company, provides a good example of adapting responsive strategies from defensive to head-on competition against Japanese challenges. During the past decade, Black & Decker enjoyed high success in the machine and power tool market in the United States and worldwide until the Japanese started invading this industry. Led by Makita Electric Works, the Japanese tool companies entered the world market by carefully identifying a high-growth market niche—the professional power tools market—which was not the main market of Black & Decker's business. The Japanese then filled this niche with new or improved power tools and charged a lower price to out-market Black & Decker. Although power tools represent only a minor portion of Black & Decker's business, they are strategically important because they have been the most profitable part of the company's business. Unlike other U.S. companies that are slow in responding to the Japanese threats, Black & Decker reacted fast because it feared that the Japanese toehold in this market niche might foreshadow an invasion into other segments. Accordingly, the company made its first response by undertaking a flank-position defense strategy to close all possible weaknesses. It has gone to great lengths to identify consumer needs through marketing research and market testing. Through these market studies, it has closed all possible vulnerable gaps of its product and improved its products' performance. Once all of its vulnerable gaps had been closed, the company moved from a flank-position defense to a head-on competitive response. The Japanese products were dissected, scrutinized, and duplicated to unravel the secrets of Japanese cost advantage and quality. Black & Decker cut its prices to match Japanese prices. It modernized its plants by introducing robots in the manufacturing lines in order to increase productivity. In the past few years, the company spent more than $250 million on these tasks. Through these competitive responses, Black & Decker slowed down Japanese advances and captured market leadership in virtually every market segment in the machine tool industry.

Xerox Company

Xerox Company is another good model of how a U.S. company launches a head-on counterattack against the Japanese challenges. Since the Japanese started invading the small copy market in the past decade by offering smaller, less-expensive machines, Xerox's market shares and profitability have been eroding. Its market share of the U.S. plain-paper copies market declined from 67 percent in 1976 to only 42 percent in the late 1970s. Xerox realized that the main competitiveness of Japanese products was cost advantage. Thus it began pursuing all the strategies expected to help reduce its products' costs.

In order to cut the cost of making its products, which in some cases ran 30 to 40 percent more than comparable Japanese copiers, Xerox copied several techniques from the Japanese. It adopted the famous Japanese quality circle in its management and production. It increased assembly-line automation and adopted less-labor-intensive product designs, with the aim of reducing costs and increasing productivity. Xerox also started changing its view of profitability by forgoing short-term results in favor of long-run profitability and market-share expansion. For example, Xerox slashed prices on many of its models in order to recapture market shares. To meet the Japanese head on, it also offered more new lines of copiers as a means of encircling Japanese products. It has strengthened its distribution networks by adding additional market channels to reach the small-business customers that are the main target of the Japanese. It has increased its investment, research, and development, since technology will ultimately determine who wins. It has spent about $600 million on R&D since the early 1980s. It executes this head-on attack not only on the Japanese in the U.S. but also on the Japanese home market. Xerox has strengthened its subsidiary in Japan—Fuji Xerox, which is a joint venture with Japanese Fuji Photo Film—in order to compete against other Japanese makers on their home front. Although the results will not be realized in the short-term period, Xerox has already made its choice to compete against the Japanese in every market segment in this industry to regain its market leadership.

IBM

IBM, the world's largest computer maker, has in the past several years shown its determination to stop the Japanese advance into the U.S. market. IBM has launched several strong counteractions to block or slow down Japanese penetration. These counteractions range from direct attack through product and pricing strategies to a joint coordination with other U.S. makers to fight the Japanese challenge.

IBM's product development strategies seem to be the most effective and the most feared by the Japanese. IBM realized that the Japanese depend on IBM's product specifications and software so that they can be IBM compatible. To thwart Japanese imitation and exploitation of IBM's technology, IBM has emphasized a quicker introduction of new-generation, higher-performance IBM systems to obsolete the old models copied by the Japanese. The Japanese find it increasingly difficult, expensive, and time consuming to keep up with the continuous flow of new IBM product developments. In the early 1980s, as Fujitsu introduced its M328, which is compatible with the IBM 370 and 3081 systems, IBM counterattacked by introducing its new 3081-K system only five months later and then announced that it would introduce new software packages that would not only substantially enhance its 3081-K system's performance but also would not be compatible with Fujitsu's system.

In addition, IBM began seriously attacking head-on the growing small-computer markets, especially the personal computer segment, which otherwise the Japanese would probably have taken over. In 1983, IBM shipped personal computers at the rate of more than twenty thousand machines per month. It has also been willing to compete against the Japanese on a price basis by launching several major price reductions in recent years. It responded to the Japanese low-priced plug-compatible computers by introducing its 4300 series of computers at prices so low that Japanese competitors could barely beat them.

In addition, IBM has reorganized its manufacturing operations to bring down its costs so that it didn't suffer a disadvantage in relation to Japanese manufacturing costs. It has also resorted to some unconventional attacks. IBM brought two Japanese producers (Hitachi and Mitsubishi) to court for their attempted piracy of confidential IBM data plans in 1982. This seriously hurt the Japanese reputation and image in the business and the public eye.

IBM is now seriously considering coordinating with other U.S. firms to strengthen the U.S. technological and market positions in the high-technology areas. IBM's announcement that it would line up with Intel Corp., the leading U.S. chip maker and major supplier to IBM, is a good example. IBM's linkup with Intel will strengthen its production line through vertical integration. A close relationship with Intel not only assures IBM of semiconductor supplies but also gives IBM access to advanced semiconductor technology. IBM also plans to strengthen its relationship with other leading U.S. chip makers such as Texas Instruments, Inc., hoping to develop high-performance chips designed to enhance IBM's computer capability. These cooperative moves reflect the abandoning of self-centered policy making in favor of close cooperation. They mark the emergence of a new strategy for meeting the Japanese challenge in this high-technology industry.

SUMMARY

The U.S. firms have four options for defense and counterattack. They can invite government protection and pressure on the foreign competitors; they can encourage the U.S. government to seek cooperative joint efforts that would benefit both U.S. and foreign firms; they can forge beneficial private cooperative arrangements with certain foreign firms; and they can restructure their private competitive strategy to compete more effectively against the rising New Competition. Most U.S. firms use a mix of these response strategies, with their emphasis changing over time.

The U.S. firms can strengthen their ability to compete by undertaking six steps. They should measure and forecast their comparative advantage; monitor the major factors affecting their current and future comparative advantage; know the Japanese success model; consider the whole range of strategy options; plan more for the long run; and develop and execute more competitively effective strategies.

The best strategy sequence for small and medium-sized firms to consider is a flank-position defense followed by a flanking attack or guerrilla strategy. The best strategies for large firms to consider in containing or offsetting the Japanese are encirclement, bypass, innovation, buying market share, and head-on counterattacks. Firms that wish to counterattack should study the steps being taken by Motorola, Black & Decker, Xerox, and IBM.

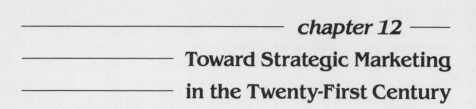

chapter 12

Toward Strategic Marketing in the Twenty-First Century

As we noted earlier, the Japanese have not invented any strikingly new concepts. Nor have they created new ways of doing business. And, until recently, they did not even invent new products. Indeed, the Japanese have simply put into practice what U.S. management has preached for years but did not widely practice.

This chapter highlights the most pivotal and pertinent strategy lessons that can be derived from an understanding of the strategies employed by the Japanese in the U.S. marketplace. For convenience, we divide the discussion into three segments: (1) understanding strategy, (2) creating and sustaining a strategic organization, and (3) managing strategy analysis. It will be evident from our discussion that these three elements of strategizing are closely interrelated. In fact, this interrelationship has become painfully evident to many U.S. firms as they have begun to respond to the Japanese onslaught.

UNDERSTANDING STRATEGY

Companies Must Manage Strategy and Operations.

The strategic management of an enterprise can be boiled down to two conceptually separate, though in practice highly interrelated, activities:

244

managing strategy and managing operations. From a marketing perspective, we can define *strategy* as the way a firm seeks to compete in its chosen product-markets to achieve some specified goals and *operations* as the execution of the tasks and activities necessary to carry out the strategy. Both strategy and operations are essential ingredients of strategic management. Neither alone is sufficient for long-term organizational success. However, most will agree that an appropriate strategy is more crucial to long-run economic performance than operations. Well-executed operations are not likely to overcome or compensate for a badly designed strategy. The discussion in this concluding chapter will be largely devoted to strategy, though most of the points made apply equally well to operations.

While both strategy and operations are necessary for successful strategic management, it is important to understand the distinctions between them. The differences in focus, scope, and mentality inherent in the distinctions are as much differences in kind as they are in degree. For example, *effectiveness* is typically viewed as how well the organization is co-aligned with its environment, that is, does the strategy fit the environment? And *efficiency* is viewed as how well the organization is managing its resources given its strategy, that is, is the organization achieving optimal performance?

Even a cursory review of the competition between U.S. and Japanese firms over the past thirty years suggests that strategic management must confront two strong driving forces: (1) the organization needs to manage today's business for results today and tomorrow, and (2) the organization needs to lay the groundwork today for its business tomorrow. Any firm must therefore fight today's competitive battles at the same time that it is preparing for the battles of tomorrow. Unless the seeds of future successes are sown today, success in the current and imminent battles may prove to be Pyrrhic victories—the battles are won, but the war is lost.

The ultimate strategic challenge is to manage successfully these opposing driving forces or organizational inclinations. Too often, it is

STRATEGIC MANAGEMENT: MANAGING STRATEGY AND OPERATIONS

STRATEGY	OPERATIONS
External focus: Setting direction	Internal focus: Attaining direction
Effectiveness	Efficiency
Doing the "right" thing	Doing things "right"
Designing the plan	Executing the plan
Commits resources	Uses resources

easier to exploit today's opportunities than it is to prepare for the uncertainties of tomorrow. This is the essence of much of our criticism of the U.S. firms' response to the Japanese invasion during the 1950s, the 1960s, and even the early 1970s: They milked the product-markets they had painfully established and committed very few resources to fending off the Japanese. To do so would have meant giving up some profits to earn or preserve future profits. This is perhaps the fundamental dilemma and challenge confronting U.S. companies as they combat the New Competition. Clearly, unless U.S. firms commit to managing strategy for the long term rather than to business operations for the short term, their chances of winning against the New Competition are slim.

Strategy Is a Choice Process That Begins in the Strategist's Mind.

In business parlance, few words are so abused as the word *strategy*. The definitions and conceptions of strategy seem endless. At a very general level, most academics, consultants, and practitioners would define *strategy* as some set of intended actions to achieve specified goals. As previously noted, our emphasis is on the choice of product-markets and modes of competition as the primary "actions" to achieve desired goals.

Implicit in this broad definition is conscious choice: The strategist chooses the actions and the goals. This choice process ultimately takes place in the strategist's mind. Strategic plans reflect but often do not reveal the choice process. Strategy therefore emanates from and resides in the strategist's mind. It is the decision maker's consciousness of the choice of decision options, their implications, and the issues surrounding these options or implications that is paramount. The aforementioned dilemma and challenge are thus ultimately resolved in the strategist's mind.

The Goal of Strategy Is to Create and Sustain Competitive Advantage.

A strategy that remains in the strategist's mind cannot succeed. It must be implemented. The heart of strategy in the military theater is to outmaneuver and defeat the enemy. On the battleground of the competitive marketplace, the only way that one business firm can outmaneuver and defeat another is to create and sustain competitive advantages—i.e., ways in which one firm favorably distinguishes itself or its products in the eyes of its customers. Unless sustainable competitive advantages are established, strategic planning, competitive intelligence, and resource generation will be for naught.

All the Japanese strategies discussed previously are heavily weighted on the belief that they must distinguish themselves in the eyes of the customer—the customer must be given reasons to discriminate in their favor. This has become especially true as the Japanese have gained in marketing sophistication. Quality, functionality, service, image, and pricing have each been used by many Japanese firms to compete against U.S. firms to make themselves more appealing to customers. Even in the 1950s and early 1960s when many Japanese firms in large measure "imitated" U.S. products, they did not simply sell the same products: They differentiated and improved on the products in numerous ways. Stated simply, U.S. firms must dedicate themselves to creating and sustaining competitive advantages in the world marketplace if they are to hold the New Competition at bay.

Competitive Advantages Are the Product of Entrepreneurial Thinking.

Generating and sustaining competitive advantages is an entrepreneurial activity. It usually requires seeing things differently and being willing to live with risks. Pursuing competitive advantage inherently involves relinquishing the status quo: introducing new products, modifying existing products, altering the conception of the product in the customer's mind, changing the modes of competition, pursuing new customers, and so forth. These efforts to change competitive dynamics reflect some degree of "entrepreneurial content." Stated differently, if a strategy is not predicated on some degree of entrepreneurial content, it is merely a replication or imitation of competitors' strategies. Such a strategy may result in winning some battles, but they are likely to be Pyrrhic victories. The war will be won by the firms whose strategies manifest an entrepreneurial element.

Competitive Advantages May Be More Than Distinctive Competences.

For strategy to result in superior economic performance, its entrepreneurial content must be of value to the firm's customers. Otherwise the firm has misfocused its entrepreneurial activity. It may have created distinctive competences that have not been translated into competitive advantages. This misdirection of the firm's efforts can only result in failure if it is not corrected. This is the core of much of our criticism of U.S. firms' responses to the New Competition.

By *distinctive competence* we simply mean the ability of a firm to do something better than its competitors. Distinctive competences include the ability to carry out innovative ideas (the capacity to introduce new products or product modifications); superior production skill (the ability to produce high-quality products and/or to produce products at the lowest cost); exceptional marketing (the ability to manage an effective sales force or to create advertising); effective management of R&D; and superior financial management skills and/or the development of superior management expertise.

However, distinctive competences do not always translate into competitive advantages. One principle is clear: As the product-markets or territory at the heart of strategic or marketing warfare changes over time, each firm must assess whether it can create and sustain the distinctive competences necessary to support and sustain the competitive advantages required to succeed in the heat of the battlefield. U.S. firms must "go back to basics." They must stringently assess what it is that they do well, or potentially do well, and that could be transformed into competitive advantages as they tackle the New Competition.

Effective Strategies Are Conditional on Firm and Market Factors.

Implicit in the discussion of distinctive competences and competitive advantages is that effective strategy is conditional: The appropriate strategy depends on the conditions facing the firm (i.e., markets, competitors, and the broader environment) *and* the conditions within the firm (i.e., its resources, capabilities, etc.). Just as the enemy's movement may require a change in the aggressor's or the defender's position, a firm's strategy must also be adapted to the conditions or circumstances relating to it. As these change, it is likely that the firm's strategy will need to change.

The conditional nature of strategy is amply illustrated in our discussion of Japanese marketing strategy. Their entry, penetration, and maintenance strategies reflect their position in the market, the responses of competitors, and their own resource base. Also, these strategies are significantly different at different time periods. For instance, the market-entry strategies of Japanese firms in the late 1970s and 1980s became frontal and bypass attacks much more quickly than they did in the 1950s and 1960s. Thus, as market, industry, environment, and organizational conditions change, U.S. firms have little option but to devise new strategies. For most U.S. firms, the strategies that won in the 1950s, 60s, and 70s will not bear fruit in the late 1980s.

Strategic Choice Is Limited to Manageable Factors.

That strategy is conditional suggests that the choices confronting an organization are not unlimited. The strategist or organization cannot arbitrarily impose its will on the environment. In fact, the contrary is the case: Much in the organization's environment must be taken "as given." These *givens* are factors outside the control of the organization: governmental policy, economic conditions, industry growth, competitors' behavior, technological developments, and so forth. The strategist or organization enacts its choices within these constraints imposed by its environment.

The implication here is that U.S. firms must carefully identify those things that are completely or partially under their control and assess the extent to which they can be managed to effect and sustain competitive advantages against the New Competition. It is particularly noteworthy how the Japanese have so frequently "managed" factors only partially under their control. Distribution channels provide a good illustration. Their effective use of U.S.-owned distribution channels provided many Japanese firms with a competitive edge, especially in their early efforts to develop a position in the U.S. marketplace.

The Firms' Goals Constrain and Direct Strategic Choice.

A comparison of the strategies of U.S. and Japanese firms in many business sectors over the past thirty years clearly demonstrates that not only are firms' strategic choices constrained by their environment but firms also constrain their choices by the goals they seek to achieve. As has long been recognized in the business strategy and marketing literatures, strategy, goals, and performance are highly interdependent.

Japanese strategic behavior in many U.S. and world markets suggests the following goals: build market share over a long time period, disregard profits as market share is being obtained and when a significant market position is finally established, then take U.S. and other foreign competitors head-on in their principal product-markets. The aim is to build market position and then worry about profitability. These goals allow the Japanese to engage in the kinds of strategic behavior described in this book: continued and gradual product and market development, a transition from imitators to leaders, initial aggressive pricing to penetrate and develop market position, followed by premium pricing. Their strategy is consistent with their goals.

The strategies of U.S. firms are also consistent with their goals. But their goals are very different from those of Japanese firms. The goals of U.S. firms center on financial targets: maintaining profitability levels, surpassing internal threshold or investment hurdle rates. Enhancing financial returns is the name of the game. Product-market development takes a decided back seat to financial returns. This is the core of the paper entrepreneurialism for which U.S. firms have been so roundly criticized.

The implication here is that U.S. firms constrain their strategy options by the goals they choose to follow. The commitment to short-run profitability precludes the thrust of the strategy pursued by so many Japanese firms, that is, long-run product-market development. Simply stated, if you seek a two-year pay-back period, it is difficult to go to battle with competitors who largely disregard short-run financial returns. U.S. firms may have little choice but to adopt goal structures more similar to the New Competition if they wish to go head-to-head with leading firms in the New Competition.

Market Structure Does Not Dictate Strategy.

Since the strategic behavior of the Japanese has often surprised U.S. firms, it should teach us to beware of conventional wisdom, rules of thumb, and accepted strategic dogma. One such "truth," which has been largely propagated by the economics profession, though frequently embraced by business strategy and marketing exponents, is the "structure-conduct-performance" paradigm: The structure of an industry (or market) largely determines the conduct or performance (i.e., market share, profitability).

As with any piece of conventional wisdom, there is a substantial element of truth in the structure-conduct-performance paradigm. The structure of an industry does influence the strategic behavior and performance of firms within it. The danger arises when we *presume* that a given market structure leads to particular kinds of strategic behavior; for example, firms in an oligopoly can only behave in certain ways. This is much too deterministic. Firms do have some strategic discretion. They can change their strategies. They can and do change the goals they wish to pursue. Japanese and U.S. firms have changed their strategies within given market structures. Witness the response of many U.S. firms to the Japanese threat in the past decade.

Latent Competitors Can Hurt More Than Manifest Competitors.

Strategy presumably is never designed in the abstract. It is intended to win customers. To do so, the strategy must entail competitive advantages; it must be superior to that of the competitors. But which competitors? The dominant competitors currently in the market? The minor or peripheral competitors? Or those not now in the market—potential competitors?

The history of the Japanese infiltration of the U.S. marketplace suggests that very often, in the interest of longer-term strategic success, it is the latent (i.e., potential and emerging) rather than the manifest (i.e., strong and current) competitors that should be the focus of competitive attention. The strategic compass of U.S. firms paid scant attention to early Japanese entrants; they simply were not seen as a threat. The U.S. firms were preoccupied with each other; they were then the major players in these industries.

However, latent competitors can also hurt you in the short run. New entrants often dramatically and quickly reshape competitive conditions in specific market segments. Such has been the result of many Japanese entries in the late 1970s and early 1980s.

The moral here is that adopting a strategic focus that addresses only the presently dominant firms is not likely to lead to long-run success. Ideally, U.S. firms must position themselves not just against current competitors but with an equally vigilant eye on emerging and potential competitors. The unavoidable trade-offs involved in positioning a firm vis-à-vis latent and manifest competitors (e.g., giving up some of today's profits to establish entry barriers against likely entrants) are a central component of the strategic dilemmas noted earlier.

Customers, Not Competitors, Determine Who Wins the War.

In military warfare, the combatants determine who wins and loses. There is not a third party acting as arbitrator or ultimate judge. There is no corollary for the role of the customer. The customer chooses among the offerings of the contestants in the competitive arena. Thus, strategies that are competitor focused to the exclusion of a customer focus may miss the ultimate target. This will be especially likely if the competitors have misconstrued the customers. A preoccupation with competitors also means that you are much more likely to be a follower than a leader in the competitive struggle.

The Japanese have clearly distinguished themselves by their attention to customers. Much of their strategic behavior reflects the Japanese as devoted adherents to identifying and satisfying customer needs. Their early efforts in entering and penetrating the U.S. marketplace are frequently built on painstakingly detailed market and customer analysis. Although these efforts were often frightfully naive, improperly focused, and poorly directed, the Japanese persisted in studying and learning about their potential customers. Furthermore, their incrementalist approach to product improvement and market development is predicated on close attention to the customer's needs and behaviors. In short, strategies designed by U.S. firms to outwit the New Competition must not forget that the customer is the object of the exercise. Competitive advantage must ultimately reside in the customer's eyes.

Continuous Incremental Changes Can Beat Occasional Revolutionary Changes.

Small changes in military combat have frequently made a substantial difference in battle outcomes. Likewise, small changes in strategy or adaptations to the environmental constraints and conditions confronting the firm may substantially affect economic performance. This is all the more likely if these adaptations are continuous: Incremental changes may cumulatively add to revolutionary change. Moreover, continuous incremental strategic change may outdo revolutionary change because a series of lesser initiatives involving less risk may outperform over the long run a strategy predicated on a single revolutionary or major initiative or change. The largely incremental nature of much of the change in Japanese product and market development strategies is testimony to the benefits of continuous strategic incremental change. U.S. firms need to pay just as much attention to continually improving the "little things" as they do to doing the "big things" right.

Strategy Timing Is as Important as Strategy Choice.

Strategy involves firms seeking to acquire and sustain competitive advantage(s) over each other. In the ebb and flow of the battlefield, firms unavoidably find themselves launching attacks on the positions of competitors or defending themselves from competitors' onslaughts. Thus, at any point in time, in any business or product-market segment, a firm is inevitably engaged in either an offensive or a defensive thrust.

Choosing the right offensive or defensive posture lies at the heart of strategy choice and strategic success. However, as the Japanese have so aptly illustrated, different offensive or defensive postures are appropriate for different competitive, environmental, and market conditions—strategy, as noted above, is conditional. There are major distinctions among the offensive and defensive strategy options in terms of the relevant conditions.

The conditional nature of offensive and defensive thrusts suggests the importance of timing in the context of strategy. A strategy must not only be appropriate for the market, competitive, and environmental conditions facing the firm, it must also be timed for maximum effect. As in the military theater, a frontal assault should be timed to catch the competitor off guard or when the competitor is least able to respond. A bypass attack when launched after a competitor has committed itself to its own strategy (e.g., built the plant, entered into contracts with distribution channels, etc.) may hurt the competitor more than if such commitments had not been made. Defensive moves should also be timed to most hurt competitors. A mobile defense may have to be initiated quickly if competitors are to be discouraged from further aggressive moves.

Successful Strategies Change the Rules of the Game.

Successful strategic thrusts almost always result in changing the rules of the competitive game. Such strategic thrusts imply that strategic initiative has been effected: Leadership in some segment of the market has been captured or extended. Strategic initiatives involve new ways of winning the war. They change the "success factors" in the competitive arena, that is, what other firms must now do to catch up with and overtake the initiator. Playing the game by the old rules means that you are destined to lose.

Japanese firms have significantly changed "the rules of the game" in every major industry segment they have entered since World War II. The invasion of the U.S. automobile marketplace is, in effect, an account of how the Japanese auto firms have altered the rules of the game for U.S. auto manufacturers. The gradual progression through flanking and frontal attacks followed by encirclement and bypass attacks changes the rules of the game in an industry broadly defined.

Significantly, the Japanese do not rest on their laurels once they have effected strategic initiatives. Their market maintenance strategies are predicated on the need for further strategic initiatives. Their dominant presumption is that nothing stands still; the competition is always in pursuit. Thus, the rules of the game must continually be changed. U.S. firms must ask how they can change the rules of the game to their advantage and, once they do, they must ask the question again and again.

Commitment, Flexibility, and Creativity: The Keys
to Successful Strategy.

Commitment embodies the "will to win," the indomitable spirit that separates winners from losers in all spheres of life. Without it, competitive setbacks become impenetrable roadblocks; with it, setbacks provide the motivation to go back to the drawing board to design better products, to market them more effectively—in short, to outperform the competition. Few will question the commitment of the Japanese to succeeding in the world marketplace over the past thirty years. It has been their invisible hallmark.

Flexibility has been the visible trademark of the Japanese. They have not engraved their strategies in stone. They have not become so committed to a specific strategy that they have been blinded by it. Rather, they have remained committed to broad strategic thrusts, and they have demonstrated tremendous flexibility in pursuing these thrusts. This is reflected in both their incremental behaviors and their revolutionary outbursts. They have continually adapted to the market and competitive environment and their evolving position within it.

Creativity has increasingly become a feature of Japanese strategy. Indeed, without creativity, strategic entrepreneurship is difficult, if not impossible. Strategic initiatives, competitive advantages, and distinctive competences must be created. Moreover, as market, competitive, and environmental conditions change, these initiatives, advantages, and competences must be challenged and reshaped—in short, recreated. Movement through a sequence of offensive and defensive postures will most likely necessitate the creation of a sequence of initiatives, advantages, and competences. It is the capacity to be creative that separates the continually successful firms from the occasionally successful.

In summary, managing the strategic behavior of an enterprise must be premised on three attributes: commitment, flexibility, and creativity. All three are necessary if U.S. firms are to continually invigorate their strategies with entrepreneurial content, whether it be in incremental or revolutionary chunks. All three lead to concerns about building strategic organizations.

CREATING AND SUSTAINING
A STRATEGIC ORGANIZATION

Strategic management does not come easily or naturally to organizations. The forces inhibiting successful strategic management are pervasive, strong, and deeply entrenched in organizations. A prerequisite to effective strategic management is therefore the recognition that the organization must manage itself to achieve strategic success, to effect a balance between strategy and operations, to manage the present and the future.

The charge that an organization must manage itself from a strategic management perspective means that it must continuously assess the relevance of its values, beliefs, and goals, how it thinks, how its members interact, what kind of leadership is provided by top management, and how it is structured. In short, the strategic organization is above all self-reflective; it is willing to critique and challenge itself.

The Major Cause of Strategy Failure Is Strategy Success.

Few things contribute so much to firms being "outmaneuvered" by competitors as their adherence to outmoded and self-serving beliefs. The specter of large U.S. firms belittling and disregarding the offerings of Japanese entrants as "inferior," "too small," or "striving after nonexisting market segments" strikes a far-too-familiar theme in too many firms, even today. All too frequently many firms believe that what won their market position yesterday will sustain it today—they do not need new distinctive competences or competitive advantages. If challenged, they may deny such beliefs, but their actions belie them. At the root of the malaise is that organizational success is a major (if not the major) cause of strategic failure. Success does indeed breed complacency. It also sustains inertia. Not only does success make the firm a competitive target, it also blinds the firm to the approach of the enemy. For many U.S. firms, it appears that this malaise was so gripping that the enemy (i.e., the Japanese) had not only firmly established beachheads but captured sizable chunks of their territory before they saw fit to mount a significant response. It is precisely when U.S. firms are successful that they must be vigilant in developing the next round of strategy, in effecting the next change in the rules of the game.

Organizations Need to Build a Strategic Culture.

The notion that strategy success leads to failure is a product of the culture prevailing in the organization. By *culture* we mean the values, beliefs, aspirations (i.e., how individuals think and what they think is important), and behavioral norms (i.e., how things get done). Organizational culture must be oriented to strategic behavior, that is, to fashioning distinctive competences that facilitate attaining competitive advantage(s) and to focusing on offensive and defensive strategies that will secure and retain strategic (competitive) initiative. Thus the ultimate test of an organization's culture is the organization's capacity in the marketplace: This is what determines whether it is a "strategic" culture. Stated differently, organizations with strategic cultures are likely to win the lengthy wars that are fought in the competitive battlefield.

By *strategic culture* we do not just mean "superordinate values and goals." We also intend it to encapsulate how the organization thinks: the elements in the mind-set of the organization such as what beliefs drive management's thinking, what criteria (values) are used in day-to-day decision making, what management considers important, and what risks are deemed acceptable and strongly shape the strategy options considered and the choices made.

It is in this context that the strategic mentality of Japanese firms plays such an important role in explaining their strategic behavior. What they do in the marketplace reflects the mind-set within their organizations. The incremental and emergent nature of much of their strategic behavior reflects a belief that success in the marketplace is not won overnight. It is an accumulation of minor victories, winning a long series of local wars. Continual product and market development emanates from a belief that the competitive arena is ever shifting; competitors and customers do not stand still. Commitment to these types of strategic behavior in the absence of short-run profitability will be possible for U.S. organizations when they actually believe that the long run is more important than the short run.

Strategic Cultures Are Created by Strategic Leaders.

Strategic cultures just don't happen. They are created by senior management committed to making their organization be strategic. Cultural change is a slow and tedious process. Avoiding the success that leads to failure trap requires an ever-alert management, one that is committed to challenging the "conventional wisdom" long upheld in the organization and the norms of doing business propagated by consultants, academics, industry experts, and—for that matter—almost anybody who is asked. On top of that, creating and sustaining competitive advantages can only result from a commitment to entrepreneurship, which necessarily entails doing things differently and taking risks. These kinds of commitment can only occur if there is genuine strategic leadership in the organization, that is, the senior management team in the organization is willing to make decisions in the (long-term) strategic interest of the organization rather than its (short-term) operating interest.

In brief, strategic leadership reflects a number of characteristics: a commitment to effectiveness and not just efficiency; a willingness to take risks and practice entrepreneurship; actions to put in place a strategic organization; and a mind-set that relentlessly challenges others to think strategically. These attributes typify many Japanese organizations. Without these attributes, it is difficult to visualize a top-management team exerting strategic leadership within their organization. Implicit in these observations is that in the absence of strategic leadership within U.S. organizations, strategic success cannot be gained or sustained in the marketplace. Strategic leadership includes building the requisite organization to create and implement successful strategies.

Firms Need to Form Strategy Circles.

The structuring of organizations in Western management thought tends to emphasize "formalism," that is, hierarchical and reporting relationships. However, in Japanese firms, by contrast, informal relations are viewed as much more important. Quality circles are perhaps the best known of their largely informal structural mechanisms designed to get organizational members to work together on identifying and solving problems. It strikes us that the organizational technology inherent in quality circles in the form of strategy circles could very well be adapted to getting organizational members to work together on strategy-related issues.

Strategy circles essentially represent the need to go beyond conventional conceptions of formal organizational structuring to infuse strategic thinking into organizations, to get organizational members to talk to each other in and around strategy problems and opportunities. This would circumvent the existing *formal* structure so dominant in so many U.S. firms in which individuals and subunits—R&D, marketing, manufacturing, and even divisions or SBUs—frequently pursue their own interests at the expense of the overall organization.

Structure Needs to Coevolve with Strategy.

From an examination of the strategies of Japanese firms in the U.S. marketplace and the responses of U.S. firms, it is clear that how organizations are structured (i.e., their formal structuring) does make a strategic difference. The peculiar structure of the large Japanese firms greatly facilitates their worldwide strategies. Their internal structuring facilitates strategy formulation and execution.

Two points are especially worthy of emphasis. First, the Japanese have adapted their organizational structures as their firms have grown in size, as they have added new products, and as they have penetrated foreign markets. As with so many U.S. firms, these structural adjustments were frequently not smooth experiences, and yet the Japanese do not seem to wait for a crisis to effect such structural change. The lesson here is that structure needs to coevolve with strategic change; otherwise strategy execution will suffer.

Second, structure is also related to strategy creation. Their macro- and micro-organizational structures allowed Japanese firms to devise sound strategies that might otherwise have proved difficult, if not impossible. Strategies therefore can and do follow structure. The adage, so central to much of the strategic management literature, that structure follows strategy may be only half right.

In summary, creating a strategic organization is difficult. Sustaining a strategic organization is even more difficult. However, it is also evident that the formal elements of organization structuring alone do not give rise to a strategically oriented organization; they are helpful but not sufficient. The command structure and deployment of troops on the ground do not tell how well the army is led and how inspired and committed it is to the fight. Similarly, a business organization's structure provides only the engine or cogs in the machine; it is the organization's culture, thinking, and leadership that provide the grease and lubrication to propel the machine forward in a strategic direction.

MANAGING STRATEGY ANALYSIS

The strategies pursued by an organization are strongly influenced by the nature, intent, and types of strategy relevant analysis conducted by the organization. Such analysis can range from explicit, systematic, and comprehensive strategic planning systems to implicit and intuitive reasoning that is never put on paper or subjected to critical appraisal. Such analysis can also reflect the strategic thinking and critical self-reflection inherent in a strategic organization or, at the other extreme, it may be nothing more than the simple assertion that the future will be similar to the past. Analysis that creates insight and understanding leading to real organizational learning is a product of managerial attention—it must be managed.

The Purpose of Strategy Analysis Is Insight, Not Numbers.

The academic and popular business press has been inundated with decision aids, techniques, and analytical models to help decision makers perform the necessary analysis to formulate, implement, and monitor strategy. Strategic-planning models, industry analysis techniques, and decision evaluation tools are relentlessly promulgated by academics, consulting firms, and even practitioners. Yet what is often forgotten is that these aids, techniques, and models are double-edged swords: They can and do generate strategic insights, but they also lead to a narrowing of the scope of our sight or vision. Any decision tool or model, by definition, can address only some segment or aspect of reality. The trap here is that we all too often misconstrue the analytical simplicity and stability of these strategy tools for a complex and dynamic reality.

A much more devastating sin than the blinkers inherent in strategy analysis tools is that strategy analysis (with or without formal analysis aids) can so easily become reflexive rather than reflective. The analysis degenerates into a routine. It becomes simply a process of completing the required documentation. The goal of doing analysis is to get the boss or the corporate headquarters or the strategic-planning department "off our backs."

A pervasive manifestation of this type of reflexiveness in many U.S. firms is preoccupation with "the numbers." Our analytical techniques (increasingly facilitated and augmented by a burgeoning computer technology) quantify innumerable facets of strategy relevant analysis, financial pro formas, cash flow projections, market trends and shares, competitive behaviors, demographic shifts, economic forecasts, and so forth. The temptation is to concentrate on getting the numbers and then draw "obvious" inferences. What is missed is that which is driving the numbers: What fundamental competitive, market, and environmental forces underlie these projections, forecasts, and estimates? For example, what competitive dynamics or environmental assumptions underlie these financial projections? In other words, preoccupation with numbers creation and the absence of efforts to subject the numbers to organized and broad-ranging critique and challenge can subvert strategic thinking; the analysis lacks reflection and is at most a reflexive act to get the task completed.

Strategic Learning Takes Place through Action.

Since strategy is conditional and U.S. organizations presumably wish to avoid the "success leading to failure" trap and reflexiveness, strategy analysis and strategic thinking must be continuous. Stated more pointedly, U.S. firms must learn from their actions. Of course, they can also learn from the actions of their competitors and other environmental entities. This learning then becomes the basis for their next round of actions. In short, reflection becomes the norm or habit.

The incremental nature of strategy analysis implicit in this discussion mirrors the incrementalism in the strategic actions of Japanese firms. Indeed, strategic incrementalism in the competitive area presupposes organizational learning. Moreover, incremental actions may be taken to generate learning: How will customers react? How will distributors respond? What will competitors do? In the absence of incremental learning, adaptation to the environment or strategic flexibility, which we so frequently cite as sine qua nons of strategic success, are not likely to materialize.

Strategy Formulation and Implementation Require Continuous Interfacing.

Implicit in much of the above discussion is that strategy formulation and strategy implementation are much more integrated and simultaneous than suggested by prevailing models of strategic management. We typically view formulation and implementation as sequential steps in managing strategy. In many respects this is correct; a strategy is broadly conceived and then actions are taken to bring it to fruition.

However, this view misses two key points. First, as the broad strategy is implemented, that is, as ideas are tested and as actions are taken, results accrue, and consequently learning and insight are accumulated. Specific elements of the original strategy are often, as a consequence, reformulated. Thus, (re)formulation and implementation go hand in hand. As we saw in the case of Japanese entry and penetration of the U.S. marketplace, an accumulation of reformulations can lead to significant strategy changes.

Second, this view of formulation and implementation as a linear and sequential process is premised on strategy as a set of organizational actions (frequently referred to in the strategic management literature as "implemented strategy") and not strategy as the strategic decision makers' consciousness of strategy choices and their implications. In the strategist's mind, as he distills and synthesizes the organization's current strategies and their results, competitors' strategies and the array of opportunities and threats facing the organization, the feed-forward and feed-back loops between formulation and implementation are much more instantaneous than in the reality of organizational actions. A major danger in missing this point is that we attribute too much importance to the creation of "plans" and "programs" and then compound the original sin by attributing too much significance to them once established. The plan and its implementation become the organization's preoccupation, not intelligent responses to the changing conditions in the environment.

This view is consistent with the apparent Japanese antipathy toward elegant strategy statements and formal, comprehensive strategic plans.

Management Must Identify and Manage Issues.

Not all things under the control of an organization or events external to it are of equal importance to strategy, that is, the pursuit of competitive advantage. Not everything is equally worthy of managerial attention and organizational resources. Moreover, management has limited time and resources. What is necessary, therefore, is for management to identify and manage those issues of most substantial import for the organization. By *issue* we mean any trend, event, or phenomenon that in the judgment of management is likely to seriously affect (positively or negatively) the performance of the organization. Indeed, issues management is becoming increasingly prevalent in U.S. organizations.

The significance of the identification and management of strategic issues is that it provides a focus for the organization's analysis efforts. It helps ensure that the organization's strategic thinking is channeled in directions of potential benefit to the organization. Once again, the Japanese have shown a remarkable capacity to identify, monitor, and manage issues facing their organization in each decade.

TOWARD STRATEGIC RENEWAL

In the last five years, increasing evidence has emerged that the New Competition has, among other things, begun to spawn strategic renewal among many large U.S. corporations. As discussed in chapter 11, some U.S. firms have (re)dedicated themselves to competing against the mainstream of the New Competition (and, in the process, of course, against other U.S., European, and other international firms). They have (re)discovered the importance of the customer; they have effected structural changes to facilitate focused strategic efforts; they have reoriented their mentality and culture to longer-term strategic game-plans; they are searching for ways to infuse themselves with the historic American spirit of entrepreneurialism. Above all, they are positioning themselves to attain and sustain competitive advantages in the marketplace.

While the results of this bout of strategic renewal are not yet fully in, it is clear that some U.S. firms have begun to stem the tide of the New Competition. However, now is not the time for false bravado. Efforts toward effecting and enhancing strategic renewal and development must be intensified. The New Competition is not standing still. The exhortations expounded in this and the previous chapter will not be easy to implement. They require truly committed, dedicated, and imaginative strategic organizations. But, they are truly necessary to meet the challenge of the New Competition.

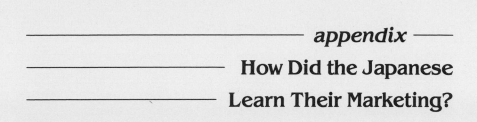

appendix ——

How Did the Japanese
Learn Their Marketing?

THE ORIGIN

Japanese marketing thought had its beginnings around 1650 in an era known as the Tokugawa period. Marketing thought was developed by Japanese merchants, a social class considered to be the lowest class of Tokugawa society because they were characterized as being socially unproductive. These merchants gradually evolved a complex commercial system that included means for collusive actions to protect their interests. This commercial system was dominated by wholesalers and retailers, who by that time played the pivotal roles controlling the entire distribution system in Japan.

As the commercial activities expanded, many commercial centers emerged, such as Osaka. A number of prominent merchants, known as "city merchants," appeared in these commercial centers and established large commercial organizations. The first member of the Mitsui family, a well-known city merchant, established the so-called merchant house in Edo (now Tokyo) and behaved like a buyer for his customers, determined what they needed, and chose products for them. According to Drucker:

> Marketing was invented in Japan around 1650 by the first member of the Mitsui family to settle in Tokyo as a merchant and to open what might be called the first department store. He anticipated by a full 250 years basic Sears, Roebuck policies: to be the buyer for his customers; to

263

design the right products for them, and to develop sources for their production; the principle of your money back and no questions asked; and the idea of offering a large assortment of products to his customers rather than focusing on a craft, product category, or a process.

MARKETING THOUGHT IN TRANSITION

After the collapse of Tokugawa, when Japan was opened to the West by Admiral Perry's ships in 1853, Japan underwent a major transformation in what is known as the Meiji period. The Meiji reforms stemmed from a desire to develop Japan so that it would be strong economically and militarily in order to protect it from the increasing influence of Western invaders.

The new government encouraged industrialization, especially in large-scale industries such as steel and textiles, whereas consumer industries were less emphasized. By this time, large city merchants began to extend their activities into the production areas instead of focusing only on distribution, as they had before. These powerful city merchants formed large-scale manufacturing and commercial groups known as "Zaibatsu." These business groups became more and more powerful as their business activities expanded. By 1890, they owned at least 55 percent of all leading manufacturing firms. Until the end of World War II, these business groups managed their business activities through a family approach, stemming from the traditional style of Tokugawa traders.

Western marketing thought did not have much influence on the Zaibatsu until the 1930s. At that time, U.S. marketing textbooks were beginning to be translated into Japanese, notably *Principles of Marketing* by Fred Clark and *Market Organization* by R. S. Vaile. American marketing thought, particularly as it applied in the consumer product sector, gradually influenced Japanese business practices. During this period, an American-style department store emerged for the first time in Japan and started using the newly acquired marketing tools, such as pricing policy, merchandise display, and advertising and promotion, in its operation.

THE PERIOD OF MARKETING REVOLUTION

The major flowering of Japanese marketing thought occurred after World War II. During the 1950s, the Japanese government pursued various policies geared toward economic recovery and gave various forms of support to those industries that seemed essential for economic recovery. One consequence resulting from the economic policies was the emergence of a mass-consumption society. During this period, per capita income rose substantially and led to an increase in consumption and a demand for an improved standard of living. As a result, consumer goods industries expanded rapidly. A large number of Japanese companies entered the consumer arena. This led to not only intensive competition among Japanese companies for market share but a great demand for more modern and sophisticated marketing tools than those traditionally used. Marketing became an important subject of interest and discussion in both business and academic areas.

In the academic field, the Japanese relied on translations of American marketing textbooks and casebooks, particularly those dealing with marketing management and theory and practice. Philip Kotler's *Marketing Management* and Phillips and Duncan's *Principles of Marketing* were the most frequently used in classrooms. Japanese scholars also translated more-specialized marketing books bearing such titles as *Product Policy, Marketing Research,* and *Advertising.* Though Japanese professors began to publish their own marketing textbooks, most of them repeated U.S. marketing theory. Few original contributions were produced by the Japanese academic establishment.

In the area of business practices, the Japanese were also influenced by the United States. During the 1947–55 period, the U.S. Supreme Command provided training to develop Japanese experts in business management. American teaching methods such as case studies and group discussions were adopted by large companies, which also gradually established their own managerial training centers. At the instigation of the United States, the Japanese Productivity Center (JPC) was formed in 1955 and became the most important institution introducing modern management techniques, including marketing, finance, production, and so on, into Japanese business practices. The center's objective was to modernize Japanese practices. Top Japanese management teams visited the United States to learn advanced techniques in various areas. They brought back the most modern American business management techniques, including modern marketing tools and strategies already practiced among leading U.S. companies.

In 1955, the first top-management team returned from the United States and introduced the concept of modern marketing in Japan. In 1956, this was followed by another team specializing in marketing. More than twenty thousand Japanese, mostly businessmen, have been sent abroad for similar purposes. At the same time, experts were invited to Japan to teach and advise Japanese business managers. In 1950, Dr.

Edward Deming was invited to Japan to teach marketing research techniques and quality control. After his visit, the importance of marketing research and the concept of quality control became two of the most important marketing elements adopted by Japanese companies. The first marketing research seminar in Japan was held in 1952, and in the same year the first marketing research agency was established. Since then, numerous research agencies have been established to provide research work for the government, companies, and trade associations.

THE IMPACT ON MARKETING CHANGES

Since 1960, Japanese companies, especially those in consumer product industries, have endeavored to absorb Western marketing thinking into their operation. Large U.S. companies in particular became a marketing model for the Japanese. Japanese business managers read U.S. marketing literature and made regular visits to the United States. The main issues occupying their attention have been those of organizing the marketing function, improving procedures for product development, and establishing effective controls over marketing channels. Even though not all of the U.S. practices were accepted, many of them were introduced. As a result, the leading Japanese firms evolved from being production oriented to being marketing oriented.

In firms with a limited product line, the functional organization structure was used and the marketing function was considered as important as the other functions, such as production and finance. In those large-scale manufacturing firms with highly diversified product lines, the product division concept was widely adopted to strengthen marketing capabilities in each product line. In companies such as Hitachi and Toshiba, wholly owned separate subsidiaries were established to undertake marketing activities and to market their product line. To cope with the increasing business activities in international markets, international divisions were developed within companies. These international divisions adopted marketing strategies familiar in U.S. firms, such as product line stretching, product proliferation, and product improvement.

Retail institutions also underwent a transformation, moving toward a mass-merchandise orientation and chain operation. American-style supermarkets and discount stores began to appear. American techniques such as high volume, low margin, high turnover, a broad line of merchandise, and an aggressive promotion policy were employed in these Japanese stores.

Eventually, the Japanese firms began to seek ways to improve control of their distribution channels and to market their rapidly growing output more effectively. They adopted modern American concepts such as vertical marketing systems (VMSs) and franchising. Japanese auto producers are a good example. After the war, Toyota brought independent dealers under its control by adopting a franchise system as well as a fixed price policy. Each dealer was assigned to sell in each prefecture and dealt exclusively with Toyota cars. Later, when Toyota started adding new car models to its product line, it reorganized the dealership system by type of vehicle and model, a system in which a dealer carries only one or two of a manufacturer's model lines—Corona dealers, Corolla dealers, etc. According to Kamiya, a marketing executive who had had much experience with the American dealer system, this format was adopted from those used by Americans.

In addition to these organizational and distributional changes, the Japanese adopted modern marketing tools like advertising and sales promotion for demand creation and stimulation. Advertising agencies were founded and expanded rapidly. For example, Dentsu is now the world's largest advertising agency.

The aforementioned factors describe only a few of the many changes undergone by Japanese marketing. Japanese marketing style was developed in the course of time as the result of an interplay between Japanese traditional marketing and Western-style marketing. In this evolutionary process, Japan applied modern American marketing concepts and techniques but did not copy them totally, instead choosing the ones that suited its needs. The Japanese know how to learn from others and how to turn the better ideas into practice, both in the domestic and in the international market. As a result, Japanese firms such as Toyota, Sony, Matsushita, Hitachi, Fujitsu, Casio, and Honda are now highly marketing oriented. These Japanese firms know marketing as well as the Western firms do, and they appear to have the edge in applying it, and applying it more strategically.

"That which is honored in a country will be cultivated there." So important is marketing in Japan that each year the Japan Management Association calls for nominations to select the fifteen best marketing companies. They ask two hundred experts to nominate the three companies that show overall excellence in customer orientation, in every marketing function, and in profitability. The top three winners in 1983 were Suntory Ltd., Toyota Motor Sales Co., and Matsushita Electric Inc. This list continues with Honda, Ajinomoto, Nippon Electric Co., Shiseido Cosmetics, Fuji Photo Film, Sony, Hitachi, Sharp, Otsuka Pharmaceutical, Fujitsu, Kao Soap, and Nissan Motor.

Clearly, other countries wishing to cultivate stronger marketing capabilities must begin by honoring the marketing function, as the Japanese have done.

NOTES

CHAPTER 1: WORLD CLASS MARKETERS—THE JAPANESE

Page

8 Japan's economy: Bank of Japan, *Comparative International Statistics,* 1966, 1977, 1980.

9 The increased saving rate: U.N., *Monthly Bulletin of Statistics,* June 1981; and Science and Technology Agency, *Japan: Indicators of Science and Technology,* 1981.

9 Productivity increased: MITI, *White Paper on International Trade,* 1980; and Japan, Prime Minister's Office, Statistics Bureau, *Statistical Handbook of Japan, 1982.*

10 Japanese labor's productivity: See Dale Jorgenson, "U.S. and Japanese Economic Growth, 1952–1974: An International Comparison," *Economic Journal,* 88, No. 352 (1978).

11 In 1955: *JETRO, Stages of Development of the Japanese Economy,* 1979.

11 Japan's *dependency ratio*: Dependency Ratio = Import/domestic demand.

12 Japan's postwar export expansion: Bank of Japan, *Balance of Payments Monthly,* April 1970 and April 1981.

13 Meanwhile, exports: Japan, Ministry of Foreign Affairs, *The Japan of Today,* 1982.

14 In the U.S. market: *World Auto Trade: Current Trends and Structural Problems* (Washington, D.C.: Government Printing Office, 1980), p. 1.

14 The Japanese success: Harvard Business School, *Note on the Motorcycle Industry,* 1975; and *Nippon: A Charted Survey of Japan,* ed. Tsuneta Yano Memorial Society (Yano-Tsuneta Kinenkai) (Japan, 1983–84), p. 177.

15 By 1968: Japan Tariff Association, *The Summary Report: Trade of Japan.*

15   By 1963: See Northwestern University, Center for the Interdisciplinary Study of Science and Technology, *The U.S. Consumer Electronics Industry and Foreign Competition.*

16   In the field: "Seiko's Smash," *Business Week,* June 5, 1978, pp. 86–97.

16   Japan has also achieved: Nippon Steel Corporation, *Nippon: The Land and Its People,* pp. 68, 70, and 252.

17   In just a few years: "Like a Dose of Medicine," *Forbes,* June 8, 1981, pp. 72–76; and *Wall Street Journal,* November 10, 1981, pp. 1, 20.

17   In the semiconductor market: *Industry Week,* April 20, 1981, pp. 63–70.

17   In the United States: *New York Times,* September 9, 1980, pp. D1, D24.

18   In robots: "The Robots Are Coming," *Focus Japan,* 8, No. 6 (June 1981).

18   Western industrial planners: "Surveys on Aerospace," *The Economist,* August 20, 1980.

19   The value of: Japan, Ministry of Finance; the data are as of March 31, 1981.

20   Japan's tremendous gains: Douglas Frazer, "The Myth of the Over-Privileged Autoworkers," *Wall Street Journal,* April 27, 1981.

21   "Know the enemy": Sun Tzu, *The Art of War,* trans. Samuel B. Griffith.

CHAPTER 2: THE NEW COMPETITION'S SUCCESS FORMULA

22   We saw evidence: The term *Japanese miracle* was introduced by Professor Hiromi Arisawa, one of the leading formulators of Japan's postwar industrial policy. See his earlier book, *The Control of Japanese Industry* (Tokyo: Yuhikaku, 1937).

22   Several learned explanations: The authors who advanced early analytical explanations include Ralph Hewins, *The Japanese Miracle Men* (London: Secker & Warburg, 1967); P. B. Stone, *Japan Surges Ahead: The Story of an Economic Miracle* (New York: Praeger, 1969); Robert Guilain, *The Japanese Challenge* (Philadelphia: Lippincott, 1970); Herman Kahn, *The Emerging Japanese State; Challenge and Response* (Englewood Cliffs, N.J.: Prentice-Hall, 1970); Richard E. Caves and Masu Uekusa, *Industrial Organization in Japan* (Washington: Brookings Institution, 1976); Herman Kahn, *The Japanese Challenge, the Success and Failure of Economic Success* (New York: Crowell, 1979); and G. C. Allen, *The Japanese Economy* (New York: St. Martin's Press, 1981).

22   Many scholars attribute: Eugene J. Kaplan, "Japan: The Government-Business Relationship" (U.S. Department of Commerce, February 1972), pp. 56–72.

22   Some scholars have emphasized: Alexander K. Young, *The Sogo Shosha: Japan's Multinational Trading Companies* (Boulder, Colo.: Westview Press, 1979); Chalmers Johnson, *MITI and the Japanese Miracles: The Growth of Industrial Policy 1925–1975* (Stanford, Calif.: Stanford University Press, 1982); and Hugh Patrick, "The Future of the Japanese Economy: Output and Labor Productivity," *Journal of Japanese Studies,* 3, Summer 1977.

23   The most prevalent: See Rodney Clark, *The Japanese Company* (New Haven, Conn.: Yale University Press, 1979); William G. Ouchi, *Theory Z: How American Business Can Meet the Japanese Challenge* (Reading, Mass: Addison-Wesley, 1981); Shimada Haruo, "The Japanese Employment System," *Japan*

Industrial Relations, Series 6; Richard Tanner Pascale and Anthony G. Athos, *The Art of Japanese Management: Applications for American Executives* (New York: Simon & Schuster, 1981); and M. Y. Yoshino: *Japan's Managerial System: Tradition and Innovation* (Cambridge, Mass.: MIT Press, 1968).

26   "The company starts": Mitsuyuki Masatsugu, "The Modern Samurai Society; Duty and Dependency in Contemporary Japan," *AMACOM* (New York: American Management Association, 1982).

27   American scholars: Ezra F. Vogel, "The Challenge from Japan" (statement before the U.S. Senate Finance Committee's subcommittee on International Trade, Washington, D.C., December 10, 1980); and William W. Lockwood, *The Economic Development of Japanese Growth and Structural Change* (Princeton, N.J.: Princeton University Press, 1968).

28   In the mid-1950s: Johnson, *MITI and the Japanese Miracles,* pp. 230, 236–37.

29   In 1980: "Oriental Economists," *Japan Company Handbook,* second half, 1981.

30   Perhaps the greatest service: See details in JETRO Marketing Series 2, *The Role of Trading Companies in International Commerce,* 1980.

31   In the postwar period: Bank of Japan, *The Japanese Financial System,* p. 7.

31   In the mid-1960s: See Yoshino, *Japan's Managerial System,* pp. 139–47.

31   The Japanese government: See Johnson, *MITI and the Japanese Miracles,* p. 200.

31   Nissan Motor Company: John B. Schnapp, *Corporate Strategies of the Automotive Manufacturers,* Vol. 2, pp. 182, 187.

33   Existing firms: See Yoshino, *Japan's Managerial System,* pp. 163–67.

33   During the 1970s: Kenichi Ohmae, "Japan: From Stereotype to Specifics," *McKinsey Quarterly,* Spring 1982, p. 6; and J. Hirschmeier and T. Yui, *The Development of Japanese Business* (Cambridge, Mass.: Harvard University Press, 1975).

35   The consensual style: Gail M. Makinodan, "Japan: The Decison Making Process," *The Interpreter,* published by the Japan Institute.

35   When a decision: See Yoshino, *Japan's Managerial System,* p. 255; and *NIPPON: The Land and Its People,* p. 75.

36   In Japan: Yoshimatsu Aonuma, *A Japanese Explains Japan's Business Style,* p. 45.

38   In 1959: "How Nissan Deals with Competition and Devaluation," *Business Week,* April 7, 1973, p. 68.

38   When Sony: Akio Morita, "How Sony Did It" (speech delivered to the Trade Expansion Committee of the American Chamber of Commerce in Japan, May 31, 1977).

CHAPTER 3: THE MARKET-TAKEOVER PROCESS: HOW THE WEST WAS WON

39   In 1958: *Toyota—The First Twenty Years:* (Calif.: Toyota Motor Sales, USA Inc., 1977), p. 7.

40   Ford (1925): Shotora Kamiya, *My Life with Toyota* (Calif.: Toyota Motor Sales, USA Inc., 1976), p. 102.

Page

40   Unable to compete; Tokyo Gas & Electric, Tokyo Ishikawajima Shipbuilding, and Datto Motor Company.

40   In 1936: Kamiya, *My Life with Toyota*, p. 108.

41   In the immediate years: Daniel L. Spencer, *Military Transfer of Technology: International Techno-Economic Transfers vis Military By-Products and Initiative Based on Cases from Japanese and other Pacific Countries* (Washington D.C.: Air Force Office of Scientific Research, AFOSR-67-0231, 1967), p. 59. Original reference provided by Chan Sup Chang, *The Japanese Motor Vehicle Industry; A Study of the History of the Japanese Motor Vehicle Industry and the Impact of the Japanese Motor Vehicles on the U.S. Market* (Ph.D. dissertation, The American University, 1974).

41   These American: Seiji Nakamura, *Gijutsu Kakushi to Gendai* ("Technological Renovation and Modern Times") (Tokyo: Sanichi Shobo, 1959), p. 96— original references provided by Chang; and Spencer, *Military Transfer,* pp. 60 and 79.

41   In the government's paper: P. Bayres and A. J. Sanders, *Japan: Its Motor Industry and Market* (London: P-E Consulting Group Limited, 1971), Report to the British National Economic Development Office, pp. 2, 63–64.

43   *Direct assistance:* Ibid., p. 68.

43   Financing measures: John P. Hartley, "Why Japan's Ahead: The View from Tokyo," *Automotive Industries,* March 1982, pp. 34–37; and Joseph M. Callahan, "Why Japan's Ahead: The View from Detroit," *Automotive Industries,* March 1982, p. 36.

43   Teams of government: Leslie Darbyshire, *The Competitive Position of Imported Automobiles in the American Market* (D.B.A. dissertation, Department of Finance, University of Washington, 1957)—original reference provided by James Rader, *Penetrating the U.S. Auto Market: German and Japanese Strategies—1965 to 1976* (Ann Arbor, Mich.: UMS Research Press, 1979).

43   Prior to 1955: *Statistical Abstract of the United States,* 1977, Table 1474, p. 867; and Bayres and Sanders, *Japan: Its Motor Industry and Market,* p. 50.

43   In the world market: Nobuyori Kodaira, "Position of the Japanese Automobile Industry in the World," pp. 16, 17.

43   Japan did not win: Bayres and Sanders, *Japan: Its Motor Industry and Market,* p. 2.

44   Although not the target: *Toyota—The First Twenty Years,* pp. 26–27.

45   Toyota commissioned: "How the Japanese Blitzed the California Auto Market," *Forbes,* September 15, 1971, p. 29.

46   For the Japanese: David P. Ahern, "The Auto Industry and the Big Three," *Financial Analysts Journal,* May-June 1968, p. 99.

47   Speaking to: Thomas O'Hanlon, "GM Takes the High Ground in the Battle of Detroit," *Fortune,* May 1, 1969, p. 74.

47   General Motors': Dan Corditz, "Autos: A Hazardous Stretch Ahead," *Fortune,* April 1971, pp. 69–136; and O'Hanlon, "GM Takes the High Ground," p. 74.

48   As Donald Peterson: Corditz, "Autos," p. 71.

48   In 1960: Bayres and Sanders, *Japan: Its Motor Industry and Market,* p. 73.

48   Compact auto sales: *Toyota—The First Twenty Years,* p. 33.

48   Japan's product strategy: Chan Sup Chang, *The Japanese Motor Vehicle Industry,* p. 130.

48   The new Toyota Corona: *Toyota—The First Twenty Years,* pp. 28–33, 76.

49   The Japanese pursued: Sanford Rose, "The Secret of Japan's Export Prowess," *Fortune,* January 30, 1978, pp. 56–63; and *Toyota—The First Twenty Years,* pp. 33, 37.

49   Both Toyota and Nissan: Bayres and Sanders, *Japan: Its Motor Industry and Market,* p. 54; and *Toyota—The First Twenty Years,* p. 37.

49   Toyota recruited: *Toyota—The First Twenty Years,* pp. 37, 38.

49   Toyota could not: John R. Stuteville, "The Buyer as a Salesman," *Journal of Marketing,* 32 (July 1968), 214–18.

50   Effective penetration: Stefan H. Robock and Kenneth Simmonds, *International Business and Multinational Enterprise* (Homewood, Ill.: Richard D. Irwin, 1973), pp. 416–18—original reference provided by Rader.

50   The Corolla series: John B. Schnapp, *Corporate Strategies of the Automotive Manufacturers—Vol. II: Strategic Histories* (Boston, Mass.: Harbridge House, 1978), p. 150. Prepared for the U.S. Department of Transportation, National Highway Traffic Safety Administration, pp. 150, 157.

51   At Nissan: "How Nissan Motor Deals with Competition and Re-evaluation," *Business Week,* April 7, 1973, p. 69.

51   As a result: Louis Kraar, "Japan's Automakers Shift Strategies," *Fortune,* August 11, 1980, p. 108.

51   Referring to: John P. Hartley, *Automotive Industries,* March 1982, p. 36.

52   The results of this: Bayres and Sanders, *Japan: Its Motor Industry and Market,* p. 41.

52   Over the same period: John B. Schnapp, *Corporate Strategies of the Automotive Manufacturers—Vol. III: Panorama of Selected Economic and Operating Information,* (Boston, Mass.: Harbridge House, 1978), p. 40. Prepared for the U.S. Department of Transportation, National Highway Traffic Safety Administration.

53   For example: *Business Week,* February 6, 1971, p. 20.

53   From the 384: *Toyota—The First Twenty Years,* p. 7.

53   The company signed up: "The Fast Pace of Japanese Cars," *Business Week,* August 8, 1970, pp. 42, 44.

53   Toyota's growth: *Toyota—The First Twenty Years,* pp. 43, 44, and 69.

54   Toyota fostered: "How the Japanese Blitzed the California Auto Market," p. 29.

54   Nissan: "The Fast Pace of Japanese Cars," p. 42.

55   On July 1, 1971: Bayres and Sanders, *Japan: Its Motor Industry and Market,* pp. 127–31.

55   On August 14: "How Nissan Motor Deals with Competition and Re-evaluation," p. 68.

55   While these events: *Automotive News,* February 23, 1981; and Takahie Hatori and Takeshi Soda, "Toyota's Product Planning Forces," *Wheel Extended,* IV, No. 4 (September 1975), 43–45.

55   Toyota continued: Yoshino Miwa, "The Development Process of Japan's Automobile Production Technology," *Wheel Extended,* VII, No. 1 (Summer 1971), 11.

56   An import manager: *Toyota—The First Twenty Years,* p. 44.

56   Barnes estimated: Callahan, "Why Japan's Ahead," p. 35.

56   Meanwhile Japanese: "How Nissan Motor Deals with Competition and Re-evaluation," p. 69.

Page

57	As late as 1974: "The Small Car Blues at General Motors," *Business Week,* March 16, 1974, p. 79.
57	Henry Ford II: "How the Japanese Blitzed the California Auto Market," pp. 28–29.
57	As *Newsweek*: "Japan's Big Drive Autos," *Newsweek*, May 3, 1971, p. 76.
57	When GM: Considerable discussion of the Vega story is given by John Z. DeLorean, *On a Clear Day You Can See General Motors* (New York: Avon Books, 1979), pp. 187–203, written by Patrick J. Wright.
58	Japanese strategic thought: Musashi Miyamoto, *A Book of Five Rings* (Woodstock, N.Y.: Overlook Press, 1974).
58	It is difficult: Ibid., p. 78.
58	If the enemy: Ibid., p. 48.
58	However, the object: Ibid., p. 80.

CHAPTER 4: IDENTIFYING OPPORTUNITIES

66	The last provision: Chalmers Johnson, *MITI and the Japanese Miracles: The Growth of Industrial Policy 1925–1975,* (Stanford, Calif.: Stanford University Press, 1982), p. 218.
68	Should Japan: "Organization for Economic Cooperation and Development," *The Industrial Policy of Japan* (Paris, 1972), p. 15.
75	The Japanese entered: "Note on the Motorcycle Industry," Harvard Business School, pp. 16–17.
75	The Japanese invaded: "The New Lean, Mean, Xerox," *Business Week*, October 12, 1981.
75	We believe that: "The Wild One," *Forbes,* September 15, 1966, p. 15.
77	The development: Jack Baranson, *The Japanese Challenge in U.S. Industry* (Lexington, Mass.: Lexington Books, 1981), p. 43.
77	Sony's Walkman: Interviews with Akio Morita, president of Sony, in *Playboy*, August 1982.
78	If we compare: See "Canon Takes Aim at the Snapshooter," *Fortune,* July 26, 1982, p. 38; and "Japan's Canon Focuses on America," *Fortune,* January 12, 1981, pp. 83–84.
78	It was a big gamble: Kenichi Ohmae, *The Mind of the Strategist: The Art of Japanese Business* (New York: McGraw-Hill, 1982), pp. 128–29.
79	In contrast: Baranson, *Japanese Challenge in U.S. Industry*, pp. 108–9.
80	The following example: Robin H. Leaf, "Learning from Your Competitors," *McKinsey Quarterly,* Spring 1978, pp. 52–60.
81	Each of the nine: Johnny K. Johansson, *Japanese Export Management* (Stockholm, Sweden: Marknadstekniskt Centrum, 1981), pp. 16–17.
81	Perhaps most significant: Lawrence A. Walker and Hanns-Martin Schoenfeld, "The Role of Governments in Promoting Exports: A Survey of Official Meas-ures in Five Major Countries," *Export Marketing: Lessons from Europe,* ed. Jagdish N. Sheth and Hanns-Martin Schoenfeld (Champaign: College of Commerce and Business Administration, University of Illinois, 1980), pp. 49–75.

CHAPTER 5: ENTRY STRATEGIES

87   Before entering the United States: "Meet Mr. SONY," *Atlantic,* pp. 36–38.

87   Matsushita has stationed: Yasuo Okamoto, "Matsushita Electric in the International Market," *Wheel Extended,* X, No. 2 (Autumn 1980), 8–10.

88   They would send: *Tokyo News Letter,* Mitsubishi Corp., October 1978.

89   Toshiba, for example: "Japan: Undercutting the West in Medical Electronics," *Business Week,* April 27, 1981.

89   Casio's strategy: Kenichi Ohmae, "Japan: From Stereotypes to Specifics," *McKinsey Quarterly,* Spring 1982, p. 6.

90   Quality is a multidimensional: Hitoshi Kume, *Quality Control in Japan's Industries,* Wheel Extended, IX, No. 4, 20–27.

90   The entry of Japanese: "Japanese Chip Challenge," *Fortune,* March 23, 1981, pp. 115–22.

91   Nissan digested: *Datsun News,* May-June 1969, p. 2.

91   Service departments: John B. Rae, *Nissan/Datsun, A History of Nissan Motor Corporation in U.S.A., 1960–80* (New York: McGraw-Hill, 1982), pp. 225–31.

91   However, as Kotler: Philip Kotler, *Marketing Management: Analysis, Planning, and Control,* 4th ed. (Englewood Cliffs, N.J: Prentice-Hall, 1981) pp. 381–82.

91   Very often the pricing: Somkid Jatusripitak, "Exporting Behavior of the Firm: A Study of the Decision Making Processes of U.S. Manufacturing Firms" (Ph.D. dissertation, Northwestern University, Evanston, Ill., 1984.

92   Japanese firms introduced: *The U.S. Consumer Electronics Industry and Foreign Competition,* Northwestern University, Center for the Interdisciplinary Study of Science and Technology, p. 24.

92   Seiko entered: "Seiko's Smash," *Business Week,* June 5, 1978, pp. 86–92.

94   The entry of Japanese banks: Stephen Bronte, "The Japanese Attack on Corporate America," *Euromoney,* September 1982, pp. 195–207.

95   Japanese apparel: "Now Japan Unveils High Fashion," *Business Week,* June 14, 1982, p. 85.

95   In cosmetics, Shiseido: "Shiseido Scents Profits," *The Japanese Challenge in Europe,* prepared and published by Business International S.A. Geneva, reprinted from *Business Europe,* September 22, 1972.

99   Joint ventures: Marvin J. Wolf, *The Japanese Conspiracy* (New York: Empire Books, 1983), pp. 139–43.

100   Honda's motorcycle: *Note on the Motorcycle Industry,* Harvard Business School, 1975, pp. 11–12.

101   This was followed: *New York Times,* June 3, 1979, pp. F1, F4.

102   Whereas the main: "Japan's Strategy for the '80's," *Business Week,* December 14, 1981, pp. 53–54.

102   The Japanese—led by: "Computer Warfare: Beating Back Japan," *Newsweek,* March 8, 1982, p. 80.

102   A survey showed: "The Japanese Chip Challenge," *Fortune,* March 23, 1981, p. 116.

102   In just one year: *Industry Week,* April 20, 1981, p. 64.

102   Even though price: "Japan Is Here to Stay," *Business Week,* December 3, 1979, p. 85.

102   Automation was adopted: "The Japanese Chip Challenge," *Fortune,* March 23, 1981, pp. 115–22.

Page

103   Reportedly, the Japanese: "The Micro War Heats Up," *Forbes,* November 26, 1979, p. 56.

CHAPTER 6: PENETRATION STRATEGIES

105   Kawaski also launched: Harvard Business School, *Note on the Motorcycle Industry,* 1975, pp. 16–17.

105   The copier market: "The New Lean, Mean Xerox," *Business Week,* October 12, 1981, p. 128.

106   During the same period: "Japan: Taking on the Swiss in Luxury Watches, "*Business Week,* June 15, 1981, p. 49.

106   Worldwide, Seiko: "Seiko's Smash," *Business Week,* June 5, 1978, pp. 86–92.

106   Canon's success: *Fortune,* January 12, 1981, pp. 87–88.

107   For example, Honda: NADA, *Motorcycle Appraisal Guide,* April-July 1975.

107   During the 1965–76 period: James Rader, *Penetrating the U.S. automobile Market: German and Japanese Strategies* (Ann Arbor, Mich.: UMI Research Press, 1980).

108   Canon continued to: *Wall Street Journal,* December 1, 1981, p. 37.

109   In the air-conditioning industry: "Air Conditioner Study's Implication Worrisome," *Chicago Tribune,* November 21, 1983.

109   A Japan Trade Council: Japanese Trade Council Report, March 7, 1980.

109   In the words: "Japan Is Here to Stay," *Business Week,* December 3, 1979, p. 85.

110   Nippan Kohan: *Wall Street Journal,* December 1, 1981.

113   Under MITI's leadership: "Japan's Strategy for the 80s," *Business Week,* December 14, 1981, p. 68.

115   In their attack: *JEI Report,* December 18, 1981, p. 4; and *Business Week,* December 14, 1981, p. 78.

115   "First we must": Hitachi in the 80s: A Focus on Computers," *Business Week,* March 2, 1981, p. 38.

118   Many of the elements: This description of Toshiba's penetration of the medical equipment market is drawn in part from published sources. It primarily depends on interviews with a number of Toshiba's personnel.

118   In April 1981: "Japan: Undercutting the West in Medical Electronics," *Business Week,* April 27, 1981.

120   The Toshiba philosophy: "The Japanese Chip Challenge," *Fortune,* March 23, 1981.

CHAPTER 7: CONFRONTATION STRATEGIES

123   This chapter uses: Military concepts and language have long been used in competitive business strategy literature. For some of the classic works in military strategy, see Carl von Clausewitz, *On War* (London: Routledge & Kegan Paul); B.H. Liddell Hart, *Strategy* (New York: Praeger, 1967); and J.F.C. Fuller, *The Conduct of War, 1789–1961* (London: Eyre & Spottiswoode, 1961).

CHAPTER 8: MAINTENANCE STRATEGIES

Page

cial Times, December 12, 1983, p. 9; and "Watch What They Do, Not What They Say," *Forbes,* March 17, 1980, pp. 69–70.

160   In motorcycles: *Marubeni,* No. 104, February 1982.

162   *Mechatronics:* Takeshi Higuchi, "Mechatronics Sweeps Japan," in *The Wheel Extended,* XII, No. 1 (January-March 1982).

162   Nippon Steel: Saburo Iwai, "Strategy for Progress: The Case of Nippon Steel," in *Corporate Strategy & Structure: Japan and the U.S.A.,* ed. John Vandenbrink (Chicago, Ill.: 1983), pp. 87–97.

169   In textiles: "Japanese Textile Industry: Hope for Growth by Diversifying," *Financial Times,* December 12, 1983, p. ix.

171   In European markets: "Aero-engine: British Technology, Japanese Case," *The Economist,* August 18, 1979, p. 66; and "Japanese Investment: Made in Europe," *The Economist,* May 1, 1982, p. 63.

CHAPTER 9: BUILDING A GLOBAL POSITION

173   Japanese firms put: Yoshi Tsurumi, *The Japanese Are Coming: A Multinational Interaction of Firms and Politics* (Cambridge, Mass.: Ballinger Publishing, 1976), pp. 82–83.

173   In contrast: U.S. Department of Commerce, Industry, and Trade Administration, *Seven Surprising Facts about Exporting* (Washington D.C., n.d.), p. 1.

175   Meanwhile the Swiss: Shinya Ishikawa, *Marketing of Imported Goods in Japan; Problems to Beat,* in Dentsu's *Japan Marketing/Advertising.*

176   The Japanese makers: Johannes Hirschmeier and T. Yiu, *The Development of Japanese Business* (London: George Allen & UNWIN, 1981), pp. 301–2.

176   The major portion: G. C. Allen, *The Japanese Economy* (New York: St. Martin's Press, 1981), pp. 161–63.

177   In 1954: Bank of Japan, *Economic & Statistical Annual.*

178   Europe now absorbs: "The Japanese Juggernaut Lands in Europe," *Fortune,* November 20, 1981, pp. 108–22.

178   *Passenger cars:* This section is largely based on Geoffrey Shepherd, "Japanese Exports and Europe's Problem Industries," in *Japan and Western Europe,* ed. Loukas Tsoukalsi and Maureen White (New York: St. Martin's Press, 1982), pp. 141–45; and "Japanese Car Makers Shift into High Gear in Drive on Europe," *Business Europe,* August 25, 1972.

179   *Watches:* This section is largely based on "Seiko's Precise Timing," *Business Europe,* September 8, 1972.

180   The global expansion path: See details of Japanese strategy in Europe in "Bulldozers Roll In," *Business Europe,* July 28, 1972.

182   The Japanese relied: "It's the Response That Counts," *Forbes,* November 23, 1981, pp. 123–29.

182   As the Japanese: "A Worldwide Strategy for the Computer Market," *Business Week,* December 14, 1981, p. 65.

182   In Thailand: "Japan's Lone-Wolf Tactics in Computers," *Business Week,* September 21, 1981, p. 50.

183   Sewing machines: Tsurumi, *The Japanese Are Coming,* pp. 31–32.

183   The Japanese ascendancy: The major contributions to this section are from Shiro Takeda, "How Japanese Corporations Develop International Markets:

Page

Product Differentiation and Marketing Efforts," in *Wheel Extended,* X, No. 2 (Autumn 1980), pp. 2–7.

184   For example, Seiko: "Seiko's Smash," *Business Week,* June 5, 1978, p. 92.

185   One solution was: J. W. Vaupel and J. P. Curban, *The World's Multinational Enterprises* (Cambridge, Mass.: Harvard University Press, 1973), p. 122.

185   Japanese manufacturers: See details in Noritake Kobayashi, *Japan's Role in Southeast Asia,* Institution of Southeast Asia Studies (issues seminar series No. 3, 1973).

185   The products made: M. Y. Yoshino, *Japan's Multinational Enterprises* (Cambridge, Mass.: Harvard University Press, 1976), pp. 75–76.

191   In the TV market: *The U.S. Consumer Electronics Industry and Foreign Competition* (Evanston, Ill.: Northwestern University, Center for Interdisciplinary Study of Science and Technology, May 1980), pp. 52–57.

191   After attaining leadership: This section is based on *ibid.,* Chap. 3.

195   Research has shown: James C. Abegglen, ed., *Business Strategies for Japan* (Tokyo: Sophia University, 1970), p. 67.

195   The Japanese motorcycle industry: Harvard Business School, *Note on the Motorcycle Industry,* 1975, pp. 21–22.

CHAPTER 10: LINKING STRATEGY, ORGANIZATION, AND DECISION MAKING

199   For example: Ako Horita, "How Sony Did It" (speech delivered to the Trade Expansion Committee of the America Chamber of Commerce in Japan, May 31, 1977).

199   NEC, for example: "A Worldwide Strategy for the Computer Markets," *Business Week,* December 14, 1981.

200   Shiseido: "Japan Plants a New U.S. Crop," *Ad Forum,* September 1982, p. 5.

200   Over the past few decades: David E. Brown, "Growth Analysis of the Electric Industry," a report for the Toshiba Summer Internship Program, 1982, p. 12; and Ryuei Shimizu, *The Growth of Firms in Japan* (Tokyo: Keio Tsushin, 1980), p. 192.

201   A flanking strategy: Sun Tzu, *The Art of War,* trans. Samuel B. Griffith, pp. 96–101.

202   A rising tide: Shimizu, *Growth of Firms in Japan,* p. 105.

204   The Konzern: Mamoru Tsuda, "Big Corporations and Business Groups of Japan Today," in Third World Studies Discussion Paper, No. 8 (paper presented during the weekly research seminar-workshop with the multimedia on August 27, 1977 at Vinzon Hall, U.P.).

204   At the same time: Ibid., pp. 17–19.

205   The GTCs: Alexander K. Youmg, *The Sogo Shosha: Japan's Multinational Trading Companies* (Boulder, Colo.: Westview Press, 1977), pp. 39–41.

205   The industrially linked: Johnny K. Johansson and Ikujiro Nonaka, "Japanese Export Marketing: Structures, Strategies, Counter Strategies," *International Marketing Review* (Winter 1983).

206   These sales subsidiaries: M. Y. Yoshino, *Japan's Multinational Enterprise* (Cambridge, Mass.: Harvard University Press, 1976), Chap. 5.

206   Automobiles: U.S. Department of Commerce, Economic Development Administration, "The U.S. Consumer Electronics Industry and Foreign Competitors,"

Page

May 1980; and "A Worldwide Strategy for the Computer Markets," *Business Week,* December 14, 1981, p. 54.

207   However, the rapid: Shimizu, *Growth of Firms in Japan,* p. 94.

208   These ad hoc teams: Ibid., pp. 89 and 105.

209   An important point: "Japanese Corporate Decision Making," *JETRO: Business Information Series 9,* pp. 20–21.

209   The second category: Friedrich Furstenberg, *Why the Japanese Have Been So Successful in Business* (London: Leviathan House, 1974), Chap. 15.

210   The product development process: Robert E. Cole, "The Japanese Lesson in Quality," *Technology Review,* July 1981, p. 31.

CHAPTER 11: RESPONDING TO THE NEW COMPETITION

235   As suggested by: See Johnny K. Johansson, and Ikujiro Nonaka, "Japanese Export Marketing: Structures, Strategies, Counterstrategies," *International Marketing Review,* (Winter 1983).

235   Kotler has suggested: Philip Kotler, *Marketing Management: Analysis, Planning, and Control,* 5th ed. (Englewood Cliffs, N.J.: Prentice-Hall, 1984), p. 411.

237   Warner-Lambert—which: "Beating the Japanese in Japan," *Forbes,* April 27, 1981, p. 46.

237   Undertaking a strong push: C. M. Watson, "Counter-Competition Abroad to Protect Home Markets," *Harvard Business Review,* January-February 1982, pp. 40–42.

240   Black & Decker: Marc C. Particelli, "The Japanese Are Coming," *Outlook* (Booz, Allen & Hamilton, Spring, 1981); and "Black & Decker Meets Japan's Push Head-on in Power-Tool Market," *Wall Street Journal,* February 18, 1983, pp. 1 and 15.

241   In order to cut: *Wall Street Journal,* July 30, 1982, p. 32; and "Counterattack: Xerox Slashes Prices," *Fortune,* July 26, 1982, p. 8.

241   Xerox has strengthened: *Wall Street Journal,* July 30, 1982, p. 32.

242   In the early 1980s: Thomas A. Pugel, Yusi Kimura, and Robert G. Hawkins, "Semiconductors and Computers: Emerging Competition Battlegrounds in the Asia-Pacific Region," in *Research in International Business and Finance,* Vol. 4 (Part B), ed. H. Peter Gray (Greenwich, Conn.: JAI Press 1983), p. 263.

242   In addition: *Business Week,* January 10, 1983, p. 98, and December 14, 1981, p. 74.

242   It has also: *Wall Street Journal,* June 25, 1982, p. 4.

242   IBM is now: *Business Week,* January 10, 1980, p. 98.

CHAPTER 12: TOWARD STRATEGIC MARKETING IN THE
TWENTY-FIRST CENTURY

245   Unless the seeds: Peter Drucker stressed this point thirty years ago. See *The Practice of Management* (New York: Harper & Row, 1954).

246   At a very general level: This broad conception of strategy underlies the defini-

tion of strategy in most strategic management and marketing textbooks. See, for example, Charles W. Hofer and Dan Schendel, *Strategy Formulation: Analytical Concepts* (New York: West Publishing Co., 1978).

246   The aforementioned dilemma: This point has been forcefully argued by Lewis J. Peelman. See "The Strategy Revolution", *Strategic Planning Management,* January 1984.

247   Stated differently: Competitive advantage is receiving increasing emphasis in almost all discussions of strategy and strategic management. See, for example, George S. Day, *Strategic Market Planning,* (New York: West Publishing Co., 1984), and William E. Rothschild, *How to Gain and Maintain the Competitive Advantage in Business* (New York: McGraw Hill, 1984).

248   Distinctive competences include: This discussion of distinctive competence draws heavily from Liam Fahey and Kurt Christensen, "Building Distinctive Competences into Competitive Advantage," *Strategic Planning Management,* February, 1984.

249   A comparison of the strategies: Some of the strategy literature separates strategy and goals. Other theorists regard goals as part of strategy. The point we wish to make here is that whether or not goals are viewed as part of strategy, strategy, organizational goals, and performance are highly interrelated.

250   This is the core: Robert B. Reich has recently done much to popularize the term "Paper Entrepreneurialism." See *The Next American Frontier* (New York: Time Books, 1983).

250   One such "truth": For an excellent discussion of the structure-conduct-performance paradigm, see F. M. Scherer, *Industrial Market Structures and Economic Performance,* 2nd edition, (Chicago: Rand McNally College Publishing Co., 1979).

255   In short, the strategic organization: We have found it useful to contrast reflectiveness with "reflexiveness," when the latter is depicted as mostly "knee-jerk" reactions to surrounding stimuli.

255   By *culture* we mean: For more detailed discussion of culture and its many linkages to strategy, see Stanley M. Davis, *Managing Corporate Culture* (Cambridge, Mass.: Ballinger Publishing, 1984).

256   By *strategic culture* we do not just mean: We want to emphasize that culture is much more embracing than what is often referred to as "superordinate values and goals." It goes much beyond a sense of purpose and direction for the organization.

257   The structuring of organizations: For an instructive discussion of many different aspects and models of organization structure, see Henry Mintzberg, *The Structuring of Organizations* (Englewood Cliffs, N.J.: Prentice-Hall, 1979).

258   The edge, so central: That structure follows strategy has been generally accepted in the strategic management literature since Alfred D. Chandler's seminal work, *Strategy and Structure: Chapters in the History of American Industrial Enterprise* (Cambridge, Mass.: MIT Press, 1962).

261   Indeed, issues management: Issues management has emerged as a recognized organizational function in many firms in the past five years. There is now an Issues Management Society with a membership in excess of 500 individuals.

Page

APPENDIX: HOW DID THE JAPANESE LEARN THEIR MARKETING?

263   Japanese marketing: Peter F. Drucker, *Management: Tasks, Responsibilities, Practices* (New York: Harper & Row, 1973), p. 62; and M. Y. Yoshino, *The Japanese Marketing System: Adaptation and Innovation* (Cambridge, Mass.: MIT Press, 1971), Chap. 1.

263   Marketing was invented: Drucker, *Management: Tasks, Responsibilities, Practices,* p. 62.

264   At that time: R. S. Vaile, *Market Organization* (New York: Ronald Press, 1930).

265   In the academic field: Yukichi Arakawa, "On the Development of Marketing Studies in Japan," in the *Analysis of the School of Business Administration* (Kobe University, 1971), pp. 39–42.

265   In the area of business practices: Ibid., p. 46.

265   In 1955: Joji Yokota, "Japanese-Style Marketing: Some Examples of Product Policy," in Dentsu's *Japan Marketing/Advertising,* p. 64; and Kohei Goshi, "Japanese Management and Productivity" (speech delivered at the Conference on Productivity Research, Houston, Texas, April 23, 1980).

265   In 1950: Arakawa, "On the Development," pp. 45–50.

266   Retail institutions: Yoshino, *Japanese Marketing System,* Chap. 3.

267   According to Kamiya: Shotaro Kamiya, *My Life with Toyota* (Calif.: Toyota Motor Sales, U.S.A., 1976), pp. 65–67.

INDEX